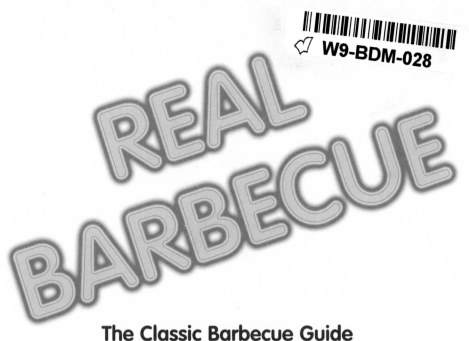

REAL BARBECUE

The Classic Barbecue Guide
to the Best Joints Across the USA—with
Recipes, Porklore, and More!

Vince Staten and Greg Johnson

The Globe Pequot Press

GUILFORD, CONNECTICUT

To buy books in quantity for corporate use
or incentives, call **(800) 962–0973**
or e-mail **premiums@GlobePequot.com.**

Text design by Casey Shain
Spot art © Clipart.com

Library of Congress Cataloging-in-Publication Data is available.
ISBN: 978-0-7627-4442-8

Manufactured in the United States of America
First Edition/First Printing

Contents

The
First Course

Introduction

The best thing to do with a book about barbecue is wipe your hands on it.

That's how we began the first edition of this book twenty years ago, and another thousand barbecue joints later, we feel the same way. No matter how brilliant the prose (and some of it is darned brilliant), reading about barbecue is like hearing about a hot date: It's interesting, but it's nothing like being there. The whole point of *Real Barbecue* remains to bounce you out of your Barcalounger and into the delicious world of great eating, from America's best barbecue joints to your own backyard.

After publication of that first edition, Willard Scott called us the Masters and Johnson of barbecue. *Playboy* labeled us barbecue's Rand McNally. We prefer to think of ourselves as the Lewis and Clark of barbecue, blazing new trails, exploring the back roads of barbecue, and discovering places previously known only to natives who lived in the neighborhood. When we headed out to find the great joints, there was nothing to guide us but smoke in the air and recommendations from friends.

It has been two decades since we first published *Real Barbecue*. In the interim our little ode to the slowest of the slow foods has become a cult classic. Which means it didn't sell very well first time out. But that was before Amazon.com and the Internet.

Now we're back to tell you that real, slow-smoked, pit-cooked, fall-off-the-bone barbecue isn't a lost art. Finding the real thing isn't always easy, and preparing it yourself requires a little effort, but it's there to be had. And it is truly the pinnacle of culinary creation, the most coddled and cared-for food in the world. Eating it is the goal; reading about it just gets you there.

Luckily, your loyal and hard-working authors are back to assist you. We logged 40,000 miles for the first edition, visiting nearly 700 barbecue joints, and burning the hair off a couple of knuckles rounding up and testing the very best this country has to offer. This expanded and revised edition incorporates eighteen years of leisurely sampling and another twelve months of serious swallowing, involving another 10,000 miles (not including air miles).

It was a lot of eating, but it was worth it. We found sauces so rich and luxurious that we wanted to climb in the pot and bask in them. We found sauces with more snap than a set of new suspenders. There were ribs that had people speaking in tongues, and sandwiches that had businessmen sneaking them home in briefcases. In the end we regretted that we had but one gall bladder each to give to the cause.

Besides the barbecue itself, there were the barbecue chefs—a friendly, entertaining, and colorful bunch of folks who have dedicated their lives to a food that gets them up at four in the morning to stand in a sweltering room. Their determination to produce a product they can be proud of, no matter how demanding the effort, is evident in every steaming bite. It is what elevates barbecue joints, despite their modest means, above restaurants staffed with Cordon Bleu chefs and decked out in designer finery.

Although this is called a travel guide, we prefer to think of it as more.

We consider it a cultural anthropology of barbecue. And as much as barbecue is about great food, it is also about great stories.

We ended the original introduction this way: Barbecue is more than a meal; it's a way of life.

Twenty years later we can only add: Amen.

The History of Barbecue—or as Much of It as You'll Ever Need to Know

About 160,000 years ago, according to paleontologists, man discovered fire. Later that same day, along about suppertime, it's very likely that he invented barbecue.

Like all great ideas, barbecue came out close to perfect to begin with. And unlike the wheel, which was another good idea, man has had the sense to leave barbecue pretty much alone. In the intervening eons, civilization has taken the wheel and frittered it away on inertial guidance systems, roulette tables, and fertilizer spreaders that take up both lanes on Sunday afternoon. Barbecue, on the other hand, is still the same mystic communion between fire, smoke, and meat familiar to *Homo sapiens idaltu* as he knelt over a smoldering hippo bone with his chef's hat on.

For your average twenty-first-century American guy or gal, barbecue is a ticket back to simpler times, when men were men and women had hair on their knees. Surely it's not necessary to detail the animal attraction of gnawing at a slab of shortbacks, and the subject of lasciviously licking sauce-drenched fingers would bring a blush to any maiden's cheeks. So let discretion rule. Let us just say that there are primal pleasures involved in enjoying barbecue the likes of which aren't legal, except maybe in Nevada.

Good barbecue now is like good barbecue always: simple and slightly sinful. After all, that whole man-woman thing can be traced back to a spare rib in the Garden of Eden. In its early days, the saga of barbecue is a bit hard to trace, partly because the chefs were just as likely to be the main course on any given prehistoric evening.

The ancient history of barbecue is mostly made up of old wives' tales, the most famous of which is the oft-told story of its origin set down by the cockney Charles Lamb in his 1822 "Dissertation Upon Roast Pig." According to Lamb's flowery account, partaking of porkers was unknown in the world until its accidental discovery by Bo-bo, a "great lubberly boy" and eldest son of Ho-Ti, a swineherd in ancient China. Left in charge of the swineherd's humble cottage, Bo-bo took to playing with fire and set ablaze the "sorry antediluvian makeshift of a building" and the pigs within. Fearing his father's wrath, Bo-bo poked a hot porker to try to revive it, burnt his finger, and popped it into his mouth to cool it. Well, Bo-bo may have been lubberly, but he was no dope. "O father, the pig, the pig! Do come and taste how nice the burnt pig eats," he shouted, simultaneously discovering roast pork and restaurant criticism. Soon it seemed that Ho-Ti and Bo-bo's little shack was burning down fairly frequently, once or twice a week, even. Called to trial for such misdeeds at Peking, the pair saw their secret get out among the judge and jury and the population at large, and soon "there was nothing to be seen but fire in every direction." Humanity moved on into the Age of Barbecue, and the Chinese stopped fooling around with gunpowder and got busy inventing Wetnaps.

Unfortunately, the march of progress led mankind away from the simple pleasures of cooking out. Across Europe, cooking was done in fireplaces hung with cast-iron griddles and pots that started the whole process of moving food away from fire, an insidious historical movement that continues to this day and can be seen at its most soulless during Early Bird Special time at Golden Corral. Eventually, after too many years away from a hot fire, a good meal came to mean a couple of suitably "ripe" fowl simmered in the depths of a dank inn and served in a dim room full of guys who hadn't rinsed out their leathers lately. It might have stayed that way, too, with unenlightened modern man blithely wolfing down centuries of truly terrible food, if it hadn't been for one fortunate accident: America.

Despite its origins in the misty dawn of man, barbecue never really hit its stride until it was rediscovered along the shores of what turned out to be the You Ess of Ay. In fact, reliable sources (as reliable as sources get on the subject of barbecue) tie the name itself to a portable frame of green sticks used by the Arawaks to smoke and roast game and fish over an open fire—an early form of barbecue pit discovered in the West Indies by the first Spanish explorers. In their version of the native inhabitants' Taino language, *barbacoa* referred to that frame of green sticks. To the explorers, it translated as "Oh, boy! Takeout!"

In classic conquering-hero fashion, the Europeans ended up claiming the invention of barbecue—or at least the word—for their own. A common shaggy-pig story gives the French credit for coming up with the idea, based on the phrase *barbe a queue*, which translates roughly as "beard-to-tail," referring to whole-hog (or goat, as the case may be) cooking. Most serious scholars, including those of the barbecue-loving *Oxford English Dictionary*, allow themselves a discreet snicker at that one, the dictionary once pooh-

poohing the story as "absurd conjecture." Europeans can claim credit for one thing, though: They brought the domesticated pig to North America.

With a combination of steamy climate, Spanish explorers selling secret recipes, and lots of easy labor, the South got a head start on the new American art of barbecue. Southerners settled on a common technique of digging pits in the earth, filling them with aromatic hardwood, and then tending a slow fire of hot coals beneath a pampered but uncomfortable guest of honor.

The first European settlers of Virginia, pretty much a salt-pork-and-

PORKLORE

Lamb on Pig

"There is no flavour comparable, I will contend, to that of the crisp, tawny, well-watched, not over-roasted, crackling, as it is well called—the very teeth are invited to their share of the pleasure at this banquet in overcoming the coy, brittle resistance—with the adhesive oleaginous—O call it not fat! but an indefinable sweetness growing up to it—the tender blossoming of fat—fat cropped in the bud—taken in the shoot—in the first innocence—the cream and quintessence of the child-pig's yet pure food—the lean, no lean, but a kind of animal manna—or, rather, fat and lean (if it must be so) so blended and running into each other, that both together make but one ambrosian result or common substance."
—Charles Lamb,
"A Dissertation Upon Roast Pig,"
London Magazine, 1822

scurvy bunch of sailors, probably adopted the Native American techniques over the decades, adapting them to hogs and other creatures of choice. Outdoor barbecues reportedly were common along the James River in Virginia. The rediscovered thrill of the barbecue was adapted by colonists in their kitchens, as well. Pieces of meat sometimes were hung by twine in the fireplace and twisted so they'd unwind slowly in the smoke. Spits were common fireplace accessories, often with pans underneath to catch juices for basting.

Spanish settlers who encountered the barbecue stands of the Creeks and Cherokees in the Carolinas and the Gulf Coast area were taking notes, too. Eventually they became a barbecue migration that followed the establishment of herds and ranches farther west into strange lands like Mexico, and real strange lands like Texas. As time passed, such carriers of the barbecue flame added their own variations, like tomatoes, garlic, and hot peppers. Tomatoes had been shunned by early barbecuers along the East Coast because they were thought to be poisonous aphrodisiacs, called "love apples." It was not until September 26, 1830, when Col. Robert Gibbon Johnson publicly bit into a basket of tomatoes on the courthouse steps in Salem, New Jersey, and didn't die, that many Easterners believed they were safe to eat. That may seem hopelessly dense to present-day barbecuers, but the road to rib tips has been littered with less-than-overwhelming thinking. In the 1700s and 1800s, for instance, New York had its chance to go down in the history books with a regional style all its own. What did the bead-and-trinket sharpies of Manhattan Island come up with? Turtle barbecues.

At some point, barbecue more or less stopped having a national history and broke into an interrelated mess of local and regional histories. In many rural areas of the South and Midwest, big outdoor barbecues became associated with political get-togethers and church meetings. Catholic churches, short on members in many areas of the South, used the tempting smoke of an all-day barbecue wafting across the countryside to attract scores of sniffing Protestants eager to make a small contribution in exchange for some prime pig. By the turn of the century in Texas, barbecue had become a common feature out behind butcher shops, as a way to make less highfalutin cuts of beef more salable.

From such backwoods roots, barbecue hitched a ride across America. It followed various migrations to various cities, moving up the Mississippi to Kansas City, for instance, where the beef-and-spicy-ketchup traditions of Texas mingled with the vinegar–hot pork of the Carolinas and a multitude of other variations. Barbecue mosied into Chicago and Cleveland and Los Angeles. Even if anyone had been trying to keep track of all this, it would have been pretty near impossible. Tradition and invention became mixed in a delicious confusion.

Sometimes, powerful interests tried to harness barbecue to their own ends. Giant barbecues were one technique Boss Tweed used to wrangle votes for Tammany Hall. Lyndon Baines Johnson, Jimmy Carter, and both George Bushes tried the same thing. But all the while, barbecue kept its essential character. After the occasional vote-getter blow-out, it would return to its

Barbecue Insults

"Shakespeare wrote 'Much Ado About Nothing' after sopping his white bread through a batch of Georgia pork sauce."
—Caleb Pirtle III

natural state, smoldering away in relative obscurity, tucked into country crossroads and big-city street corners, generally ignored by the nice folks of America, who were busy developing gelatin molds and meat loaf.

In recent times, there have been a couple of barbecue booms, one associated with the nation's first flirtation with automobiles and highways (and hence roadside stands) in the 1920s and '30s, and another in the post-war suburban '50s, when backyard barbecuers by the millions rediscovered the thrills of pyrotechnic hamburger patties, if not exactly traditional barbecue.

Now Americans are surrounded by multinational corporations and sophisticated image manipulators, many of whom are more than passingly interested in parting the Average Man from his hard-earned dining dollar. The twenty-first-century image-and-eating machine coughs out fast-food franchises at such a rate that it became mathematically impossible to build more, for fear that there would be more people working in them than eating in them. Convenience stores battle to match their microwaves against chicken joints that buy birds raised in fowl factories where the light's on all night long.

And yet, the chuffing, ramshackle barbecue joint endures. Like crabgrass, it pops up through the cracks of corporate America. The mom-and-pop gro-

Barbecue Insults

"In Wisconsin, they think a Sloppy Joe is barbecue."
—Bill Schuetze, a Wisconsin native
who moved to Louisville, Kentucky

cery is dead; the little roadside motel is staggering. Mystery Spots and Indian Caves gather cobwebs while people seek out theme parks. So why does the barbecue joint remain, boisterous and boastful, while all the rest vanish? The answer lies in its very nature. Despite the fact that you can walk into a rib joint and walk right out with a slab of ribs, barbecue is not "fast food"; it is the very opposite. Barbecue is slow food, laboriously smoked even when prepared in the most "modern" electric ovens, and it's a cuisine that looks to the past. The care and craftsmanship of the pitman recall a simpler time when pride meant more than profit. You can see it in the names of America's barbecue joints themselves, always harking back to their individual histories for the touchstone of better days, for the purest style and the ultimate taste: "Texas barbecue" in New York City and "Oklahoma-style barbecue" in Los Angeles, "Southern-style" in Kansas City and in Fort Collins, Colorado.

At such outposts of good eating, and in backyards and parking lots across the nation, there is a vast flickering ritual, a shadow play of flame and smoke that can envelop a modern cook and whisk him for a moment back to the barbacoa, lost in the simple satisfactions of the evening's meal. At such times, the history of barbecue is present in every pit, with thousands of years of human history flavoring the meat. No modern corporation can hope to fake a flame like that.

Barbecue in Other Countries

Phil Fisher traveled all over the world for the Brown & Williamson Tobacco Co., teaching farmers in other countries how to grow tobacco. And when dinnertime arrived, the locals usually invited him to their favorite eating establishment. Oftentimes that establishment served barbecue. And that suited Fisher just fine, because he was a barbecue fanatic. "I've eaten barbecue all over this country, all over the world," he told us two decades ago. He had tasted the local cuisine in fifty-five countries and eaten barbecue in many of them.

One of his most memorable barbecue-eating experiences came in Spain. "We were in Jarandilla, Spain, my boss and me. It's in the backcountry. We were staying in a castle turned into a resort hotel. The locals said, "How'd you like to sample the local cuisine?" I always believe when in Rome . . . So we walked down the hill to this place." This place was called *La Cueva Puta*, which translates to "Cave of Bad Women." That's right, a combination barbecue joint and whorehouse. That beats the hell out of Ace's, which was Atlanta's combination barbecue joint and taxi stand, and out of Cafe Tattoo, which was Baltimore's combination barbecue joint and tattoo parlor. "We walked in, and the owner chased the girls out. Then he put what looked like a door across two nail kegs and brought out the food. There was octopus cooked in black ink, raw squirrel, and barbecued goat. Because it was the only thing really cooked, I ate it. It was good, really saucy. And it was an experience."

The story of Spanish barbecue reminded him of the time he had barbecue in Turkey. "We were in a small village, and they took us to the mayor's house to eat. They had a whole lamb there that they were cooking over a spit barbecue. They told me that because I was the honored guest I got choice part of the lamb. Then they reached over and stuck a toothpick through the eyeball and handed it to me. Now in a situation like that, you can't turn your hosts down. So I ate it." And what does a barbecued lamb's eyeball taste like? "I don't rightly know, because I swallowed it whole."

Barbecue Architecture:
From Bauhaus to Sowhaus

How different things might be if Frank Lloyd Wright had taken the road less traveled, the one with the barbecue joint on the right, just past the trailer court. Wright's fondness for concrete would have suited fire-conscious barbecue men just fine. Wright came along at the right time, when health departments were forcing sidewalk barbecue stands to clean up their acts and put up buildings. But Wright and other architects didn't take an interest in barbecue places. So the Memphis style has nothing to do with the debate over wet or dry ribs. The Chicago School isn't where Leon and Lem learned to cook barbecue. And Art Deco isn't the guy who owns Art's Bar-B-Que out on the bypass. Barbecue men were left to their own designs, and they have created an architectural style all their own. Believe us.

In the beginning there was no barbecue-joint architecture. Barbecue was an outdoor food, served at political rallies and picnics, sold in pastures and backyards. It was around the turn of the twentieth century that barbecue moved to the street corners and, in rural areas, to roadside stands. "These locations they picked, particularly the street corner locations, were crucial," says Grady Clay, urban environmental expert and author of *Close-Up: How to Read the American City*. "They had visibility; they could be seen from four directions. The smell attracted from four directions. Smoke signals were very important to success. There was always a little commotion. Commotion is an absolute necessity for success in this kind of business."

Then came the health department inspector. He had more to do with creating barbecue architecture than all the design firms combined. He required tin sides. Then he wanted the sawdust floors replaced with concrete. The barbecue men pondered the health requirements and saw that the only thing left of the old days was the tent top, so they added a tin roof, and the barbecue joint was born.

That was the original barbecue joint: corrugated tin sides, bare concrete floors, and a tin roof. We call the first wave of barbecue-joint architecture the Greasian style. The focus of the place was the grease-caked pit. For a number of years that was all there was to barbecue architecture: a shack built around a pit. But that great American business force, competition, entered. Just as lawyers find that when there is only one in town, there isn't enough work, but when there are two there is more than either can handle, so too did barbecue men discover that competition created more barbecue eaters. And soon that little six-stool shack wasn't big enough. So the first barbecue man expanded. He built a wing on the side. As business continued to increase, the building took on a life of its own—a new wing on the other side, a take-out window out back, a picnic area, indoor restrooms. And thus was born the Sowhaus style: The place has grown in all directions, like a sow fattened up.

When Fred the grocer down the road saw how well Jim Bob and his new competitor Joe Frank were doing selling barbecue, he built a little pit out back of his store and started selling sandwiches. And people started buying them. That old competitive machine was at work again. Pretty soon Fred was selling more sandwiches than soap. So he cut out the soap section and set up a dining table there. And before he knew it, he was out of the grocery business and into the barbecue business. He still had the little one-pump country store building, but he was a full-fledged barbecue joint. This kind of evolution was happening everywhere. In one town it might be a service station, in another a meat market. But all began as one business and then shifted. The old building remained, and maybe even remnants of the old business. George Hooks in Milledgeville, Georgia, still sold a few groceries when we visited twenty years ago. Owens Barbecue in Lake City, South Carolina, started out as a grocery store, but five years after opening the store, Mellon Owens decided to start cooking barbecue. Soon the barbecue just took over. The building still had the basic characteristics of a country store, but with a screened pit out back. It was an example of the Remodeling School, an architectural style characterized by minor changes to major structures.

As competition heated up, a new guy moved into town. When the Laundromat closed, he took over the lease, built a counter, set up booths where the washers used to be, and began cooking out back. On the outside it still looked like a Laundromat. On the inside it was a barbecue joint. Scholars of architecture call this "adaptive reuse," taking old structures and using them for new purposes instead of abandoning them. We call it the Bizarrantine style because the results are bizarre: barbecue joints in former residences, where they probably burn stacks of zoning and fire regulations instead of hickory; barbecue joints in former gas stations, where one can only hope they washed out the underground tanks a bit before they started lighting fires. Pratt's Barn, which serves one of the best barbecue pork sandwiches in east Tennessee, is housed in a barn-shaped building. But out front, standing guard over the door, is a 20-foot-tall cement Indian. Don't ask what Honest John (that's the Indian's name) has to do with barbecue. He has nothing to do with barbecue. But he used to draw a lot of gawks from tourists back in the days when Pratt's was Honest John's and a gift shop.

Probably the most common Bizarrantine barbecue joints are in former fast-food restaurants, where barbecue men scurry like hermit crabs when an old marketing concept dies. When a Burger Heaven franchise goes out of business, hungry citizens dreaming of barbecue will gather, drawn by still-unexplained forces, and stand in the parking lot surrounding the place until a pit opens there; it is the central process of Darwinian dining, the survival of the fittest cuisine.

Actually, the great forces of history make the direction of all this quite clear: Left unattended, structures will tend to experience the rapture, becoming born-again barbecue joints almost overnight, sprouting rusty smokestacks and misspelled mottos where once an architect trod. Eventually absolutely everything in America will be a barbecue joint.

What a wonderful world that will be.

Barbecue Is Where You Find It:
Here's How . . .

The problem:

It is a dark and stormy night. You have been all day on the road. You're tired. The wife's tired. The kids are irritable. And you are all starved.

The solution: Barbecue.

Nothing can turn a day around like hot barbecue and a cold drink. But how do you find a good barbecue joint in a strange town? It's for sure you won't find it by calling the AAA. They can plan your journey and pick your motel and get your car towed. But they are not the Rand McNally of the rotisserie.

Begin by asking. It helps if you know someone. Even people who can't stand barbecue invariably know someone who loves it. Get an introduction, call the barbecue fanatic, and ask for a guided tour. That's the ideal situation. But even if you only remotely know someone in the strange town, give him or her a call. Vince knew someone who knew Bill Powell, a retired newspaperman living in Paducah, Kentucky. He called Powell up, explained that he was looking for a good barbecue place, and spent a delightful twenty minutes talking barbecue with Powell. And his recommendation, Starnes', turned out to be so good that it made our top one hundred list.

But what if you don't know anyone in town? "Ask at the grocery store or the filling station," advised former Tennessee congressman Robin Beard, a barbecue fanatic if there ever was one. Beard admitted to having eaten barbecue for breakfast. On more than one occasion. His former press secretary, Rusty Brashear, said that they had to arrange their campaign stops to coincide with barbecue joints. We've taken Beard's advice and found it right on target. The boys who pump gas may not know French cuisine, but they know pig sandwiches. A dusty-faced fellow at a Gulf station on U.S. Highway 60 steered us to the Marion Pit Barbecue in Marion, Kentucky, and we still thank him for it. Marion Pit is so good that restaurants from all over the country have been known to order up some of the sauce. Locals call the place "Jack's," after the owner, Jack Easley. And when we asked a filling-station attendant in Jackson, Tennessee, for directions to a nearby joint, he gave us a dissertation on the local barbecue scene. "What do you want to go there for?" he challenged, pulling himself upright. We told him we'd heard they had good barbecue. He shook his head and allowed, "Oh, they've got good barbecue. But they don't want to give you any of it. They're tight with it, give you these little old sandwiches. You want some good barbecue, you go back up this road to the bank and then look over to the left. You'll see this little trailer. That's Bill Case. Now, he's got good barbecue, and he's not so tight with it, either." We followed his advice and enjoyed a delightful meal and conversation with Bill Case.

If you can't get a recommendation anywhere, grab a phone book. Don't just look under "Barbecue" in the Yellow Pages. Some of the best barbecue joints don't know there is a separate listing. Check under "Restaurants," too. Check the names. You can tell a lot from a barbecue joint's name. If the owner was sure enough of his product to lend his last name to the place—say Allman's Barbecue in Fredericksburg, Virginia, or Lindsey's in Little Rock—that's a good sign.

"There are some fairly good places in the cities that are institutional-type barbecue places that will have some kind of fancier names," said

Beard. "But in the country, it's good to have that guy's name on it. It means he takes pride in his barbecue." If he is sure enough of his product to use his first name, then you can almost bet on a winner: Emmett's in Gadsden, Alabama. Angelo's in Fort Worth. And surest of all is the barbecue man who will lend his name to something stupid sounding. Take Maurice's Piggy Park in West Columbia, South Carolina. Can you imagine the ribbing Maurice would take if his "Piggy Park" were to serve inferior sandwiches? Fortunately for Maurice, and for you, Maurice serves barbecue that is *real* good. Given a choice between a joint named Fred's Barbecue and a joint named Swiss Chalet Barbecue, go for the first name every time.

Sometimes the phone-book listing will tell how long a place has been in business. Generally, the longer the better. There are exceptions to this rule, towns with such poor taste that they have kept a mediocre barbecue joint going. And sometimes a place may have been in business too long. The original owner, the one who created the sauce and built the reputation, may have died or sold out. It is rare indeed for the new owner to be as careful and good as the original. For a rule of thumb, use this tip from Wayne Monk, owner of Lexington Barbecue No. 1 in Lexington, North Carolina. He said, "The life span of a barbecue joint seems to be twenty to forty years."

Now get on the phone. Ask for directions. A really good barbecue joint usually is slightly, if not impossibly, difficult to find when you're a stranger in town. If giving directions comes second nature to the person who answers the phone, good. It means they've done it before. If that person answers by saying, "Yeah?" instead of "Good evening. How may I help you?" start driving.

Now comes the real test: the drive-by. How does the joint look? Don't be leery of a run-down exterior. As the saying goes: "It's not much on the outside, but . . . " The "but" is usually followed by a testimonial to the quality of the meat, the heat of the sauce, the freshness of the bun, and the gusto of the beans. Beard said, "If it looks too slick, then I'm worried. I don't want

Good barbecue joints often aren't much to look at.

them spending a whole lot of time cleaning tables and shining windows. If it's a small operation, I want that guy spending time with his barbecue."

Beard said the reason many rural barbecue joints are nothing more than shacks is because the owner didn't start out with the intention of opening a barbecue restaurant. "It usually started out with a farmer raising pigs, and when he had too many he'd pull out a few and put 'em on a spit. It would be too many for the family to eat, but if he had the right touch and his wife could come up with a tangy sauce, the neighbors would drop over—and, first thing you know, he'd dig a pit, build a shack for the smoker, and start cooking them by the batch, as a side business. He wouldn't have any overhead. He had the property; he had all the raw products right

The parking lot can tell you a lot about a barbecue joint.

there. Then when the crop went bad, there was always the sandwich trade to fall back on. When the farmer found he was making more money out of barbecue than farming, he knew he'd found his true calling."

A good barbecue joint is seldom in a building built for it. The best barbecue joints seem to open up in abandoned Laundromats, burned-out Dairy Queens, and failed Burger Chefs. Remodeling is usually minimal. To make up for spare interiors, good barbecue joints sometimes use bright, even gaudy colors outside.

The parking lot can tell you a lot, too. Is there a bizarre mixture of cars, say a Mercedes, a Chevy with a flame paint job, and an animal-control dump truck? That's good; it means that the cooking crosses cultural lines.

Do you realize how good barbecue has to be to get a Mercedes owner to park next to a dump truck? Also, look for mail-delivery vans. Mail carriers can stop anywhere on their routes; if the food wasn't good, they'd be tired of it already.

Now it's time to give the place a closer look. Check the front window. Is the owner advertising other products? "Anybody that's looking for barbecue who stops at a place that has barbecue on the sign but hamburgers and hot dogs advertised in the window is going to be disappointed," said Beard. "That's not a very good place, and you're not going to get very good barbecue. I just want to see a place that does nothing but barbecue." Jack Sweat, who used to run a place called Sweat's Barbecue in Soperton, Georgia, told us years ago about a time a family of Yankees returning from a vacation at Hilton Head stopped by his place and ordered fried shrimp.

Next, look around back. It is a serious mistake to walk directly in the front door of a barbecue joint without making a lap of the place. The front is showbiz; the back is where the truth hangs out. What should you look for?

Wood. "Always look for that stack of wood," emphasized Beard. "And if it's a real neat stack of wood, you'd better watch out. Some people will put wood out there for aesthetics. If they are really using it, the stacks are going to be a little messy, a piece lying here and there. Because if they are really cooking barbecue, they are going to be going out in the middle of night to grab some wood, and they aren't going to be taking time to stack it back neatly."

Backup smokers. Out behind many good barbecue joints it'll look like a used-car lot—a real bad used-car lot—with piles of rusting iron parts, barrels, sheet metal, and mobile smokers with or without flat tires. These are experimental models, and a pretty good sign the place isn't experimenting on you.

A guy leaning against a wall. At barbecue joints, guys leaning against walls aren't goofing off; they're working. Tending a good pit takes years of experience, boundless patience, expert knowledge, and the ability to lean

The messy woodpile: a sign of a good barbecue joint

against a wall. Leaning against a wall in a cloud of hickory smoke and puffing on a cigarette is worth style points.

Flies. If it's summertime and there are no flies hanging around, you should ask yourself, "What do the flies know that I don't?" Actual flies aren't required, however, if you can spot a flyswatter on a windowsill somewhere.

If the joint has passed the drive-by and the closer-look tests, you are ready to park and get out. Time for one last test. (Robin Beard again): "Look for the smokestack and sniff the air for the smell of hickory or whatever wood they're using. If it's a weak, almost nonexistent smell, then they're not cooking it right. If there's a good heavy smell, then that's just another indication you've stopped at a good place."

If the joint has passed all these tests, then go on in. Don't be alarmed by a plain interior. Remember, any barbecue joint with a pit on-site probably has had its share of fire problems. No point in complicating matters with a lot of wooden shelves and seats or tacky plastic doodads that will just fuel the flame.

Jim Dodson, a North Carolina native and barbecue fanatic, once told us, "I prefer a place with cheap plastic tablecloths and mismatched utensils and hard-plastic section plates that are the color of an old schoolhouse bathroom wall. It helps if there is no printed menu. It helps if there is a sink located right in the dining room and there is a friendly but bored gum-chewing waitress with her name scripted in frilly pink letters above her left, ample breast. It helps if her name is Wanda. Or Trixie."

Look around. Lewis Grizzard, the late Georgia humorist, believed, "If there are any religious posters on the walls, you can usually count on the barbecue being good." We could make a list of barbecue places that fit that description, including Maurice's Piggy Park in South Carolina and Otto's in Houston. The Old Plantation House in Birmingham had a genealogical chart tracing Jesus's lineage all the way back to Adam and Eve. If there aren't posters, look for calendars—the local ones, from slaughterhouses and farm-implement dealers. The more calendars, the better the barbecue. Louie Mueller's in Taylor, Texas, once boasted a nine-calendar wall, and the brisket backed it up.

What should you order in a strange barbecue joint? For starters, order something small. A half-slab instead of a slab of ribs, a sandwich instead of a dinner plate—and even a small sandwich at that. Barbecue aficionado Beard: "What I'll usually do is get the smallest sandwich they've got, and then if I like it, I go in for the kill." If the clerk asks you a question, like "Do you want it hot?" answer in the affirmative. If they ask, that probably means most customers get it that way. If most get it that way, that's the way you want it, too. Another tactic: If there's something on the menu that you've never heard of, order it. It doesn't matter if it's "soaks," "pit-cut," a

"C-B Joe," "burnt ends," or even "snoots." The fact that it's there means the locals demand it, even if the tourists don't have a clue. Nine times out of ten, whatever it is, you'll love it—and you'll get a smidgen of respect for having given it a try.

We could give you other barbecue rules. Over the years we've heard them all. But these are the ones that seem to be most important. And remember: These are only guidelines. We have found exceptions to every one. "You can take all these things that I have said and still get blasted out of the water," says Beard. "Barbecue just defies rules."

Pig Pickin': How We Selected the Hundred Hot Barbecue Joints

We don't use the star system to rate barbecue places. We're not even sure we understand the star system. What is the difference between a three-and-a-half-star place and a four-star place? Nothing else in life is rated on stars. When you go in for a salary review, your boss doesn't say you had a three-and-a-half-star year. And he doesn't rate you on a 1-to-10 scale, either. He just tells you how you did. So that's the way we're going to rate barbecue joints, the way the people who eat there rate them. No stars, no grades, no 1-to-10 scale.

Our ratings scale is derived from hours and hours of conversations with barbecue connoisseurs, people who drive 100 miles out of their way to a new barbecue joint. To begin with, there is no low end of the scale, no barbecue equivalent of a one-star restaurant. They just don't survive. A barbecue joint that is fair to middling is called "Pretty Good" by barbecue connoisseurs. One step up the ratings ladder is the joint that does a respectable job, that might get you back again, if you want some barbecue and the better places are closed. It is rated "Good" by barbecue connoisseurs. Now we arrive at the exalted plateaus, where the barbecue is considered special, worth a far drive and a long wait. These are the places that are packed every noon and supper hour. They receive the next-to-the-highest rating: "Real Good."

Finally comes the top, the pinnacle of barbecue knowledge, where secret sauces deserve to be secret—barbecue places that are worth a special trip. These are the places that are packed at three in the afternoon. Barbecue connoisseurs have a special term for them: "As Good As I've Ever Had." In barbecue conversation, that is the ultimate compliment. Why won't a true barbecue connoisseur just come out and call a place "The Best"? We wondered about that for a long time. And after much conversation and much thought, we have arrived at the answer. The barbecue purist, the true connoisseur, knows that out there right now, at this very minute, some barbecue cook is building a pit, hand-lettering a shingle BAR-B-Q and hanging it out. And the connoisseur thinks maybe, just maybe, this one may be a little better than the place up the road or across the county line. So his barbecue fanaticism becomes an eternal quest, an unending search for the best barbecue joint in America.

What We Looked For

Here is how we judged the hundreds of barbecue joints we tried on our barbecue quest. First and foremost was the meat. Was it tender? Was it flavorful? The bottom line in barbecue is meat. Second was the preparation. Did the cook know what he or she was doing? The third was the sauce. We recognize the broad range of sauces used in American barbecue. In fact, we enjoy most all of them. But the sauce must form a perfect union with the meat. Next we noted the service. Was it cheerful? Was it fast? Was it service at all? And finally we checked the atmosphere. Would we want to return? Would we want to bring our mother? (Sometimes a place can score extra points if you wouldn't want to bring your mother.)

We used much the same testing methodology as regular restaurant critics. We arrived at each barbecue place unannounced, ate unattended, and, if the barbecue didn't stack up, left unnoticed. We didn't want special attention; we wanted to test each place under normal conditions. In short, we wanted the same kind of sandwich, the same kind of service that you would receive if you stopped in after a long day on the road. Any cook can wow you with a special meal. We were looking for the places that can wow you day in and day out, eat-in or takeout.

Where We Went

We didn't eat at every barbecue joint in America. That would be an impossible task considering all the barbecue places there are and all that modern medicine has discovered about the link between cholesterol and good health.

There are 8,728 barbecue restaurants in the United States, according to the Yellow Pages (once owned by Ma Bell, now owned by InfoSpace). That's not very many in the scheme of what consulting groups like to call "restaurant concepts." There are four times as many Mexican restaurants and almost ten times as many pizza places. It's less than 2 percent of the 626,724 restaurants in business in 2006, just a drop in the sop bucket. It's also a number that would probably not be accepted by any except the guy who owns the Yellow Pages. A Texan would look at that number, rub his chin, and say, "Texas is a big state, but it's not that big." A Tennessean would ask, "Does that include places in Texas?" and when the answer was yes, reply, "Then that number's too high." And a barbecue purist of any origin would sniff, "I bet 90 percent of them cook with gas or electric. And that's not barbecue."

So what is barbecue? That is a question that will start an argument in most any bar in the country. Finding an answer was our dilemma when we began this book. We toyed with the idea of "when in Rome." If the locals call it barbecue, then we would call it barbecue, too. Then we mentioned that idea to our friend Bill Schuetze, a Wisconsin native. "In Wisconsin they think a Sloppy Joe is barbecue," he said. His answer convinced us that that was not the right way to go. In the end we adopted the U.S. Department of Agriculture's definition, even though it applies to packaged foods and not restaurants. The USDA says barbecue is "[meat that] shall be cooked by the direct action of heat resulting from the burning of hard wood or the hot coals there from for a sufficient period to assume the usual characteristics . . . which include the formation of a brown crust . . . The weight of barbecued meat shall not exceed 70 percent of the weight of the fresh uncooked meat."

The definition has several appeals for us. It's been in use since the early part of the twentieth century. It conforms pretty closely to what purists think of as barbecue. And it guarantees that whatever goes on the grill, be it hog or heifer, will come off as barbecue, no matter what kind of baste has been mopped on during the cooking and no matter what kind of sauce has been slathered on afterward. With that definition we also could eliminate many of the Yellow Pages's 8,728 so-called barbecue restaurants.

We still didn't make it to every wood-burning pit in the country. We each have but one gall bladder to give to this cause. But over the last twenty years we have eaten at more than one thousand barbecue joints, more than any man alive and quite a few who are dead.

For this update we began by scouring the Internet for recommended barbecue places. And we abruptly quit because we soon figured out that we couldn't trust many of those recommendations. We read one proclamation that the best barbecued ribs in the Northeast were at Frank's. Then we noticed in small print at the end of the post "Submitted by Frank." So we went back to the same method we used first time out: recommendations from barbecue connoisseurs. We call them our "barbecue army." We sent out letters and e-mails describing our update project, compiled the results, and hit the road. In addition to trying new places, we revisited our old favorites to make sure they were still on their toes.

If your particular barbecue choice isn't on our list, don't despair. It could have been having a bad day when we passed through. A good barbecue joint can have a bad day. But we have confidence in our selections because we don't think the converse is true: A good place can have a bad day, but a bad place can never have a good day. If you think there is a barbecue joint that is as good as you've ever had that we might have missed, e-mail us at vincestaten@gmail.com. We'll stop by the next time we're in the neighborhood. We might even take you along.

We don't claim our selections for the Hot One Hundred as the absolute last word. Close, but we like to think that somewhere out there at this very moment, some young barbecue cook is hanging out that first hand-lettered sign, and his barbecue is a little bit better than "as good as we've ever had." So our quest for the best barbecue joints isn't over. It's still continuing.

The South

We begin our tour of America's great barbecue joints in the South because that's where barbecue joints began, and it's still the heart and soul of barbecue country.

North Carolina: East

Pittsboro

Allen & Son Pit-Cooked Bar-B-Que

In North Carolina barbecue is right up there with basketball as the thing people argue about. That's because North Carolina has developed two distinct barbecue styles, and practitioners of each are divided along geographical lines. In the coastal region of the state is Down East barbecue, the oldest style of barbecue in this country. It originated in the days when people thought tomatoes were poisonous and refused to eat them. When the early settlers wanted a seasoning for their barbecued pig, they chose English ketchup, a vinegar seasoned with oysters and peppers and other spices but containing no tomato. That's still the sauce they use Down East. In the Piedmont area is Lexington style, named after its town of origin, Lexington, North Carolina.

Let's begin with the most elementary question: Where is Down East? Dennis Rogers, who was a columnist for *The News & Observer* in Raleigh, once told us, "A lot of people will tell you U.S. Highway 1 that cuts through Raleigh is pretty much the dividing line between eastern and western North Carolina. From Raleigh east, including Raleigh, is Down East. From Raleigh west is Lexington style."

Down East they cook the whole hog, with no baste, over hickory coals, then "pick" the meat off the bone, chop it into fine hunks, and coat it with a thin, hot vinegar–based sauce. The traditional side dishes are Brunswick stew, boiled potatoes cooked with paprika, coleslaw, and corn bread. "Our folks around here eat an enormous amount of barbecue," said Rogers. "It is a standard at social gatherings. What the politicians call the rubber-chicken circuit, around here is pig pickin'. You can even rent cookers from U-Haul. Rufus Edmisten lost the governor's race, and I'm sure it was

Allen & Son

because he made the statement right before the election that he was sick of barbecue. There ain't no way in hell you're going to be governor of North Carolina if you don't love barbecue."

You wouldn't think that an area with a barbecue tradition that dates from pre–Revolutionary War days would break so easily with that tradition. But Rogers said, "We're having a real problem here in eastern North Carolina because so many of the places have gone to gas. They'll lie to you and tell you it's because of the health department, but it's because it's easier."

Melton's in Rocky Mount, the first place to sell barbecue on the street, has gone to gas; so have many, many other Down East barbecue joints. But a few still cling to the old ways. Brenda Allen described the "old ways" to us when she was working in the Allen & Son restaurant almost two decades ago:

PORKLORE

Barbecue Bowl

In 1981 North Carolina's 6th District Representative Gene Johnston and South Carolina's 6th District Representative John Napier got in a barbecue feud. Johnston charged, "What little barbecue South Carolinians produce, they ruin with that awful mustardy sauce they drown it in down there." And Napier countered, "Hogwash." Johnston and Napier decided to settle the matter with a duel. But not with pistols. With barbecue. And thus was born the Congressional Barbecue Bowl. The first one was held on April Fools' Day 1981 with a dozen entrants from each state. A panel of impartial congressmen from Georgia and Virginia were asked to serve as judges. And they offered a typical political solution, declaring it a draw. So everyone kissed his sister and went home. And the politicians, as usual, got a free lunch.

But this barbecue feud wouldn't die. So the next year Johnston and Napier conducted a second Barbecue Bowl. This time a dozen stands from North Carolina and eleven from South Carolina shipped in entries. And this time there were eight Congressmen serving as judges. Doug Clark, Johnston's press secretary, said at the time, "It's probably the toughest decision these Congressmen will make all year." By a unanimous vote, the judges picked Short Sugar's of Reidsville, North Carolina, the winner, with Big D's in Hemingway, South Carolina, second. "North Carolina barbecue is the real thing, clearly superior to the mustardy concoction prepared in the lower Carolina," crowed Johnston. But the Barbecue Bowl didn't really settle the matter. Napier claimed foul, pointing out that two of the judges, Representatives Charles Whitley and Bill Hendon, were from North Carolina.

"We cook over red-hot coals that we fire up every thirty minutes. We use hickory wood only. We have it delivered in logs, and my brother saws it, splits it, and chops it." Her brother is the Son. Her late father, James Allen, started Allen & Son in 1968. To incorporate he needed at least three people, so he used himself, his wife, and his son, hence, Allen & Son. Brenda said she wasn't offended. "My brother was at home, and I was going to college. I'd always intended to do something else anyway." Her father died in 1977. But at Allen & Son they still cook the meat his way. Jimmy Stubbs runs the Allen & Son in Pittsboro. Keith Allen oversees the Allen & Son in Chapel Hill. You can taste the freshness in the sandwiches. The finely chopped pork, as white as a preacher's hair, is piled on an offering-plate-size bun, and then baptized with a trademark Down East pepper-vinegar sauce. The meat will melt in your mouth if you try to savor the flavor too long.

Because both Allen & Son restaurants are within a 20-mile radius of Chapel Hill, they are a favorite of University of North Carolina students and faculty. But since UNC attracts people from all over the world, the Allen & Son restaurants are sometimes patronized by people who aren't that familiar with barbecue. Brenda used to laugh at some of the things she was asked. One man wanted to know, "Can I get some barbecue that isn't frozen?" Another one ordered a "hush puppy sandwich." Once someone even asked her to put some barbecue on top of a cheeseburger.

Brenda spent most of her time at the restaurant in Pittsboro, which she swore had a ghost. "We've decided it's Dad looking over everything, making sure we're doing it right." And at Allen & Son, they still are.

RATING: Real good.

LOCATIONS: Highway 15-501, Pittsboro; (919) 542-2294. Highway 86, Chapel Hill; (919) 942-7576.

Goldsboro

Wilber's Barbecue

When the fish were running off Emerald Isle, North Carolina, Eddie Williams would start getting antsy. Williams, who was a longtime industrial recruiter for the Johnson City, Tennessee, Chamber of Commerce, kept a trailer at Emerald Isle for those fishing urges. But it wasn't just the fishing that attracted him to that part of the world. It was also a barbecue place, Wilber's. Williams, a Tarheel by birth, moved to Tennessee in the early fifties, but his barbecue heart always remained in eastern North Carolina. He told us before his death in 1995, "They've got some good barbecue around here in Tennessee, but they use that sweet sauce. I like Wilber's 'cause it's hotter."

Williams wasn't afraid to step into the North Carolina barbecue feud that has been simmering for decades. He said the Down East style was best, and he thought the people of the western part of the state would agree, if they wouldn't let their pride get in the way. That's because he saw them with their guard down. "My sister's son had a wedding in High Point, and Wilber catered it from Goldsboro." The distance between High Point and Goldsboro is only 140 miles, but it's a lot farther than that in the barbecue world. You see, High Point is on the buckle of the western North Carolina barbecue belt, 18 miles from Lexington. And Goldsboro is almost the center point of the Down East barbecue area. And never the two shall agree, especially when it comes to barbecue. Williams cackled when he recalled, "Most of the people at the wedding were from around High Point, but they didn't slow up eating that Wilber's."

Wilber's reputation extends far outside of North Carolina. Rick Patterson, who lives in Marietta, Ohio, still has the book of matches he picked up at Wilber's in 1979. "I have kept it to this day in case I came near Goldsboro again. Wilber's is the best I've ever had, and I was raised on the Ridgewood barbecue (in Bluff City, Tennessee)."

Wilber's Barbecue

Wilber Shirley, owner and founder of Wilber's, works hard at holding on to that reputation. "My wife says I married the restaurant and left her."

Wilber cooks twenty-eight whole hogs at a time over live oak coals. He built a special cookhouse out back, some 50 or 60 feet from the restaurant. It means a little more running back and forth from cookhouse to restaurant, but Wilber says, "It keeps fire insurance premiums down." Insurance premiums are one of the few places Wilber cuts corners. He still cooks with wood even though Goldsboro passed new air-quality regulations that effectively eliminate cooking barbecue over wood. But Wilber got grandfathered in. He can keep cooking with wood, but when he passes on to tend that great barbecue pit in the sky, his joint has to convert to gas.

Wilber's sunburned sauce is almost straight vinegar, as thin as rainwater, with red pepper for tone and black pepper for fire. Wilber's isn't a flavoring sauce, it's a flavor-enhancing sauce that soaks into Wilber's creamy chopped pork and seems to disappear. Don't miss Wilber's long, worm-shaped hush puppies. They may not look appetizing, but once you start eating them, you can't stop. And top it all off with Wilber's banana pudding.

Wilber has fixed up the inside over the years. He's even paved the parking lot, our only complaint last time. But it's still not high-class; it looks more like a Rod and Gun club with its knotty pine paneling, high-pitched ceilings, and exposed wooden beams. He's had to keep on adding to the dining area. Wilber says he can seat "328 or 329, depending on how fat the 328th person is."

RATING: Still as good as we've ever had.

LOCATION: 4172 U.S. Highway 70 East; (919) 778–5218. (He now has two other locations around Goldsboro, but this is the one you want to visit.)

P.S. While you are in the neighborhood, you might want to try Parker's in nearby Wilson (25 miles away). There are plenty of people in the eastern part of the state who think Parker's is better than Wilber's. Of course, there are also a lot of folks who think Wilber's is better. We say: You can't go wrong with either one.

Parker's

When Parker's opened in 1946, it was an instant hit with the tobacco-warehouse folks, of whom there were many at the time. You don't have to close your eyes to imagine what it must have been like back then. Just look around at the waiters in paper hats.

PORKLORE

The Case of the Saucy Thief

1957. Sometime after midnight. Scott's Famous Barbecue in Goldsboro, North Carolina. A neighbor spotted a thief climbing in the window and alerted police. But when officers arrived, nothing. No burglar, only a broken window. They were ready to leave when they heard a thud in the storeroom. They eased open the door and peered in. Two eyes were peering back. There, hunkered down in Scott's sauce barrel, was the burglar. He had almost evaded capture, but now he was stirring because he was very uncomfortable.

"He was in the hot sauce barrel," laughed Jim Scott, grandson of the restaurant's founder, "and that hot sauce is hot. It'll blister your hands if you work in it very long without rubber gloves." Police rolled the man out of the barrel and carted him downtown to spend the night in jail. The next morning owner Martell Scott dropped by. He wasn't going to press charges, he said. He asked only that his broken window be replaced. The man was released. There was no prosecution. But the crime didn't go unpunished. Police handed out their own, albeit unintentional, punishment. All night they refused to let the barbecue burglar shower. He spent his night in jail marinating in Scott's Famous Hot Barbecue Sauce.

This joint is as plain as your unmarried cousin, a simple lunchroom that specializes in pork barbecue. There's fried chicken and fried fish on the menu, but that's just so folks can eat here every day and get an occasional change of pace. You won't need one with barbecue this good: Real good. Parker's is located at 2514 Highway 301 South in Wilson; (252) 237-0972.

New Bern

Moore's Olde Tyme Barbecue

Why are so many barbecue places Down East converting from wood to gas? Tom Moore, the manager of Moore's and son of the founder, offers some insight and some hard figures. It's a dollar decision. "We cook lots of meat two or three times a week rather than a little bit every day," says Tom. "That's because the wood's so expensive." The reason Moore's holds out for wood is because Tom thinks it's worth it. "The secret to cooking barbecue is using live oak coals."

It was a lot simpler when Tom's dad, Big John Moore, first got into the barbecue business in 1945. "Dad borrowed $35 to buy a pig and got someone to cook it," says Tom. "When he sold the barbecue, he paid off the cook and bought another pig." Big John kept plowing his profits back into his business until he was able to open a small restaurant in a converted filling station. Over the next three decades Moore's moved from place to place, finally settling into its current location in 1972. It's nothing fancy, a brick building with an order counter in the center and dining rooms on each side.

It's all self-serve: You order at the counter, grab your drink out of a case by the door, and carry your food to one of the long family-style tables. "There's no table service and no tips," says Tom. "That's so you can have a good meal for under $3.00."

The specialty of the house is the chopped pork sandwich, lightly seasoned with a Down East–style sauce. "We don't use ketchup because it has a distinct flavor of its own," says Tom. "These are all flavor enhancers. And we use red pepper instead of black because it's not as hot and it's digestible. Black pepper isn't digestible."

It is a memorable meal, and that's the way founder Big John Moore wants it to be. Big John, who got his nickname because he was 5-foot-10 and 220 pounds, told us twenty years ago, "I like to tell my customers, 'When you think of a pig, think of me.' That way they remember me and my barbecue." Big John died in 1989, but to commemorate him and his cooking methods, still in use after all these years, they have tweaked the joint's name. It's now Moore's Olde Tyme Barbecue.

RATING: Still real good.
LOCATION: Highway 17 South; (252) 638–3937.
WEB SITE: www.ncbbq.com

North Carolina: West

Lexington

There's a sign on the road into Owensboro, Kentucky, proclaiming the town as the "Barbecue Capital of America." But wait. Memphis claims the same title for itself. As does Kansas City. And the entire state of Texas.

They are all great places to eat great barbecue. But when it comes to the title of Barbecue Capital of America, there is really only one choice: Lexington, North Carolina. Sure it has only twenty-one barbecue joints (Memphis and Kansas City each have more than a hundred; Texas must have a thousand), but it also has only 19,953 residents. That's one barbecue joint for every 950 residents for those who don't do math. No place else is even close.

Hog Wild

The winner of the 1984 Cheer-Off at the Lexington Barbecue Festival, Lexington Senior High, won out over four other squads with this cheer:

> Get pork, big bones and ribs,
> Get extra lean,
> Lexington's home barbecue is really keen.
> So chow down everybody,
> Get in with the best,
> The barbecue from Lexington outshines the rest.
> Hey, outshines the rest.
> Are you ready to chow down?
> Yes, we are.

Lexington has a barbecue style so distinct that it derives its name from the town, and so pervasive that when people talk about western North Carolina barbecue, they are talking about the Lexington style: pork shoulder, pulled and chopped; smeared with a red sauce made from vinegar, pepper, salt, sugar, and tomatoes; crowned with a red slaw made with the sauce; and served on a hot bun.

Why is barbecue so popular in this small town 20 miles south of Winston-Salem? "Tradition," says Wayne "Honey" Monk, owner of Lexington Barbecue. "It just got rooted so long ago. People here know what good barbecue is."

Lexington barbecue started in the late 1910s with Sid Weaver and Jesse

Swicegood, who began cooking under pitched tents in a vacant lot across from the courthouse. All of Lexington barbecue is descended from these two men and their disciples. "At first they only cooked when court was in session and they had a crowd in town," says Monk. Davidson County was farm country, and the farmers would come to town during "court week" to watch the goings-on and trade horse stories. By the mid-twenties the farmers were coming to town every Saturday, and Weaver and Swicegood and their tents were there to meet them. Soon factory workers and schoolkids were eating barbecue, and it became an all-week proposition. In the thirties health regulations forced Weaver and Swicegood to add tin sides to their tents. Swicegood trained Warner Stamey and Conrad Everart (the original owner of Lexington Barbecue); Weaver trained Alton Beck and J. B. Tarleton. Every current barbecue restaurant owner in Lexington was trained by one of these four or by someone who was.

We decided that this time out we would try to eat our way through Lexington in one day. To guide us we took along Vince's cousin's husband, Arnold. Who better to pig out with than a man named Arnold?

To ensure fairness for all, we didn't make out a list. We decided to let fate be our guide. We would drive into Lexington and stop at the first barbecue joint we found. From there we would wander around town, eating randomly. In addition to ensuring fairness, it also would give our stomachs an opportunity, however brief, to do a little digesting.

The short story of a long, long day—we started at 10:00 A.M.—is this: It can't be done. You can't eat your way through Lexington, North Carolina, the Barbecue Capital of America, in one day. Allow three. And stock up on Tums.

We began at Smokey Joe's. Because that was the first joint we chanced upon driving in from the north, where Arnold lives.

Smokey Joe's has much to recommend it, including Cheerwine, an indigenous North Carolina cherry-flavored soft drink, on the menu. The barbecue is chopped fine and topped with red slaw, like most barbecue

Barbecue Center

sandwiches in town. It is very good, but in Lexington "very good" isn't quite good enough.

We moved on. And on.

We were at barbecue joint number four for the day when Arnold finally had to ask. "How do you tell it apart? It all tastes great!"

That's when we explained: "Arnold, we are parsing the difference between a 9.5 and a 9.8. It may seem impossible, but stay with us."

He did, and that's when we hit the Barbecue Center, a downtown diner with cheery cherry-red booths and loud crimson-colored counter stools.

And that was when Arnold first caught on. "This really is great. This is better than any of the other places. The meat is tender, it has a great taste, and the sauce is great."

Arnold fell in love with Lexington barbecue, and the word *great*, at the Barbecue Center.

We moved on.

Cook's

Speedy's had the biggest sandwich. But not the best.

Jimmy's had the neatest decor, a green fifties drive-in, but not the neatest sandwich.

Whitley's was fun, and Smiley's was neat.

But it wasn't until we rolled into Cook's, an out-of-the-way rustic-style joint, that we found a place to equal the Barbecue Center in, to use Arnold's word, *greatness*.

Joint number ten on our tour, Tar Heel Q, distinguished itself with barbecue so fresh it oinked. We could see into the kitchen from our counter spot, and we watched as the cook pulled the shoulder off the fire, rolled it, pulled the meat, then chopped it and piled it on the bun.

It was after six, and we were feeling full of barbecue, but we knew we had to make one more stop. And we knew where it was. It's a regular stop on our trips through North Carolina. Last time we rated it tops in town. We wanted to make sure that Lexington Barbecue was still holding its reputation.

Tar Heel Q

If you really want to sound like a native, call it "Honey Monk's." That was its original name. Honey was owner Wayne Monk's nickname. Monk is a barbecue purist. "We do everything basically the same way I was taught years ago." Monk is a descendant of the Swicegood School. He learned from Warner Stamey, who bought Swicegood's business in 1938. "When you start cutting corners, finding a faster way to do it, you're hurting yourself." That's why Lexington No. 1 doesn't switch to gas or electric cookers. That's why it doesn't make sauce in an eighty-gallon kettle. That's why it doesn't leave cabbage out of the refrigerator. "We make the sauce in small pots because we can control the quality better. And if you let cabbage sit out, you get an acid taste in your slaw." Lexington's sauce, which Monk

Lexington Barbecue

sells in the restaurant under the Smokehouse label, is Lexington-style sauce in its purest form: vinegar-thin, with peppers for sizzle and ketchup and sugar to temper the spices and hold down the lawsuits. The Hot & Tangy version puts out more heat than a trailer fire.

After eating barbecue all day we were still compelled to down the entire sandwich at Lexington Barbecue—it's that good. We always dine incognito, but at the end we sometimes lift our veil. When we finished, we asked our waitress if Wayne was around. "He's back in the kitchen," she replied. After all these years, Wayne still keeps his finger in the saucepot.

Like Swicegood and Stamey before him, Monk is training his descendants and competitors. "I don't know how many have left here and gone into business." No matter how many leave and open up competing restaurants, Monk says, it doesn't make any difference. His business just keeps on growing. "I'm serving about all I can cook. They moved my interstate on me. I lost the tourists but picked up local business. The only thing that affects my business is ice on the road." Neither rain nor snow nor dark of night keeps the locals from turning into Honey Monk's. Just ice. That's quite a compliment from the barbecue connoisseurs of Lexington, North Carolina. Frankly, if we lived in Lexington, we'd try to make it through the ice, too.

LEXINGTON BARBECUE RATING: As good as we've ever had.
LOCATION: 10 Highway 29-70 South; (336) 249-9814.

COOK'S BARBECUE RATING: Real good.
LOCATION: 366 Valiant Drive; (336) 798-1928.

THE BARBECUE CENTER RATING: Real good.
LOCATION: 900 North Main Street; (336) 248-4633.

TAR HEEL Q RATING: Real good.
LOCATION: 6835 West U.S. Highway 64; (336) 787-4550.

PORKLORE

Big Pig

The grand marshal of the 1986 Lexington Barbecue Festival Parade was Norma Jean, a two-year-old, 600-pound, housebroken Duroc pig, who lived in a room in the home of Dr. and Mrs. Norman Sattler of Lumberton, North Carolina. Norma Jean got so large by pigging out on her favorite foods, Godiva chocolates and champagne.

Short Sugar's Pit Bar-B-Q

Reidsville

Short Sugar's Pit Bar-B-Q

"If they were to film a remake of *American Graffiti,* this would be the place to film it," says Reidsville native Roger Carter. "It hasn't changed since I was a teenager in the fifties." That was fifty years ago. When we revisited in the summer of 2006, it *still* hadn't changed. But that's a good thing with barbecue this good.

Short Sugar's, which opened the summer of 1949, is still in the same location; it's still a drive-in, and it still has curb service. There is even a curb boy who looks old enough to have started there when the place opened.

When Short Sugar's opened its doors and parking lot in '49, Reidsville's teenagers quickly descended. It was soon the teen hangout. It was also a teen hangout parents could approve of. "Johnny wouldn't sell alcohol and wouldn't open on Sunday," says Mrs. Biddie Overby, widow of one of the cofounders. "He said, 'If you can't make a living in six days, you'd better quit.' He also said, 'If I don't want to go to church myself, I don't want to keep anyone else from going.'"

Short Sugar's got its odd name from Johnny's late brother, Eldridge. They were originally going to call the place the Overby Brothers Drive-In, named for Johnny, Eldridge, and Clyde Overby, who had decided they wanted to open a pit-barbecue restaurant. But in June 1949, two days before the grand opening, thirty-four-year-old Eldridge was killed in a car wreck. So the two surviving brothers decided to honor Eldridge and name it after him. Eldridge's nickname had been Short Sugar. There are varying tales about how he acquired such a moniker. One thing all the stories agree on is that he was short. They diverge on the "Sugar" part. It was either because of his infectious laugh or because of his reputation as a ladies' man or because he wasn't a ladies' man and the ladies liked to tease him: "Come on, Short, come on, sugar."

Short Sugar's has expanded a bit over the years. But the place still has the look of the fifties. And Carter says the sandwiches they make are just the way he remembers them from the fifties. Mrs. Overby credits that consistency to "the sauce and the care we take cooking the meat." The sauce is the same one created by Johnny Overby in 1949. It's a thin concoction, about the color and consistency of prune juice, but with considerably more firepower (and without the aftereffect). The recipe is still known only to Biddie and one of her daughters, but we can tell you it has that undeniable Lexington-style taste, an immediate blast of vinegar with a lingering sweetness, kind of like dipping a dill pickle in ketchup.

There's no hiding the care they take in cooking the meat. The pit is in plain view behind the counter. They serve their barbecue chopped, sliced, or minced; heaped on a Merita bun; seasoned with the thin vinegar-and-ketchup sauce and topped with slaw. And for an after-sandwich treat there's an out-of-this-world lemon pie with vanilla-wafer crust.

Reidsville is off the beaten interstate path, but that hasn't prevented Short Sugar's from getting the recognition it deserves. In 1982 it was the winner in a Congressional barbecue contest. And people from all over make the detour to get some of Short Sugar's barbecue. David Wilson, a son-in-law of Johnny Overby and one of the current owners, says the most famous customer is probably Lash LaRue, the old cowboy, who whipped by on occasion. Or did before he rode off into that sauce-colored sunset in 1995.

But the most unusual customer came by a few years ago. A hearse led a funeral procession in for curb service. Everyone inside bolted to the windows to see what was going on. "Did someone die from the barbecue?" a prankster asked. "Maybe it was his last request: He wanted to take some with him," another quipped. That wasn't it. Nor was it a barbecue-famished hearse driver stopping in for a quick sandwich before the trip to the cemetery. It was the twenty-year reunion of the local high school class. The teenagers of Reidsville can't get Short Sugar's out of their system, no matter how old they get.

RATING: Real good.
LOCATION: 1328 South Scales Street; (336) 349-9128.

Shelby

Bridge's Barbecue Lodge

The most impressive woodpile in America belongs to Bridge's Barbecue Lodge, a place that really does look like its name. The place's neatly stacked hickory wood stretches for what seems like as far as the eye can see, particularly if you are like us and are nearsighted. It's a good 50 yards from one end to the other, and it's clearly visible when you park and stroll in. It's better than a billboard in our nearsighted eyes. The woodpile isn't just for show. Bridge's cooks all night over hickory mixed with oak.

The inside more closely resembles a roadhouse with plenty of booths around the edges.

(Above) The giant woodpile at Bridge's
(Below) The interior of Bridge's Barbecue Lodge

Bridge's chops its meat the western Carolina way, with a few chunks left in, so you know you're eating barbecue. The sauce is a tad darker and thicker than other Piedmont-style joints.

Bridge's Barbecue Lodge was founded by Red Bridges, a disciple of Warner Stamey up in Lexington. Alston Bridges—no relation—has a competing barbecue place just across town. It's not as much to look at, but the barbecue is the equal of Red's. Flip a coin.

RATING: Real good.

LOCATION: Bridge's Barbecue Lodge is at 2000 East Dixon Boulevard; (704) 482-8567. Alston Bridges is at 620 East Grover Street; (704) 482-1998.

Cleveland

Keaton's Barbecue

With the closing of Hook's Barbecue in Milledgeville, Georgia, Keaton's inherits the title of most out-of-the-way barbecue joint in America. Don't go looking for Cleveland. In our experience it doesn't exist. It isn't even a wide spot in the road, just a mythical address. Fortunately, there are good signs to direct you off nearby Interstate 40.

But Keaton's would be worth the trip if you got lost. It offers what we consider the perfect barbecue meal: a scrumptious pork sandwich accompanied by a Nehi Orange in a glass bottle and a Blueberry Yum Yum. You don't even have to know what a Blueberry Yum Yum is to know you want one. It's a graham cracker crust filled with cream cheese and topped with blueberries. Yum yum.

And it doesn't get any better than a soft drink in a glass bottle. We don't mind paying twice as much for half as much drink if it's in glass. A Nehi in a plastic bottle doesn't seem as cold as it does in a glass bottle. Nehi in a can doesn't taste the same. And Nehi in a cup with ice gets watered down too quickly. For our taste, and taste buds, you can't beat a

Keaton's Barbecue

Nehi Orange in a glass bottle. Maybe it's just in our head, but that's where our taste buds are, too.

We think of Keaton's as a reformed roadhouse. One sign on the wall asks PLEASE KEEP NOISE AT A MINIMUM LEVEL—ABSOLUTELY NO PROFANITY, and another sign warns NO WEAPONS ALLOWED UNLESS YOU SHOW PROPER DOCUMENTS FROM LOCAL SHERIFF.

That said, the place still sells beer.

But the barbecue is what you'll want. It has a strong, tart flavor—definitely not for wusses. But you won't be able to put it down. Except for an occasional long swig from your Nehi.

Keaton's was founded by B. W. Keaton and his brother Bud in 1953, and it's still in the family; it's run by B. W.'s daughter, Mrs. Kathleen Murray.

The day we visited she was working the cash register. "The help didn't show up," she sighed. Well the front help didn't show up. But her regular cook did, and in addition to cooking this day he was assigned to deliver trays to the table. "Be kind," said Mrs. Murray. "He doesn't know what he's doing."

He did just fine carrying out our tray. And he obviously knew what he was doing when he cooked the barbecue.

RATING: Real good.

LOCATION: The signs say Cleveland, but the mailing address is Statesville. For a mapping program use this address: 17365 Cool Springs Road, Cleveland, North Carolina. Or call (704) 278-1619. It's just north of Charlotte and well signed.

WEB SITE: www.keatonsoriginalbbq.com

PORKLORE

The Big Fix

Only in that other Cleveland—Cleveland, Ohio—would a barbecue cook-off contestant claim the fix was on. That's what Calhoun's, a Knoxville restaurant, did in 1985 when it failed in its bid to repeat as national champion. Michael Chase, owner of Calhoun's, had a bone to pick with contest organizer Gary Jacob. Chase charged that Jacob, who also tabulated the ballots, had worked as a consultant to the winner prior to the event and that one of the thirty judges was negotiating a limited partnership with the winner. Both charges were true, but Jacob said neither affected the final results. Calhoun's threatened legal action. Jacob said that all the smoke had done was give him a bad reputation. "People think I'm the Al Capone of ribs."

South Carolina

Holly Hill

Sweatman's Bar-B-Que

We've never met anyone who wasn't repulsed at the first sight of mustard-based barbecue sauce. "Yellow barbecue!" they exclaim. "Ugh!" Mustard-based sauce is a South Carolina phenomenon. In fact, it's a central South Carolina phenomenon, confined almost exclusively to a 65-mile radius of Columbia.

If you're ready to give yellow barbecue a toss, we suggest you start with the best. Years ago, H. O. "Bub" Sweatman served a bright yellow meat that was like nothing you've ever tasted, and his restaurant is still getting rave reviews from locals and out-of-towners alike. This is not ballpark mustard spread on pork. Bub's sauce is made from a century-old family recipe. The sugar, or honey, or whatever it is Bub put in it, cuts the mustard's natural pungency and meshes nicely with the pork's natural sweetness.

Truth in Barbecue

South Carolina's state legislature passed a Truth in Barbecue law in 1986, requiring barbecue restaurants to purchase a sticker that tells customers if they cook with wood or with something else, and if they cook whole hogs or part of but not the whole hog.

Years ago, Bub's wife, Margie, told us about this third-generation bar-becue man. "It's in his blood," she said. "And once it's in your blood, you can't get it out." He tried to get it out in the early seventies. He quit barbe-cuing and devoted full-time to farming his 2,500-acre spread. But by 1977 he was itching to get back to it. So he bought a dumpy old house and con-verted it into a weekend barbecue place and country restaurant. It still looks the part. The planks are weathered; the porch is swayed; the steps are worn. Out back you find the open pit, surrounded by a screen shed. They burn oak limbs down into coals, shovel them into the pit, and then cook whole hogs all night Thursday and all night Friday.

The buffet features two bins of meat, the first for what you might call regular barbecue, big white chunks of creamy pork, and the second for "close to the fire" meat, browner with sauce baked in. The locals prefer the second. You should, too.

Bub, being of farmer stock, was a practical man. He wanted to offer value. But he also wanted to clear a little profit. He changed his original all-you-can-eat buffet policy. Sweatman's became an all-you-can-eat-from-one-plate restaurant. There was even a hand-lettered sign to remind: TAKE WHAT YOU WANT, BUT EAT WHAT YOU TAKE. LET'S KEEP FOOD PRICES DOWN.

RATING: As good as we've ever had.

LOCATION: Take U.S. Highway 176 to South Carolina Highway 453. It's about 3½ miles down on the right, surrounded by ancient oak trees and an expansive field. If you get lost, call them at (803) 492–7543. If you're coming from the other direction . . . aw, don't come from the other direction. It's too much trouble to direct you that way. It's open Friday and Saturday only.

Kingstree

Brown's Bar-B-Que

Our friend Boots Duke—and isn't that a wonderful name?—first intro-

Brown's Bar-B-Que

duced us to Brown's. Boots has a house at the beach, and he discovered Brown's on his way down when he stopped to get gas in Kingstree. (We know there's an opportunity for an eat-here-and-get-gas joke here, but we pass because you won't get gas at Brown's.)

Boots fell in love, and next time we saw him he was still raving, insisting on having some shipped to us. And insisting. Normally we resist having someone overnight us barbecue because overnight barbecue is another name for day-old barbecue. We relented, and the next day at lunch we gritted our teeth and prepared to play nice. We bit in and—wow—it was wonderful, day-old be damned.

We've been fans ever since.

Brown's didn't make the first edition of this book because Tommy Brown hadn't yet given up farming for a higher calling. He was still cooking for friends on weekends, delighting them and enjoying himself. That was almost twenty years ago. Now he's at the top of our barbecue chart with his tender chopped pork and tart spicy vinegar sauce. Around these parts they call Brown's Peedee style, after the nearby Peedee River. Drive an hour north into North Carolina, and they call it Down East style.

Last time we stopped in—and we route all our easterly trips through Kingstree—Tommy's wife, Angie, was out because she was delivering their first child. That's good news for the Browns and for us. It means there's a new generation to keep the place going. We hope forever.

RATING: As good as we've ever had.

LOCATION: 809 North Williamsburg County Highway; (843) 382–2753.

West Columbia

Maurice's Piggy Park

One look at Maurice's Piggy Park might convince you that the B.B. in B.B.Q. stands for Big Business. Maurice's Piggy Park is Big Business, and Maurice Bessinger is the Colonel Sanders of Barbecue. Our first time out Maurice had two locations. Now you can't drive through Columbia without seeing one of his ubiquitous billboards. We swear he has a joint at every interstate exit.

And that's a good thing.

Piggy Park is success porcine-ified. The parking lot is full. The line is long. The service is fast. If it weren't for that smoky smell, you would swear you were in a McDonalds. Everything says Fast-Food Chain, and it is fast. But it isn't a chain. It is just successful, and we don't believe in penalizing success. We know that barbecue snobs sniff at nice places, wondering if perhaps the owner isn't spending more time on the books than on the barbecue. But facts are facts: If you beget a better barbecue sandwich, people are going to beat a path to your door. Why not pave the path?

That's what Maurice has done. He has branched out and expanded and remodeled. But he still takes care of business, barbecue, letting whole hogs smolder for eighteen to twenty-four hours over hickory coals. When the meat is done, his workers pull it, chop it, and then coat it with Mau-

Barbecue Insults

"Somehow during that great human migration that flooded south after Jamestown . . . Georgians, an otherwise agreeable race, simply never mastered the art of barbecuing a pig like their cousins from North Carolina. It may have been that all that hard journeying, coupled with the assorted perils of passing through South Carolina, caused them simply to forget the procedure by the time they got down here. Maybe as a people they were just forgetful."

—Jim Dodson, native North Carolinian

rice's "million-dollar secret sauce." It's a thick, ocher-colored sauce, definitely made from the bitter center of a mustard seed, but cut with sugar that makes it as sweet as iced tea.

If you want to try some, you can. Maurice packages what he calls "gourmet microwave barbecue," which sounds like somebody's idea of a bad joke, but it tastes absolutely delicious. All you need is a charge card and a phone or an Internet connection. Federal Express will deliver it to your door tomorrow morning. Call before midnight, so you won't forget.

For a time you could even find Maurice's trademark Carolina Gold Barbecue Sauce in your local grocery store. No more. Almost all of the large chains, including Bi-Lo, Winn-Dixie, Food Lion, and Wal-Mart, have decided the popular mustard-based sauce is too hot to handle. And it has nothing to do with the spices. It's political correctness, according to Maurice. When the Confederate flag was moved from the South Carolina Capitol building a few summers ago, Bessinger demonstrated his colors by unfurling an enormous Confederate flag over his company headquarters and moving the smaller American flag to a less conspicuous spot. Grocery chains, which don't court controversy, removed his sauce and frozen packages of his barbecue pork from their shelves. Maurice's sauce had been available in more than 2,000 stores. It's now sold only in a handful of independent groceries. Bessinger complained to the *Atlanta Journal-Constitution*, "Winn-Dixie is going to have to take that name off and call it Winn-Yankee."

RATING: Real good.

LOCATION: The original with the giant Flying Pig sign is at 1600 Charleston Highway; (803) 796–0220.

WEB SITE: www.mauricesbbq.com

Spartanburg

Beacon Drive-In

There used to be a billboard in Palm Springs, California, that read, YOU ARE ONLY 2,300 MILES FROM THE FAMOUS BEACON DRIVE IN, SPARTANBURG, S.C. And when we would see it, we would speed up. We could hear the Beacon's ringmaster, J. C. Strobel, urging us to "Move, move, move."

It's a fine line between obnoxious and humorous, and J. C. Strobel straddles that line every day as he runs the cafeteria at the Beacon, something he's been doing for half a century. When the column of customers gets slow, J. C. gets quick. "Next, next, next," he barks at the bewildered tourist. "Let's move on. Come on, come on, come on, down the line." You are standing there feeling insulted and wondering if J. C. even heard your order, when suddenly he cocks his head sideways, turns, and spits, "Hey Fred! Three outsides, two slices, five cheese, two with slaw, two chili cheese with, two without, three burgers with, one without, hash aplenty." And before you know it, he is handing you a plate that holds your order, right down to a tee.

J. C. may be the Eighth Wonder of the World, the human collator. He'll store about twenty orders in his head, sort by categories, then output them in one breath and turn back to the line, ready for more. "Let's move on, next, next, next." J. C. doesn't own the Beacon, but for regulars he is the Beacon. John White is the owner. White opened his first Beacon in 1947, three buildings ago. "We wore those other places out," he says. J. C. is the Beacon's Confucius. There are little hand-lettered "J. C. says" signs tacked on every bare spot. J. C. SAYS: IT'S FINE TO PASS IN LINE. J. C. SAYS: LET'S MOVE ON. J. C. SAYS: LET'S DON'T BOOGIE JIVE, LET'S MERCHANDISE. J. C. seems to have a one-track philosophy.

The Beacon is a drive-in of the old school: the longer the menu, the better. There are sixty-six different sandwiches, twenty-four side dishes, thirty-one plates, fifteen desserts. When J. C. says, "Chili-cheese," he wants a cheeseburger with chili on top. "With or without" is with or without bacon. "Pork-a-plenty" is a sliced pork sandwich with french fries and onion rings (which are cooked with the skin on). But the item that gets top billing on the menu, and deservedly, is the barbecue. You can order regular ("Slice"), the crunchy crust ("Outside"), or Beef Slice. It all comes the same way: mountains of meat overflowing a softball-size bun and smothered in a tart tomato-vinegar sauce.

Yes, J. C. can be obnoxious. But when you are trying to stampede 12,000 people through a cafeteria, which is how many the Beacon serves on an average Saturday night, you have to keep them moving, moving, moving; next, next, next.

And yes, we know that the Beacon is a drive-in first and a barbecue joint second. We don't care.

RATING: Real good.

LOCATION: 255 Reidsville Road; (805) 585–9387. On Easter the Beacon's sunrise service annually draws 5,000 to the parking lot. (There's free watermelon afterwards.)

Virginia

Fredericksburg

Allman's Pit Cooked Bar-B-Q

It was music to a barbecue lover's ears. We placed our order with the youthful waiter at Allman's, then listened as he called it out to the kitchen: "Mom, a minced with slaw."

Mom, a minced with slaw! Mom's in the kitchen.

That's actually a little misleading. The Mom in the kitchen wasn't our waiter's mom. It was Mary "Mom" Brown. But that makes it even better than a family joint. You see, Mom has been in the kitchen at Allman's since the sixties. Allman's had only been open six years when she set up shop. She still does the slicing and the mincing and makes the sauce and the slaw by hand. And it's a wonderful sauce and a wonderful slaw. The sauce is sweet and vinegary at the same time, the way we like it. The slaw is creamy and crunchy, a perfect match to give texture to the meat.

PORKLORE

First Barbecue

The first mention of the word *barbecue* in this country was in the Acts of the Virginia Burgesses in 1610, according to Jerry Simpson, who spent a summer researching it. The Burgesses passed a law "forbidding the shooting of firearms for sport at barbecues, else how shall we know when the Indians are coming."

There are folks in New York and California spending millions to try and re-create the ambience that accidentally flows out of Allman's: a dumpy little brick building, tables scattered around, a sticky counter for the regulars who come by themselves. If Mary "Mom" Brown could bottle this atmosphere, she could make several millions selling it to the restaurant hopefuls out in the barbecue wilderness.

RATING: Real good.
LOCATION: 1299 Jeff Davis Highway; (540) 373–9881.

Lightfoot

Pierce's Pitt Bar-B-Que

Let's say you take our advice and decide to give Pierce's barbecue a try. And let's say you are heading down Interstate 64 when you realize you've lost the directions. Never fear. You won't have any trouble spotting Pierce's. It's the only barbecue joint we've seen that's painted like a beach umbrella. "We call it U-Haul orange and Ryder yellow," J. C. Pierce, son of the founder and manager, told us. "They're our trademark colors." Those traffic-stopping colors and the enticing aroma from Pierce's hickory-fired open pit have cost many a trucker $75. You see, for years there wasn't a nearby exit. So truckers and state legislators alike would park on the interstate shoulder and jump the fence. J. C. remembered one little old lady who got her dress caught on the barbed wire, got a ticket, and still tried to get over the fence. "The policeman told her to move her car, but she refused. 'If I have to pay a $75 fine,' she said, 'I'm at least going to eat. Go ahead and tow the car!'"

Pierce's opened in October 1971 as a take-out joint. It was just a little 10-by-14-foot shack that Doc Pierce, J. C.'s father, had constructed in the middle of a vacant field. "We had a guy painting our sign for us, and we noticed he was misspelling the word *pit*. When we went to correct him, he said, 'If you don't like the way I spell, you can do it yourself.'" The Pierces decided they liked the unusual spelling—*pitt*—and had their restaurant name trademarked that way. Doc Pierce turned the business over to J. C. back in '81 after quadruple bypass heart surgery, but that didn't keep him from traipsing in and out every day till his death in 1991.

Pierce's hasn't changed its cooking method the entire time it has been in business. The butts are roasted slowly on an open pit in a building 20 yards behind the restaurant. They use mostly hickory, with a little oak mixed in. The meat is cooked for eight hours, then pulled from the bone by hand, cut in small chunks, and variegated in Pierce's spicy tomato-based sauce. J. C. promised that Pierce's would always cook with wood, even if it takes longer and costs more. "Dad used to say, 'The difference between cooking over a pit and cooking on a gas cooker is like the difference between homemade biscuits and canned biscuits.'"

RATING: Real good.
LOCATION: 137 Rochambeau Drive; (757) 565-2955.

Leesburg

Mighty Midget Kitchen

What the Mighty Midget lacks in size—and it is easily the smallest barbecue joint in America—it makes up in taste.

There's a reason for the Kitchen's midget size: It was forged from the fuselage of an old B-29 bomber. Yeah, the B-29 was a big airplane, but it gets a lot smaller when you slice off the nose cone and turn it on end. There's just enough room in the Midget's midget kitchen for a deep fryer, a grill, a refrigerator, and two cooks.

The Mighty Midget Kitchen first opened in 1947, serving diner food, burgers mostly. It was one of a couple dozen fun-looking restaurants created from mothballed wartime airplane bodies. The Kitchen was cooking right along until the early nineties when through an odd series of machinations it became the property of the city of Leesburg. But the city didn't really want to be in the restaurant business. "We're a service provider, but burgers is kind of pushing it," the deputy town manager told the local newspaper in 1994. That's when the old jet cone was sold and moved to its current location on the side deck of a kitchen-design shop.

The good news for barbecue fans is that they don't try to cook the 'que inside that midget kitchen. There's a 10-foot custom pit parked nearby for that.

The miniature size doesn't yield a miniature menu. The Midget serves all the barbecue usuals—pulled pork, smoked chicken, ribs on the weekend— but also old Midget favorites, burgers and fries. The pork sandwich is no midget; it's big and meaty, with a mighty smoky flavor.

RATING: Real good.

LOCATION: 202 Harrison Street Southeast, across from Tuscarora Mill; (703) 777-6406.

WEB SITE: www.mightymidgetkitchen.com

Tennessee

Bluff City

The Ridgewood

There's an old saying that the more things change, the more they remain the same. Perhaps no barbecue restaurant in this book has changed more since the first edition and yet has remained the same. The most important thing that has remained the same is the barbecue. But so much else is different.

Let's start with the location. It has remained the same, yet it's changed. They built a new highway from Bluff City to Elizabethton, bypassing the Ridgewood. So it's the same road, but it's different; it's no longer the main road.

The building, a long concrete diner, is the same—but it, too, is different. There's now an indoor waiting area (no more standing in the hot sun) and indoor bathrooms (no more hiking around the building in cold weather to an unheated john).

But the biggest change at the Ridgewood is in attitude.

Last time we stopped in, the Ridgewood was run with an iron hand by founder Grace Proffitt. Mrs. Proffitt, as everyone called her, died in March 2003 at age eighty-five, and the new generation of family running the place is more, what shall we call it, service oriented.

Take closing time. Two decades ago it was, for reasons known only to Mrs. Proffitt, 8:25 P.M., and this time was strictly enforced. That night twenty years ago when we pulled into the Ridgewood parking lot, our barbecue guide Bruce Haney warned, "Turn off your headlights. If Mrs. Proffitt sees those lights, she's liable to run and lock the door." Bruce explained that his wife would no longer patronize the place after a closing-time incident. "One night we stood in line for an hour, waiting to get in. It was hot. She was fussing with our year-old baby the whole time. And when we finally got up to the door, Mrs. Proffitt shut it in our faces, said she'd served all she was going to that night." That wouldn't happen today. For one thing there's the new air-conditioned waiting area. And for another the faces are friendly, not scowling. Closing time is a more logical 8:30 (7:30 on school nights).

We heard another tale of Ridgewood rudeness back then: Eight executives from nearby Tennessee Eastman Corporation had stopped in before heading to the airport 8 miles away. Four of them got there first, and the waitress seated them. When the other bunch arrived, Mrs. Proffitt put them at a table on the other side of the room even though it was early and there wasn't anybody else in the place. She left, and they got up and moved a couple of tables so they could all sit together. They waited. And they waited. And the waitress never came. Finally they looked over by the door and there was Mrs. Proffitt, arms crossed and tapping her foot. She told them, "When you'uns get in the seats I set you in, I'll serve you."

Bruce called the Ridgewood "the Don Rickles Restaurant." We

checked with him again, and he said he no longer hears stories like that. "And I miss them."

Despite the additions, or perhaps because of them, the Ridgewood has the look of something built in the days before planning commissions, a diner that has sprouted wings. You no longer have to go outside to get to the restrooms, but there's still an obstacle: You have to walk through the fog of the smoking section.

The Ridgewood has been serving up barbecue since 1948, when Mrs. Proffitt turned a lemon into lemonade. Her husband, James, had decided to open a beer joint on the Elizabethton highway below their house. He got a cement-block building up and was ready to open when voters in Carter County approved a measure to go "dry"—that is, prohibit the sale of alcoholic beverages. He remembered watching some fellows smoke fish while on vacation in Florida, designed his own smokehouse, and, poof, like smoke, a beer joint became a barbecue joint.

We remembered the heavenly pork sandwiches from our first visit, so we ordered one again with Mrs. Proffitt's barbecue beans on the side. The sandwiches are still a skyscraper of meat four layers thick, piled on a plump Kern's bun and ladled with enough sauce to drown a small dog. Last time Bruce had noted, "They have some very definite ideas about how much sauce to put on it. You will notice there are no sauce dispensers on the table." That's changed, too. There are now squeeze bottles of sauce on the tables. But it's the same lovely sauce, thick and tangy, spicy but not dangerously so, about a 5 on a 1–10 hotness scale. The beans were out of this world. There seemed to be a pound of lean meat cooked in with them.

The more things have changed at the Ridgewood, the more they have remained the same. But that's good.

RATING: Real good.

LOCATION: 900 Old Elizabethton Highway; (423) 538-7543. One more change: The area code has gone from 615 to 423.

P.S. If the Ridgewood's waiting area is packed, and it often is, you can head up the new highway, 19E, toward Elizabethton a half mile to Mrs. Proffitt's longtime competitor, chief rival, and one-time partner, Pardner's. If you detect a similarity, that's no coincidence. You see, J. Paul Bare, who started Pardner's, was Mrs. Proffitt's partner before heading out on his own. There's a real story there: a no-compete clause, a lawsuit, and . . . well, let someone at Pardner's tell you. There are people in east Tennessee who swear Pardner's barbecue is better, that the Ridgewood is resting on its laurels while Pardner's is trying to build its reputation. We disagree but respect the rights of those who think that.

While you're in the area, you might as well head over to Kingsport to see the world's only barbecue joint with an entrance guarded by a 33-foot-tall concrete Indian. The Big Indian, as he is known locally, sits out front of Pratt's Barbecue Barn at 1225 East Stone Drive; (423) 246–2500. He was once the conversation piece at a local souvenir shop. Bruce Haney says, "He may be inappropriate at Pratt's, but he sure makes giving directions a lot easier."

PORKLORE

How Do You Eat a Rib Sandwich?

Everybody knows how to eat ribs, but what do you do when you first encounter a rib sandwich, a menu item favored at many urban barbecue stands? These directions were courtesy of the Raineshaven Barbecue in Memphis, Tennessee: "First you take off the top piece of bread. Then you separate the ribs and take 'em one at a time in your hand. You run the rib this way and then back this way, sort of like eating corn on the cob. Then you go for the slaw. And you use the bread to sop up whatever is left over."

Knoxville

M&M Bar-B-Que

The rain was pouring as freely as sweet tea at an all-for-one-price buffet when we stopped at M&M Bar-B-Que, a cement-block stand located in the parking lot of the Maytag Laundry Center.

"We'll go to Noah's next," quipped Dr. LaFong, our Knoxville barbecue guide. Readers of the first edition of this book may recall that Dr. LaFong was our tour guide in Atlanta two decades ago. He returned to his hometown in 1995 and consented to lead us on our barbecue foray once again. It was a much shorter tour in Knoxville, which doesn't have near the number of barbecue joints of Atlanta.

Our drenched tour was coming to an inglorious conclusion (the four previous joints all matched the weather—not so hot) when we drove up to M&M. And things perked up.

Stan the Trigger Man was dancing in the rain. Stan Martin, who does the cooking for his cousins Precy and Natalie Martin (the M and M of M&M), was undeterred by the record rain (5 inches over eight hours, the heaviest downfall since before the first edition of this book). The clouds didn't dampen his outlook. He did a couple of steps of the hustle as he checked on the chicken. We hadn't announced ourselves or anything, just gave Stan a nod, and he offered us a half chicken hot off the grill. Or grills. M&M employs six cookers of assorted sizes scattered around the side lot.

"Try this . . . on me," Stan insisted. "You'll like it." We did and we did.

M&M is a wood-burning operation, and Dr. LaFong said that if it weren't for the rain, we would have been able to smell the barbecue several blocks up Middlebrook Pike.

Normally LaFong eats his 'que here on the concrete picnic table, but with the rain beating down, he beat a retreat into the Laundromat, and we shared a sandwich over a laundry-folding table. The smoke flavor overpowered the scent of fabric softener, and the meat was pull-apart good with a

Vince Staten and Stan "the Trigger Man" at M&M Bar-B-Que

sweet sauce that brightened up the kind of day that only a Tennessee River carp would like.

LaFong proclaimed that M&M was a worthy successor to Knoxville's longtime barbecue king, Brother Jack's. Brother Jack operated a stand near the University of Tennessee campus for almost fifty years, starting in 1947 and closing in '95. LaFong remembered how it was at Brother Jack's when he was a UT student in the mid-sixties. "Sometimes we'd take dates with us. Not only would the girls not go inside, they wouldn't even wait in the car for us. They insisted we give them the keys so they could drive around."

M&M is in a bright commercial area in west Knoxville. If Dr. LaFong could get a date, she most certainly wouldn't make him give her the keys to the car here.

Brother Jack's had a sawdust floor—honest—and a number of intriguing hand-lettered signs: NO SPITTING ON FLOOR. NO COMBING HAIR IN KITCHEN. NO PLAYING CARDS AND CUSSING. SING, BROTHER JACK. (*Sing* was really *Sign,* but Brother Jack made a typo when he was painting.)

M&M isn't that primitive—but it does have a dozen plastic coolers lined up outside in the parking lot, a nod to the fact that there isn't much storage space in their tiny building.

And to cement its reputation as Brother Jack's successor, M&M offers a hot sauce that is just as tasty and just as potent as Jack's. They don't use Brother Jack's trademark rhetorical question, "You want that hot, don't ya?" But if they did, the answer would be the same—"Yeah!"

RATING: Real good.

LOCATION: 7409 Middlebrook Pike; (865) 692–1003. At this writing, M&M is only open Thursday, Friday, and Saturday from early spring till late fall.

WEB SITE: www.m-mcatering.com

PORKLORE

Barbecue Insults

"They don't know what barbecue is in Cincinnati," said Cincinnati deejay Gary Burbank, a native of Memphis. "Some people here took me to this place they said had the best barbecue in the country, and the waitress brought me something that looked like it had grape jelly on it."

Greenbrier

Old Fashion Bar-B-Q

There's just a small sign in the front yard, one of those portable jobs like barbers use to let people know they're in. OLD FASHION BARBECUE OPEN, it reads. It's easy to miss it when you are barreling down U.S. Highway 431. The little sign gives no indication of what a treat the barbecue pilgrim has in store. Old Fashion Barbecue sells velvety chopped pork from an old metallic gray bread truck parked on blocks in the driveway of the ranch home owned by the Jones family. Richard Jones started the place. He learned the art of cooking barbecue years ago from Sam Chatman, an old church friend. Twenty years ago he told us, "I thought I had it. My friend would never tell me I had it, but he would leave me alone, so I figured I must have it." Jones knew he had it when his friend divulged his secret sauce recipe. "He was getting on in years, and he didn't want to die without someone having that recipe."

Jones had it. And he passed it along to his son-in-law, who still has it. Old Fashion's chopped pork sandwich is almost a half pound of tenderness, with a crisp vinegar flavor. A little fat woman, who was sitting in the driver's seat of the van while she waited for her order, said it best: "I used to go to that place in Springfield, but once I found this place, I quit them. His meat here is nice and moist, but it's not greasy."

Old Fashion is a weekend-only, take-out place. Jones liked it that way because, he said, "If I have to have people come in and sit down, I'd have to have two restrooms and follow a lot more rules. I'd just rather do it this way." His son-in-law still does it that way. The "old fashion" way.

RATING: As good as we've ever had.
LOCATION: 1784 Tom Austin Highway; (615) 384–5077. If you're coming from Springfield, it's about 8 miles south on Highway 431.

Hendersonville

Center Point Pit Barbecue Cafe

Twenty years ago, Dolly Loyd made us a list of all the country music stars who had frequented her barbecue cafe over the years. It read like a first draft of the Country Music Hall of Fame: Faron Young, Conway Twitty, George Jones, Alabama, Johnny Cash and June Carter, Slim Whitman, Billy Walker, Roy Orbison, String Bean, Tanya Tucker, Glenn Campbell, Ray Stevens, Ricky Skaggs, Little Jimmie Dickens, Bill Monroe, Red Foley, Tammy Wynette, Minnie Pearl, Jerry Reed, Bobby Bare, Roy Acuff, Waylon Jennings, Barbara Mandrell, the Louvin Brothers, Roger Miller, Willie Nelson, the Willis Brothers, Grandpa Jones, Jimmie Newman, Tom T. Hall, Lefty Frizzell, the Kendalls, the Oak Ridge Boys, Mel Tillis, Dolly Parton, Archie Campbell, Boots Randolph, Chet Atkins, and George Morgan. Whew!

Loyd had been a pork purveyor since 1965, when she and her late husband, Bill, opened Center Point. "Johnny Cash was one of my first customers," she said.

Over the years all these Hall of Famers and future Hall of Famers came in for one reason: Dolly's barbecue. Her chopped pork, oozing with a rich-tasting tomato-and-vinegar sauce, stood on its own. But when she served it on her corn bread pancakes, it was time to make reservations for the Barbecue Hall of Fame induction ceremonies.

Dolly has passed away, but the great barbecue, still cooked in the same way, is on the bill at owner Robert Duke's cafe.

RATING: Real good.
LOCATION: 1212 West Main Street; (615) 824–9330.

Lexington

B. E. Scott's Bar-B-Q

Of all the pitmasters we met researching the first edition, none was more serious about his barbecue than Early Scott. Mr. Scott was in his sixties at the time and already slowing down. He cooked only one night a week, on Wednesday, but when he cooked, he devoted his full attention to his barbecue. He would sleep on a cot next to the pit with a little alarm clock next to the bed to get him up every couple of hours to tend his pit.

It was a grueling method of cooking: burning hickory strips down to red-hot coals, spreading those coals evenly in the fire bed, then mopping the searing meat with a spicy vinegar varnish. There are easier ways to cook barbecue. But Early Scott didn't want to take the easy way out. Early Scott wasn't just an old-fashioned barbecue cook, he was an artist. And his was a dying art. In the sixties almost every barbecue joint cooked pretty much the same way, the Early Scott way, with patience and with pride. But ingenious manufacturers devised shortcuts: pressure cookers to cut the time, electric cookers to eliminate the smoke, gas cookers to keep the heat even. Scott rejected those shortcuts. He even grew all the vegetables he used in his sauce, mixing the sauce up in small batches so each would taste the same as the one before it.

Former Tennessee congressman Robin Beard, a longtime fan of Scott's barbecue, told us that Early once told him, "A man that won't sleep with his meat don't care about his barbecue." And that has become our credo when evaluating real barbecue: A man that won't sleep with his meat don't care about his barbecue.

But a quarter century of tending his pit the old-timey way was taking its toll, and shortly after our first edition was published, Early sold out to his longtime helper Ricky Parker. Early had told us as much the day we sat on his front porch and watched a string of cars swing through his parking lot on the off chance he might have some leftover meat. "Don't have any of that bobba-que?" each asked. He would wave and shake his head no.

Ricky has been a worthy successor to Early. He is just as serious as the master, often working 120 hours a week at his craft. (Yes, his marriage to barbecue cost him his marriage to his wife.)

Ricky carries on the old ways, cooking whole hogs for twenty to twenty-three hours over an open pit, covering the meat with pasteboard from old appliance cartons. When the hogs are done, Ricky, like Early before him, hand-pulls the meat and serves it just like that, on a plate or on a bun.

We've told the Scott's story over and over over the years, because we think his place is simply the best of the best. Once, after we told a friend the Scott's story, she asked, "So how's his barbecue?" Then she immediately withdrew the question. "What am I asking? Anybody who cooks like that has to make great barbecue."

Scott's still does. The pulled pork sandwich, hot off the grill, is so good it will make your eyes roll up in your head.

"It's a lot of trouble to cook this way," Scott told us. "A lot. Gas and electric are cheaper and not as big a mess, but it don't taste the same. It's not the same."

Ricky doesn't sleep with his meat, but he has an excuse: He doesn't sleep. He says he averages three hours a night during the week. So we give him a pass: He may not sleep with his meat, but he still cares about his barbecue.

RATING: As good as we've ever had.

LOCATION: 10880 Highway 412 West; (731) 968–0420. Ricky has installed a phone in the place, something Early always resisted. At the time of our first visit, Early's sister-in-law Tina told us, "He don't want to be bothered when he's cooking that barbecue."

PORKLORE

Is Barbecue Kosher?

"We are always allowed to eat porkfish," said Paul Skolnick, the only Jewish competitor at the 1987 Memphis International Barbecue Festival, where contestants are not allowed to cook any meat except pork.

Mason

Bozo's Hot Pit Bar-B-Q

Yeah, the name is Bozo's, and you're laughing, what does a clown know about barbecue? But no joke; the barbecue at Bozo's is serious stuff.

The original Bozo was Thomas "Bozo" Williams, who opened this joint in 1923. Then along came the clown, made famous originally on Chicago television and then licensed to local TV stations across the country in the sixties. Well, this TV bozo couldn't take a joke and actually dragged the real Bozo's into court, claiming the west Tennessee barbecue purveyor was infringing on his trademark.

In the end the joke was on Bozo the TV clown (real name: Larry Harmon) because he lost his suit. The U.S. Supreme Court—in only its second barbecue ruling (it also handed down a civil rights decision against the Birmingham barbecuer Ollie's)—ruled, rightly we think, that this Bozo was no bozo, that he had been using the name on a commercial enterprise long before there even was TV. So now Bozo's is free to practice its craft under its rightful name.

The current Bozo—and we mean that in a good way—is John Ozier, a local restaurateur who bought Bozo's from the Williams family in 1999 and has done much to preserve the legacy—although the locals aren't too happy that he switched to frozen fries.

Bozo's is still in the same unpretentious brick building it's occupied for fifty years, the one that looks like a highway patrol station from the forties.

And there are still two pits, the cook side and the warm side, one for, well, cooking, and the other for warming. Pork shoulders are still cooked for twelve hours (they are turned once, after seven hours), then refrigerated overnight, and warmed the next day for another two and a half hours before pulling and chopping. That job used to be in the expert hands of Mamie Taylor, who has passed away but devoted decades to the fine product at Bozo's. You can get your sandwich either white, brown, or mixed. The brown is the chewy outside part of the pig.

Bozo's may look like an old highway patrol building, but the barbecue is 10-4.

RATING: As good as we've ever had.

LOCATION: 342 Highway 70 West; (901) 294–3400.

Memphis

You could write a book about Memphis barbecue. In fact, Carolyn Wells did. It's called *Barbecue Greats Memphis Style* (Pig Out Publications), and it is great.

Memphis is one barbecue-crazy town. The Memphis Yellow Pages has a separate listing for "Barbecue," and there are eighty-eight restaurants listed. And many of the best barbecue places don't even know there is a separate listing for barbecue restaurants. (Some don't even have phones.)

We believe there's no such thing as a bad barbecue place in Memphis. Some are just more equal than others.

Memphis has two divergent barbecue traditions: the wet style and the dry style. Proponents of the wet style—let's adopt the style newspapers use when reporting on a mixed-drink referendum and call them the Wets—believe the secret is in the sauce. They prefer a rich-looking paste made by mixing equal parts tomato sauce and vinegar and then seasoning with onions, peppers, and anything else in the cabinet that looks spicy.

The Drys scoff at sauce on the finished product. "If it's cooked right, you don't need no sauce," said the late Lucious "The King" Newsom, who cut his teeth on Memphis rib bones. The Drys use a paprika rub on their meat before cooking, giving the finished rib a gritty crust.

When you take into account the meat debate—pork ribs versus pork sandwiches—you have four possible selections. Throw in the offbeat items, and the choice is endless. They'll barbecue anything in Memphis. Coletta's still serves a barbecue pizza. The old Brady and Lil's had barbecue spaghetti.

Memphis may have gotten more of our attention than any other barbecue hotbed. Vince is a native Tennessean, and he has been eating Memphis barbecue since his high school basketball team played in the state tournament there in 1965. In addition, we have made untold pilgrimages to Memphis over the years, checking out the latest barbecue discovery. Memphis barbecue fanatics, and this seems to be anybody in Memphis who still has his teeth and quite a few who don't, never quit searching for that Perfect Rib.

Charlie Vergos' Rendezvous

We think we have found that rib. And it's been in plain sight all along. It's at Charlie Vergos' Rendezvous. The Rendezvous has been serving ribs in this downtown rathskeller since 1948. Charlie is the Dean of the Dry School. The 'Vous's ribs are rubbed with a paprika-and-spice mixture that bakes on crispy and holds the juices in until your bicuspids set them free. There is nothing like them anywhere. For a dry rib these are the best and have been for decades. Vergos' noisy, claustrophobic cavern is a study in tacky. Every inch of the walls is gilded with old signs, old newspapers, old business cards—the kind of collection you might find at a museum with-

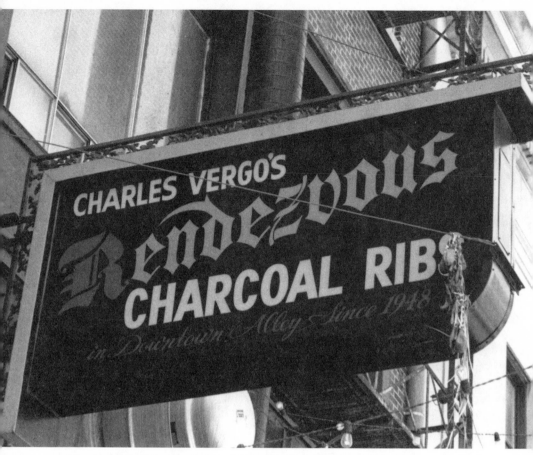

Charles Vergos' Rendezvous in Memphis, Tennessee

out a curator. Go early or be prepared to wait outside in line, where you can smell the hickory smoke and listen to your stomach rumble.

RATING: As good as we've ever had.

LOCATION: General Washburn Alley, which runs parallel to Second Street between Second and Third; (901) 523–2746.

WEB SITE: www.hogsfly.com

Leonard's Pit Barbecue

Leonard Heuberger, the man who put the *Leonard* in Leonard's, is acknowledged as the creator of the Memphis-style barbecue sandwich: chunks of pulled pork, mounded on a bun, covered with vinegar-and-tomato sauce, and crowned with coleslaw. Leonard's neon pig—MR. BROWN GOES TO TOWN, it says—was a beacon on Bellevue beginning in 1922. The original place was purchased by a local corporation in the eighties but many of the cooks stayed on, giving the place a continuity that continues today. The cooks that Leonard hired back in the days when his chief competitors were the Pig 'n' Whistle, Miss Culpepper's, and Willie King's taught the current cooks. The present owner, Dan Brown, began in Leonard's kitchen in 1961, so he knows how it's done.

RATING: Real good.
LOCATION: 5465 Fox Plaza Drive; (901) 360–1963.
WEB SITE: www.leonardsbarbecue.com

Payne's

Any Memphian, even a recent refugee from Arkansas, can direct you to the 'Vous or Leonard's. But only the true barbecue connoisseurs will send you to Payne's, a plain-vanilla place making do in a converted filling station in Mid City. Memphis native Tommy O'Brien introduced us to Payne's in 1980, and we were careful not to spread the word, until the first edition of this book. We didn't want the sweetness of success to spoil the sass of the sauce. But word is out. "You can't get in there at lunchtime," says Memphian Dennis Sigmund. "Now, I don't go by that. I rate places not by how many people are there but who is there. When you see guys leave construction sites, when you see trucks from the power company, plumbers' trucks—and they are all at Payne's every day—you know it's got to be good."

Payne's is better than good, better than real good. It's as good as we've ever had. The secret? You can't get any fresher meat. Before she passed, Emily Payne served. She would toast the meat on the rack until you ordered. Her daughter-in-law, Flora Payne, promises the same loving service that her mother-in-law provided at the restaurant.

"It's the best wet barbecue sandwich I have ever put in my mouth," says

Sigmund. "Just talking about them, I can almost taste that hot mustard coleslaw that runs down your arm. For a rib sandwich, wet ribs on a piece of a bread with mustard relish, we're talking good eating."

RATING: As good as we've ever had.

LOCATION: 1762 Lamar Avenue; (901) 272–1523. Also at 1393 Elvis Presley Boulevard; (901) 942–7433.

Corky's Ribs & BBQ

Several decades into our barbecue obsession we started to notice something about the barbecue meccas: The top-rated joints in these towns or states would remain the same, but the order of preference would change seemingly by the year.

We still think Arthur Bryant's is as good as it gets in Kansas City. But over the years we have heard these comments from our Kansas City sources: "Arthur's is not as good as it used to be." "Arthur's is back." "Arthur's has slipped in the last few months." Multiply that by years, and you get the point: Arthur Bryant's reputation ebbs and flows.

But every time we visit Kansas City—and one or both of us is there every year or so—we find Arthur's barbecue just as tasty as it was the last time. We peep into the kitchen, and it's the same folks running the pit and slicing the meat and stirring the sauce. So we've come to this conclusion: Arthur Bryant's stays the same. It's just that its reputation goes up and down.

Which brings us to Corky's. Corky's didn't make the first edition of this book for a very simple reason: It hadn't been in business long enough. When we did our original barbecue research in 1986 and 1987, we decided that we wouldn't consider any barbecue place that hadn't been in business for five years. That was because it takes a year from the time you turn in your manuscript until it is published. We wanted to make sure that every place we included would still be in business when the book was published. Corky's didn't open until 1984. It wasn't the only great barbecue joint that didn't make the age cut. Capital Barbecue in Frankfort, Kentucky, which came to be our favorite of our favorites, was also too new. That was then. Now Corky's is one of the venerables of Memphis barbecue. It's been around long enough that it has fallen victim to the Arthur Bryant Syndrome: The only thing that's changed is its reputation.

One year our Memphis operatives tell us it's the best; the next year it's fallen behind (pick one) Interstate or Cozy Corner or the Barbecue Shoppe.

We visit Memphis frequently—Vince has a cousin there—and we think Corky's pulled pork, like Corky's funky interior, is copacetic. We've never had barbecue at Corky's that was anything less than heavenly. (None of this applies to the various Corky's franchise outfits, none of which has ever measured up to the original in our opinions.)

RATING: Real good.
LOCATION: 5259 Poplar Avenue; (901) 685-9744.
WEB SITE: www.corkysbbq.com

The Cozy Corner

Our second favorite Memphis native, after Elvis, is Cybill Shepherd, and our fandom has nothing to do with her singing voice. And when Cybs is in town, she haunts this downtown lunch place. The ribs are real good, as are the chicken, the turkey, even the Cornish hen of all things.

The Cozy Corner practically defines "not much to look at," sitting as it does amid a scrum of abandoned buildings. Vince's Memphis cousin says they'd have to do a major renovation to locate a crack house there.

But we don't go to a barbecue joint to admire the architecture. We go hoping to admire the meat. And the meat here is about as admirable as it gets, the epitome of what the Wets of Memphis like, which is sauce-drenched chopped pork. If you order it hot, be sure you have your swimming suit. You're going to need to dive into something cool.

RATING: Real good.
LOCATION: 745 North Parkway; (901) 527-9158.

Georgia

Watkinsville

Hot Thomas Bar-B-Que and Peach Orchard

Barbecue has given us some wonderful restaurant names: Dr. Hogly Wogly's in Los Angeles; Dreamland in Tuscaloosa; Maurice's Piggy Park in West Columbia, South Carolina; the Moo Moo Hut in Corbin, Kentucky; the Pig Squeal in Waverly, Alabama; Short Sugar's in Reidsville, North Carolina; Bubbalou's in Orlando; and Curtis' All American Ninth Wonder of the World Barbecue in Putney, Vermont.

But none is more wonderful than the name of this plain little place in the middle of an orchard in the middle of nowhere. Hot Thomas. What wonderful images that conjures up. It's evocative but it's also simple, short, and to the point: Hot Thomas. And it turns out, it's appropriate. That's the owner's name—well, his nickname. Jerry is his real name.

Happily, the barbecue is as wonderful as the name. Mr. Thomas—we can't bring ourselves to call him Hot—offers a choice of tomato or vinegar sauce. We got both. Why not? A sandwich is only three bucks. We preferred the tomato, but we don't have anything bad to say about the vinegar-based sauce. Both were wonderful, and hot—we asked for hot, of course—it's *Hot* Thomas!

Hot Thomas Bar-B-Que is literally in the middle of nowhere. We were running low on gas and a bit concerned because there really isn't anything around Hot Thomas. We asked Mr. Thomas's son Mark how far to the nearest gas station. "Five and a half miles," he answered with a specificity that hinted he knew of what he spoke. He did; the nearest gas station was exactly 5½ miles on our odometer, just on the edge of Watkinsville, which is itself no big town. It's near Athens, which is a good-size town, thanks to its main industry, the University of Georgia.

You Want That Hot, Don't Ya?

Most barbecue joints serve mild sauce with their sandwiches. If you want it hot, you have to ask. We once heard a customer complain about the mildness and comment, "What's the point?" Does it have to be hot to be good? No. Jack Dempsey, the south Georgia barbecue king, put it this way, "It used to be hot, hot, hot—all anybody wanted was hot sauce. Now about the only ones who want it hot are the boozeheads."

There's no artifice at Hot Thomas. The place is a block building, one long room with fold-up tables and outdoor johns. It was once a country store, and there are still remnants—how many other barbecue joints sell barbecue sandwiches and monster hunting knives from the same counter?

We can only recommend the sandwiches.

RATING: As good as we've ever had.
LOCATION: 3753 Highway 15; (706) 769-6550.

Jackson

Fresh Air Bar-B-Que and Brunswick Stew

If you got directions to the Fresh Air back in 1929 and it had taken you this long to getting around to going, the directions would still hold. It has been in the same location—in fact, the same building—that long. "People bring their kids in and say, 'Your grandparents brought me in here when I was your age, and it looked just the same then,'" says owner George Barber. "Other people come in and say, 'I was here twenty or thirty years ago, and it's nice to see nothing's changed.'"

Nothing has changed. Well, a little. The last time we visited, George's grandfather, eighty-year-old G. W. "Toots" Castor, who bought the place in the forties, was still firing up the pit every morning at 4:30 A.M. He's now working for that great pitmaster in the sky. But the pit he fired up is still in plain view right behind the order counter. The cooking methods are the same: They cook fresh hams over a hickory-and-oak fire for twenty to twenty-four hours, then pull the meat, chop it, pile it on a bun, and ladle it with a tangy ketchup-and-vinegar sauce that is traditional to central Georgia. George says even the tables are the same and now going on sixty years old. "They made 'em from old 2-inch beat-up pine board, cut from trees around the area."

The Fresh Air was remodeled once, in '55. "But about all they did was pour concrete floors and add a little pine paneling on the inside, just those two changes." That's right, prior to 1955, the Fresh Air had a sawdust floor. Many old-timers remember it and still lament its passing. In the mid-eighties Barber added on a room to the side. But he made sure he left everything else, all the old stuff, intact. "Basically it's just a shack with an old rustic feel that people associate with barbecue."

The barbecue they associate it with is so good . . . How good is it, George? "It's not unusual for someone to get a plate of barbecue and Brunswick stew for breakfast."

RATING: As good as we've ever had.

LOCATION: 1164 Highway 42 South; (770) 775–3182. (It has franchises in Athens and Bogart.)

Atlanta

It's been twenty years since Dr. LaFong took us on a guided tour of Atlanta's barbecue hot spots. At the time we found Cosmic Barbecue at a quartet of Hotlanta locations. Two of them are gone, and so is Dr. LaFong, who moved back to his hometown of Knoxville, where he once worked as a copy editor on the local daily rag. (It was a low-pay, late-night, long-hours job, and his sole joy at work was taking press releases from the Mobile Home Dealers' Association and everywhere it said "mobile home," marking it out and replacing it with "trailer.")

We still remember that tour with fondness. We set our barbecue record in Atlanta, eating at fourteen joints in one day, starting with a barbecue breakfast south of town (isn't bacon just smoked pork? Then what's wrong with real smoked pork on a plate for breakfast?) and winding up with carryout ribs in Buckhead. That wasn't just popping in, taking a nibble off a sandwich, and then popping out. That was Eating with a capital *E*, giving a place a fair shake. If it happened not to measure up to our standards, we pitched the rest. No sense in wasting a good appetite on inferior barbecue.

By the end of that day we were counting potato chips as a vegetable.

This time the guide for our Traveling Barbecue Show was Mrs. McNeer, a worthy successor to Dr. LaFong and a genial companion in her own right, if you don't count the four hours we spent stranded on the side of the interstate, waiting on a tow truck.

Harold's

Our first stop was Harold's, the old-line barbecue place in Atlanta. Mrs. McNeer had never been to Harold's despite her passion for new gustatory experiences (she lives on the northside; Harold's is on the southside). On the surface nothing much has changed at Harold's. It's still the same people, almost all from the Hembree family, only they are all twenty years older than they were the last time.

Twenty years ago we ate at the bar, but not that kind of bar. Harold's doesn't serve alcohol in any form. Dr. LaFong explained to us at the time that Deep South barbecue joints seldom sell beer because most grew up as family restaurants, where you took the wife and kids after church.

You can't get alcohol at Harold's bar—
but you can get great barbecue.

Harold's is still in a low-slung brick building with bars on the windows, a nod to the nearby prison. Okay, two things are different. We didn't see the shotgun that used to be leaning up against the wall in the kitchen. And Harold's now cooks on a fancy flip-top electric pit, although they still finish the sandwich off by grilling the bread on a charcoal pit behind the bar.

The pit change at Harold's put us in a quandary. We kept places out of the last edition for cooking electric instead of with wood or wood charcoal. If someone hadn't tipped us off, we wouldn't have known that Harold's had switched. Frankly, we didn't think it tasted any different than on any previous trip. (Before our update trips in 2006, we had last eaten at Harold's in 1999.)

We still love the pork sandwich. And the Brunswick stew. And the corn bread, made from cracklin's. We had to drag Mrs. McNeer off to the next spot. She solved our problem by giving us her rating, without being prompted.

RATING: "This is as good as I've ever had." —Mrs. McNeer
LOCATION: 171 McDonough Boulevard Southeast; (404) 627-9268.

Old Brick Pit Bar-B-Q

We hit two places in Hiram and some places up north before Mrs. McNeer steered us to this former Dairy Queen where the Old South meets the New South. Literally. The Old Brick Pit employs an international staff. The day we visited the pitmaster was from Mexico, the cook was from Puerto Rico, and the clerk was from Asia. But they must have been from southern Mexico, south Puerto Rico, and Southeast Asia, because the pulled-pork sandwich tasted like good old-fashioned southern barbecued pig.

The pit is right behind the counter and seeps smoke into the counter area. If you ask nicely, they'll swing up the metal lid and let you watch that pig sizzle. And fill the whole place with sweet smoke.

RATING: Real good.
LOCATION: 4805 Peachtree Road; (770) 986-7727.

Old Brick Pit Bar-B-Q is in a former Dairy Queen.

The Swallow at the Hollow

Mrs. McNeer wanted to conclude our barbecue day with a night of music and meat. And she had just the place, a joint she frequents on a semiannual basis. It's a great name, the Swallow at the Hollow, with good 'que and good music, courtesy of traveling Nashville songwriters. Three songwriters shared the stage, two aspiring and one successful. They played the songs they wrote for the big stars, and we listened and nibbled on an array of pit-cooked meat. We liked our pulled-pork plate a lot and would have included the place in the book based on that alone. But add in the entertainment, and you have just about the best barbecue evening a fellow and a gal could have. Oh yeah, Mr. McNeer went along, too.

RATING: Real good.

LOCATION: 1072 Green Street, Roswell (an Atlanta suburb); (678) 352–1975.

WEB SITE: www.theswallowatthehollow.com

Sam & Dave's BBQ 1

Amenities are not in Sam or Dave's vocabulary. There's no public restroom—in fact, there's a threatening sign warning the weak of bladder not to even ask. And if you eat at one of the three indoor tables, you'll most likely get roughed up by folks waiting in line. After filling their dead strip-mall spot with cookers and warmers, there's hardly enough room left over for a pair of brogan shoes, much less a fancy dining room.

No, Sam & Dave's is not about amenities, it's about barbecue. The place wasn't founded by the famous Soul Men. It's just that when a Sam

Sam & Dave's BBQ 1

and two Daves team up, it's too tempting not to name the place after the great sixties soul singers. Sam is actually a lawyer (Sam Huff); Dave 1 is David Poe, from a family of caterers; and Dave 2 is David Roberts, who's done a bit of everything in the restaurant business, from selling organic vegetables to cooking at some fancy places, including the Dining Room at the Ritz-Carlton Buckhead and the Brasserie Le Coze.

We always gravitate toward pork, and Mrs. McNeer agreed with us that the giant hunks of shredded meat were worthy of a Soul Man.

We'd like to make a joke using the title of Sam & Dave's other big hit, "Hold On, I'm Coming," but Mrs. McNeer deemed it unnecessary.

RATING: Real good.
LOCATION: 4944 Lower Roswell Road; (770) 977-3005.
WEB SITE: www.lostmountainbbq.com

Kentucky

They think they are hot in North Carolina because they have two distinct barbecue styles—Down East barbecue and Lexington barbecue.

That's not hot—that's mild compared to what Kentucky has wrought when it comes to barbecue. Kentucky has three distinct styles! There's western Kentucky barbecue, where they cook pork shoulder, pull and chop the meat, and grill it on sandwich bread. There's Owensboro style, where they cook mutton and douse it with "black dip," a Worcestershire-sauce-based condiment. And there's Monroe County barbecue, where they cook sliced pork shoulder and dip it in a vinegary sauce.

No other state has created more barbecue styles than Kentucky. Maybe Kentucky is more famous for horse racing and basketball and Daniel Boone, but when it comes to unique barbecue styles, Kentucky stands alone.

Get Your Goat

Writer Jim Dodson, who worked for a time in Atlanta, recalled the time he stopped in for a couple of Jack Dempsey's renowned she-goat sandwiches at Jack's place in Ty Ty, Georgia. "I ate one and left the other under the seat of my pickup truck for three days. When I got it out and ate it, it tasted even better."

Owensboro

Mutton Mania

No one knows how Kentucky and barbecued mutton became intertwined, but it goes back at least two centuries to the wedding of Thomas Lincoln and Nancy Hanks. You've probably heard of their son, Abe. A guest at their wedding dinner, which was held in Washington County, Kentucky, noted in his diary, "We had . . . a sheep . . . barbecued whole over coals of wood burned in a pit." Kentuckians have loved slow-cooked sheep ever since.

If you haven't yet tried it, there is nothing like your first taste of barbecued mutton. To truly understand this fact, you must visit Owensboro, Kentucky, early on the second weekend in May. Looming out of a whirling haze of hickory smoke, tinged pink by a hint of dawn, you will see cement-block fire pits the size of small garages, filled with hot coals and built smack down the center of a street overlooking the Ohio River. They will be covered with hundreds of pounds of succulent, sizzling slabs of mutton that have been cooking all night long.

Mutton is the meat God meant to be barbecued. It's not at all like the milky, delicate taste of lamb; it tastes rich, grown-up. And its earthy flavor marries up with the smoke of the hickory and the fire of the dip. It's not just good; it's perfect. This is not an idly held opinion in Daviess County, where Owensboro is situated; it is a devout belief of the greatest solemnity. In these rolling hills of western Kentucky, it is a belief that has fostered a dedicated rebel band of backwoods barbecuers, men for whom the heresy of pork and beef is only barely tolerated, for whom the word *barbecue* means mutton—and nothing else. And if you can't make it in May for the International Bar-B-Q Festival, these men (and women) will be glad to sell it to you in scores of restaurants crowded into this little city. It's barbecue's quirkiest tradition: western Kentucky mutton.

The Moonlite Bar-B-Q Inn

The Moonlite wasn't the first barbecue restaurant in Owensboro. Harry Green opened a little barbecue place here in 1890. But the Moonlite is easily the most famous barbecue place in town.

"In the wintertime, Owensboro restaurants probably serve 30,000 to 40,000 pounds of mutton a week," said Ken Bosley, who (along with his family) owns the largest of those restaurants. "In the summer it probably goes up to 100,000 pounds a week." For those not mathematically inclined, that's fifty tons a week—or about two pounds a week for every man, woman, and child in town. But Owensboro isn't just any town. "We claim Owensboro as the barbecue capital of the world, and the chamber of commerce promotes it that way," Bosley added. "I think our claim is in the mutton."

Bosley's restaurant is "Kentucky's Very Famous" Moonlite, and it is not just big, it's big big—as in forklifts, delivery trucks, and Building No. 2. The restaurant got that way by combining the love of mutton with another Daviess County passion—a good deal. Much of the meat served here is in the $8.75 all-you-can-eat buffet. A price like that means the Moonlite's rambling, paneled dining rooms tend to fill up with businessmen, visitors, families, barbecue pilgrims, and the occasional uniformed softball team halfway through a Saturday double-header. There's a lot of food set out

The Road Less Traveled to Barbecue Fame

Dave and Dottye Brandon had Wall Street in their sights in college. He took his degree in international finance; she graduated in mathematics. After a dozen years of this they traded them in, an even-up swap: pork futures for pork sandwiches when they founded Brandon's Bar-B-Que in Plantation, Kentucky.

besides barbecue: potatoes, beans, chicken livers, salads, and desserts. But the typical diner's meal seems to consist of three courses: barbecue, barbecue, and barbecue. "I've eaten here often enough to know that you don't take any salad," one softball player said, although he had saved room for the homemade cherry pie and the soft ice cream served from a self-serve machine with a warning sign: MACHINE HAS A TENDENCY TO THROW FITS. USE AT YOUR OWN RISK.

The Moonlite's mutton is served chopped and simmered in a mild tomato sauce, and it runs a bit to the strong side. You'd never suspect you're eating chopped pork with this wild-eyed funky flavor. But there are three sauces you can mix into the meat to adjust its flavor, temperature, and horizontal hold. There's black dip, a watery Worcestershire number; a sweet tomato sauce; and a Vesuvian version that's appropriately named Very Hot Sauce. Use it sparingly, or you'll singe the little silk flowers at your table.

RATING: Real good.
LOCATION: 2708 Parrish Avenue; (270) 684–8143.
WEB SITE: www.moonlite.com

Sauce and Slabs

One day it was the teenage hangout in Louisville, Kentucky. The next day it was closed and the owner was going to jail. In the early thirties local police closed Ed Land's Bar-B-Que and hauled Land off. He ended up serving time in prison for putting embalming fluid in his meat. "There was no refrigeration then," recalls Thelma Tabler, who was one of the teenagers who enjoyed going to Land's. "Everyone used an icebox. He was just trying to help the meat last longer."

Old Hickory Pit Barbecue

In every great barbecue town, there's the place you have to visit and the place you ought to visit. In Owensboro, you ought to visit the Old Hickory; it serves the best mutton in town, which most likely means the best mutton on the planet Earth. Here mutton is sold the way it should be, sliced "off the pit." This is mutton the way mutton lovers eat it—no sauce for a disguise, no tricks. It is tender, touched with the ruby hues of hickory smoking and not the least bit dry. In fact, fresh, hot mutton is as rich and delicious as an aged beef steak and, cooked right, a lot more tender. It has a very faint musky aura that mixes with the hickory aroma in subtle, satisfying ways. The slices are lean and absolutely luscious. Sometimes outsiders will think of the meat of the mature sheep as "gamy" or "icky." These are people who simply have never eaten mutton this good. Toss your Four Seasons fillet in the trash; this makes steak superfluous.

Actually, getting masterful mutton at the Old Hickory is something akin to destiny. Owner Harl Foreman Jr. is a fourth-generation barbecuer; his family started in the business in 1918, when great-grandfather Charles cooked for one of the churches and ran a blacksmith shop. The wisdom of pit-tending is a family heirloom: "It's passed down," Foreman says. The Old Hickory place may look a bit modern and rootless, but Harl says the cooking hasn't changed a bit. "We cook all night," Foreman says. "I designed my own pit, and I built this building for barbecue."

RATING: As good as we've ever had.
LOCATION: 338 Washington Avenue; (270) 926–9000.

Paducah

Starnes' Bar-B-Q

It was midafternoon of a mild February day almost two decades ago: not lunch time, not barbecue season. Starnes' Bar-B-Q was busy. Both the booths were full. And there was only one seat left at the counter. Starnes' Bar-B-Q was simplicity defined. A U-shaped counter surrounded a drink case and candy counter. There was a booth wedged in on each side where the counter meets the wall. On a cold day you might be able to squeeze thirty people in.

"Me and daddy started this when I was twelve," said Larry Starnes. When Starnes' Bar-B-Q opened its doors for business in 1954, a filling station was the only other business on Joe Clifton Drive. Now the street has been widened and turned into a Miracle Mile. It's surrounded by fast-food restaurants. But on this day, the only one with a full parking lot was Starnes'. "Every time they opened a new one, I figured it would cut into our business," said Starnes. "But it hasn't yet." Now Larry's son Tim runs the business, and it still is busy.

Starnes' is the best example going of western Kentucky- (or Paducah-) style barbecue. The meat is cooked in a pit out back over red-hot coals of hickory wood, for its distinctive flavor. Larry believes that slow cooking is the only way. But he doesn't believe all the stories he hears about barbecue fellows cooking meat for hours on end. "Anybody says they get up at 4:00 A.M. to start the fire, I just shake my head. I read this one story where the fellow said he cooked his meat twenty-four hours. I drive by his place every day, and I know better. We cook ours ten or twelve hours. But I don't get up at 4:00 A.M. to start it. We Starneses are lazy."

Starnes' meat is pulled from the bone and chopped fine, then piled on a piece of Bunny-brand white bread. Another piece of bread is stacked on top, and then the sandwich is grilled. At first blush the grilled sandwich looks like something you would order at an airport coffee shop. It takes a couple of bites to get used to barbecue on toast, but once your taste buds accept the difference, you're hooked. There's only one sauce available, a hot, tomato-based one developed years ago by Larry and his father. It's not ninth-ring-of-hell hot, but it does make a statement. If the waitress asks if you want any of it on your sandwich, the best answer is "yes." It's just a sprinkle, but it's plenty enough to heat up the meat. "Other areas they use the sauce like gravy," said Starnes. "Ours you use it like a seasoning."

Starnes' offers pork, beef, and mutton sandwiches. Paducah, after all, isn't far from the mutton country of Owensboro. "I just sell mutton as an accommodation for a few folks who ask for it. I don't really believe in it." Drinks come in the bottle straight out of the drink case. People in Paducah will tell you Starnes' is the best barbecue anywhere in the world. None of the people who say that have been all over the world, but they know barbecue.

RATING: Real good.
LOCATION: 1008 Joe Clifton Drive; (270) 444–9555.

Kevil

Leigh's Barbecue

They were barbecuing in western Kentucky before Leonard Leigh opened his place shortly after World War II. But it was Leonard who showed folks that barbecue could survive in a restaurant as opposed to the roadside stands that operated only in warm weather. His homely little place, 12 miles due west of Paducah, may be the oldest continuously operating barbecue joint in the state.

Leonard partnered with local lawyer Roy Vance—who would go on to head Kentucky's Supreme Court—to create not only great barbecue but a great barbecue dynasty. Leonard's son Eddie Ray went on to take over after Leonard died in 1971. Meanwhile, Roy's son Newton moved along with his judge dad to Frankfort and opened Capital Barbecue, so Frankfort's citizens could have some real western Kentucky barbecue and so his dad would have a place to eat lunch. Newton, who once told us he had barbecue sauce in his blood, ran his place for twenty years, closing in 2004 after the state built a new highway that detoured around his spot. Eddie Ray, who was cooking barbecue before he could spell it, is carrying on the Leigh tradition in the same location and in the same way: pork shoulders cooked low and slow—generally eighteen hours—over hardwood, then pulled, chopped, and squirted with a thin, puckering sauce. Eddie Ray must still have barbecue sauce in his blood.

RATING: Real good.
LOCATION: 9405 U.S. Highway 60 West; (270) 488-3434.

Kutawa

Knoth's Bar-B-Q

Is it kuh-NO-th's or Kuh-nawth's or what? How do you pronounce it?

"They pronounce it every which way," says owner Hugh Knoth. "It's NOth's. But we don't care how they pronounce it as long as they keep coming."

They've been coming since 1966, when Hugh's parents opened Knoth's. "It was just about the time Barkley Dam was finished. Dad had a guy come down from the Old Kutawa Springs Barbecue—it's closed now—and show him how to cook. The guy worked with dad just one day. You can't really

Barbecue Insults

"In eastern Kentucky you can ask for barbecue, and you are apt to get roast beef," said the late Bill Powell, a retired newspaperman who just happened to live in Paducah, Kentucky, in the western part of the state. "That silly bunch up there in Owensboro, they don't know what they're doing. They're kidding themselves. And Texas doesn't even have barbecue."

learn barbecue in one day. It's really something that takes time. You've got to do it a lot to learn how. And the more patience a person has, the better job he does. So dad kept at it and taught himself how to cook it right."

And like father like son. Knoth's cooks up the sweetest meat we found anywhere. Then they lather it up with a sauce that is as sweet as the meat. Knoth's cooks pork shoulders and beef over wood coals in a low-heat open pit for about fourteen hours.

The one time it did matter if they got the pronunciation right, they did. It was 1969. Knoth's had only been open three years, when Ed McMahon mentioned to Johnny Carson on the *Tonight Show* that he had eaten some real good barbecue from a place called Knoth's in Kentucky. "Supposedly he had been here," says Hugh, "although we didn't know about it at the time. The next day after he said that on TV there were ten carloads of people down here from Princeton [Kentucky] to tell dad about the show. Dad always said that was what broke it open for the business."

From then on everybody in western Kentucky knew about Knoth's. It became so famous that Hugh acquired the nickname Hot Pig. "I was in fourth grade, and my little league basketball coach said, 'Knoth, why didn't you bring me some of that hot pig?' And from then on everybody called me 'Hot Pig.' I was kind of heavy anyway, and people would yell, 'Sooeey, sooeey, Hot Pig.' I didn't like it then. And it kind of wore out when I got to be a senior in high school. But I wouldn't mind if people called me that now."

RATING: Real good.
LOCATION: 728 U.S. Highway 62; (270) 362–8580.

Gamaliel (Monroe County)

Bugtussle Bar-B-Q

Getting from the parkway or interstate to Owensboro is an inconvenience. Getting from the interstate to Monroe County is a task. But a worthwhile task. The county's isolated circumstance has produced a barbecue that is closer to that found on the shores of North Carolina than to either of its Kentucky cousins. It is almost as if some early barbecue pioneer got lost from his wagon train, ended up in Monroe County, and stayed. Monroe County barbecue is similar to the stuff they were serving George Washington in the days when settlers feared that tomatoes were poisonous. There is no tomato in Monroe County barbecue sauce. Former sheriff Beverly McClendon, a longtime observer of the Monroe County barbecue scene, says it's "just vinegar, lard, and spices all cooked together." If you are used to the Open Pit–style sweet sauce you find on supermarket shelves, Monroe County barbecue will be an eye-opener. And if you opt for dipped barbecue over sprinkled, it will also be a sinus-opener. ("Dipped" means your barbecue is dunked into the sauce, giving it a healthy dose of the hots. "Sprinkled" is more like an uptown Presbyterian baptism: just a little sauce dribbled on.)

A Monroe County barbecue sandwich looks for all the world like a pork-chop sandwich: a cut of pork as thick as a steak, dipped (or sprinkled, if you are faint of heart) in a hot vinegar-based sauce and served on white

Movieque

Barbecue has made an appearance or two in the movies over the years. Liz Taylor fainted over barbecued steer brain in *Giant*. Henry Gibson kicked off his political campaign with a celebrity barbecue in *Nashville*. Dan Aykroyd suggested a trip to Leon's in *Dr. Detroit*. And let's not forget the choice of meat for the barbecue in *The Texas Chainsaw Massacre*. (On second thought, let's do forget it.)

But as best as we can determine, only one barbecue joint has ever made it big on the big screen: Hutchens Bar-B-Q of Benton, Kentucky. Okay, technically Hutchens didn't make it. But a radio commercial for Hutchens was used in *Coal Miner's Daughter*, the big-screen biography of country singer Loretta Lynn. Loretta and her husband, Mooney, were making the rounds of radio stations, trying to get a little airplay for her self-produced first record, *Honky Tonk Girl*. Their first stop was WCBL in Benton, Kentucky. The deejay was trying to shoo them out of the studio when his record ended and he had to do some announcing. "You're listening to Tri-State country with your deejay, Bobby Day. Now here's a word from our friends down at Hutchens Hot Pig. Oink, oink, oink, oink. Tell 'em all about it, Hutch and all them little piglets." While Day continued his argument with the Lynns, you can hear bits and pieces of the Hutchens' commercial in the background. "This is Hutch Hutchens down at Hutchens Hot Pig saying bring the whole family down for our mouthwatering ribs . . ." That isn't the real Hutch Hutchens on the commercial. He died several years ago. And that isn't a real Hutchens commercial. But Hutchens Hot Pig is still operating in Benton, still serving up good barbecue six days a week. (They're closed Wednesday.)

bread. It may look like a pork chop sandwich, but the smoky, fiery taste is definitely barbecue.

At one time Fountain Run was the place for Monroe County–style barbecue. Sarah Tooley's was located on Highway 100, and a half mile down the road was daughter Ova Kirk's place. And it was not friendly competition. But mother and daughter both died in 1993, and the center for Monroe County style has shifted to Gamaliel, home of Bugtussle Bar-B-Q, a longtime local favorite. (It's named for the hometown of the Clampetts on *The Beverly Hillbillies*.) It is by no means the only place serving Monroe County style. McClendon says there are a half dozen top-notch places, from Francis' on the border near Celina, Tennessee, to Sam Graves' in Tompkinsville and Paul and Nora's just outside town. "It's like anything else; people have their different tastes. Lots of people down here go to a particular place for the slaw."

RATING: Real good.
LOCATION: 6117 Bugtussle Road; (270) 457-3868.

Prospect

Vince Staten's Old-Time Barbecue

When Vince returned home from the barbecue trail in 1987, after eating at more than 400 joints in a year, he was asked repeatedly, "When are you going to open your own barbecue place?" His answer was always the same: "Never. I've seen how hard those guys work."

But his resistance gradually eroded, as the memories of old barbecue men tending a pit at 4:00 A.M. became romanticized in his brain, and in November 1992 Vince and his neighbor, Dave Jenkins, along with their wives, Judy Staten and Trish Jenkins, opened a twelve-seat joint in their little town northeast of Louisville. Their philosophy was simple and based on Vince's experience of eating all styles of barbecue: "We don't tell you what kind or how much sauce to put on your meat. We slow-cook pork, beef,

Vince Staten's own Old-Time Barbecue

and chicken, hand-pull it from the bone, chop it, and serve it sans sauce." Vince came up with six different regional sauces—a thick sweet Texas sauce; a thin, tart North Carolina sauce; a Worcestershire-based Memphis sauce; a hot Texas-style sauce; a sauce with Jack Daniels in it; and a hot sauce, Legal Limit, which was the legal limit that their attorney David Vish would allow them to sell. Liability and all that. They also offered a dry-style Memphis rib that customers could sauce themselves if they wanted. From eastern North Carolina they borrowed the idea of serving banana pudding; from Vince's wife's family they borrowed a coleslaw recipe based on neither mayonnaise nor vinegar, but whipped cream.

Vince Staten's Old-Time Barbecue has been in business since 1992 and is still going strong. After twelve years, Vince's place moved into a one-hundred-seat space that he decorated in what he calls Early Tacky, including his favorite political poster of all time, from southeastern Kentucky: Jerry "Round Daddy" Parsons for Jailer.

RATING: We'll let you be the judge.
LOCATION: 13306 West U.S. Highway 42; (502) 228-7427.
WEB SITE: www.statensbbq.com

PORKLORE

Sheep Dip

Harold P. "Big Bubba" Stainback of Jeffersontown, Kentucky, on barbecued mutton: "The only way I'd have sheep in my pit is if one happened to fall in there. I thought we must have eaten up all the sheep in World War II, but there must have been two left someplace."

Alabama

Decatur

Big Bob Gibson Bar-B-Q

In north Alabama one name is synonymous with barbecue: Gibson. There's Gibson's Bar-B-Q in Huntsville, David Gibson's No. 2 in Huntsville, and Big Bob Gibson's in Decatur, three barbecue places that trace their lineage back to the aptly named north Alabama barbecue giant, Big Bob Gibson. (He was 6-foot-2 and 300 pounds.)

Big Bob started cooking in a pit he dug back in 1925. "Back in those days, they killed their own hogs and used the bones for stew," recalled his daughter Catherine McLemore, who took over his Decatur restaurant when he died in 1972. (Her son Don now operates the place.) "On Saturdays, people would come from miles around to eat. And he would have tables built from tree to tree." Soon there weren't enough trees to shade all Big Bob's hungry customers. That's when he decided to open a restaurant. As his business grew, so did his dining room. He kept jumping to bigger places, finally settling into the Sixth Avenue location in 1952. A year later Catherine joined the company. And in 1975 her son Don quit the computer business and returned to the family business. The continuity from generation to generation is important at Big Bob's. Catherine said, "Just a few weeks ago, we had a guy come in and tell his waitress, 'I haven't been here for twenty years, and you're the same girl who waited on me then!' Sure enough, the waitress had been with Big Bob's for thirty-two years!"

What keeps the employees is the family atmosphere; what keeps the customers is Big Bob's barbecue. The pork sandwich is a mound of shredded meat bathed in a flimsy tomato sauce that bites but doesn't sting. Big Bob's uses only pork shoulders and only hickory wood.

Big Bob would be proud of Catherine and Little Don. Business is booming, forcing Big Bob's to move across the parking lot to larger quarters. In fact, Big Bob would be proud of all his heirs. "He had five children, and every one of them went into barbecue," said Don. "And now all of those places have passed down to the grandkids."

RATING: Real good.
LOCATION: 1715 Sixth Avenue Southeast; (256) 350–6969.
WEB SITE: www.bigbobgibson.com

Tuscaloosa

Dreamland Bar-B-Q Drive Inn

What a wonderful name for a barbecue joint: Dreamland Bar-B-Q Drive Inn. It stirs images of puffy clouds with pig faces hidden in them, of '55 Chevys with hula-skirted pigs dancing in the back window, of old men napping to barbecue dreams. The Dreamland is located in idyllic surroundings (if you don't glance across the road at the trailer park). Nestled off the road in a stand of pine trees, it looks like an Elks Club that has gone to heaven. For a barbecue lover, it *is* heaven.

John Bishop Sr., known as Big Daddy, opened Dreamland in 1958. He had begun turning over the daily operation to his son, John Jr., when we first visited twenty years ago. The family sold out to Jasper dentist Bobby Underwood in 1992, and that usually means the beginning of the end for a barbecue joint. But Underwood understood what he was buying, and he preserved the legacy, meanwhile expanding the brand into other cities. Don't worry about the chain stores. Go to the original where they still serve ribs—Big John had a sign that said, DON'T EVEN ASK for side dishes—and white bread. The Dreamland still serves dreamy coffee-brown ribs with very white bread.

It's still the same simple place. The menu is so simple that they don't even have a printed version: All you can get is beer, white bread, and ribs. It's what Bishop always called an "inside picnic." The ribs are served hot off the grill, just asking to be devoured. The meat doesn't fall off the bone; it just oozes off. Bishop told us, "You can pull your dentures out and eat my ribs."

Dreamland's sauce has a unique taste, a nip that is hard to pin down. What is the secret ingredient? We had heard turnip greens. When we asked Big John years ago, he merely shook his head no. There is a theory, first explained to us by some of the newsroom staff at WVMT-TV in Birmingham, that Big Daddy put moonshine in his sauce. We decided not to ask. If the answer was yes, he couldn't tell us. And if the answer was no, we didn't want to know.

John Bishop Sr. died in 1998, but his wonderful, tasty legacy continues.

RATING: As good as we've ever had.
LOCATION: 5535 Fifteenth Avenue East; (205) 758-8135.
WEB SITE: www.dreamlandbbq.com

P.S. We have friends, respected friends, who prefer Archibald's when in Tuscaloosa. We respect their opinion, and on some of our Alabama visits we agree with them. Archibald's has been a favorite barbecue haunt of famous Alabamans from governors to football coaches. It's at 1211 MLK Boulevard. Call (205) 345-6861.

Dora

Green Top Cafe

George Gillis remembers well his boyhood visits to the Green Top. "It was the only decent barbecue you could find in Alabama." Gillis grew up in Memphis, a town that considered Alabama a poor relation when it came to barbecue. And it was poor relations that took Gillis to Alabama. "We'd visit my cousins in Sumiton, which is right across the street from Dora. They're sort of the twin cities. They were big rivals, Sumiton and Dora, but they were both crummy towns. We used to say they ought to combine them into one and they could call it Dumb-iton. The Green Top was on the Jefferson–Walker County line. And in Walker County, which at that time was dry, the bootlegger would take a check. That's the kind of place Dumb-iton was."

But the thing Gillis remembers most about the Green Top is Leo, Leo Headrick. "Leo and Susie ran the Green Top. They lived in a trailer out back. And if you hung around the Green Top long enough, Leo would bring out his guitar and sing, without any encouragement at all."

Leo died in 1996, but the Green Top is still around. And it's the same old Green Top it was when it opened in 1951. The top is still green. "Every time we reroof we have to get green shingles," said Preston Headrick, Leo and Susie's son, who is now a preacher. Miss Susie owns the restaurant, and Preston's brother Richard, and Richard's son Tomy, run the place. It still looks like a fifties roadhouse. The main dining area is stucco with fifties-style booths. "These booths were made in the fifties, though, not made to look like they were made in the fifties." Leo and Susie's oil-tinted portrait still hangs on the wall, alongside those of celebrities who have frequented the Green Top over the years: Auburn football star Bo Jackson; boxer Marvelous Marvin Hagler; politician George Wallace; astronaut Gene Cernan. ("We told him he'd been everywhere now—the moon and the Green Top," said Preston.) And, best of all, there is still Leo & Susie's Famous Barbecue Sandwich, a peerless pork production with crunchies in the middle and a tart, medium-hot vinegar-and-tomato-based sauce with a jolt that doesn't hit you until it is too late to turn back. If you want even more kick, you'll have to get it from a store-bought hot sauce that they keep on every table.

The only things that had changed at the Green Top twenty years ago had changed for the better. "Prior to '78 the bathrooms were outside," said Preston. "We're a lot more popular with the women now that we have indoor restrooms." And there was a new portrait of Big Jim Ferguson, two-time governor of Alabama and a frequent customer at Green Top. Preston recalled, "Whenever Big Jim would come in, him and Daddy would sing together, and one of them would use a bottle of hot sauce as a microphone."

RATING: Real good.

LOCATION: 7530 Highway 78; (205) 648–9838.

Birmingham

Golden Rule Bar-B-Q

For many years they made up the Twin Towers of Birmingham barbecue: Ollie's and Golden Rule.

Ollie's had the national reputation. But Golden Rule was the local favorite. Ollie's achieved its repute, or disrepute because of a 1964 lawsuit when Ollie's became a test case for the newly enacted Civil Rights Act. It was a simple suit: Ollie said he would allow blacks in the kitchen and at the take-out window but not in the dining room. The Attorney General of the United States said, "If you employ blacks in the kitchen and sell to them at the take-out window, then you serve them in the dining room." So Ollie McClung Sr. and Ollie McClung Jr., co-owners of Ollie's, filed suit against the U.S. government, claiming the public accommodations section of the 1964 Civil Rights Act was unconstitutional. And thus began *Katzenbach v. McClung*, or, as we prefer to call it, U.S. vs. Ollie and Ollie. The case turned on whether or not Ollie's Barbecue was a part of interstate commerce. The case went back and forth, but in the end the U.S. Supreme Court ordered Ollie's to comply with the law. And on December 16, 1964, after six months and a large legal bill, Ollie and Ollie gave up the fight and went back to selling barbecue.

And that's the way it went for forty years. Ollie's and Golden Rule fighting it out for local supremacy. Then in 1989 Ollie the Elder died and Ollie Junior moved the place to the suburbs. While Golden Rule was expanding—it now has twenty restaurants—Ollie's was struggling and finally closed for good in 2000.

And then there was one.

But it's a good one, a real good one.

Or twenty real good ones.

As always, we recommend visiting the original, and in the case of Golden Rule that's the Irondale location. It isn't the original original. But it's only a few yards from where the original Golden Rule opened in—hold your breath—1891. Golden Rule was a popular roadside store that sold beer, cigarettes, and pork plates, and as time passed and automobiles began passing, it expanded into auto repair.

The current owners are the third family to own Golden Rule. It was opened by the Williams family, who ran the place for forty years, selling out in the late thirties to the Stones. When Jabo Stone decided to retire in 1969, he made a deal with Michael Matsos, who already owned a popular downtown Birmingham steak house. Matsos bought the business and the building for $10,000. Legend has it that he later worried that he had been taken.

Today Golden Rule is run by Michael's son Charles, although the elder Matsos, now in his eighties, is still involved in the business.

RATING: Real good.

LOCATION: 2504 Crestwood Boulevard, Irondale (a suburb of Birmingham); (205) 956–2678.

WEB SITE: www.goldenrulebbq.com

Mobile

The Brick Pit

For every barbecue rule, there is an exception. Take our rule that the closer you get to the ocean, the worse the barbecue is. Then explain the Brick Pit, which sits 10 miles or so from Mobile Bay.

We'll explain it. Owner Bill Armbrecht does it right, way right. Take his pulled pork. He cooks pork butts for thirty hours—most places top out at sixteen—then hand-pulls the meat apart, peeling away as much fat as humanly possible. By the time a pork sandwich reaches your plate, it has been saturated with tender loving care . . . and a distinctive tomato-onion sauce.

The Brick Pit opened in 1994 because native Mobilian Armbrecht couldn't find a barbecue place in his hometown that measured up to the places he had eaten while traveling as a yacht captain. He wanted serious barbecue, and that's what he offers, carefully watching every step of the operation, right down to the blend of wood. He prefers pecan, loading up his fire with 75 percent pecan versus 25 percent hickory. He doesn't apply a rub before cooking, preferring, he says, to let the smoke do the flavoring.

Even his chicken and ribs are serious. He cooks chickens for six hours—it's three or so at most places—and ribs for twelve, twice as long as the average 'que joint.

You'd think that would be enough, but the TLC continues right on through to dessert, Mrs. Iona Waits's banana pudding. Mrs. Waits comes in daily to make her signature pudding, and it is as sweet as her disposition.

RATING: Real good.
LOCATION: 5656 Old Shell Road; (251) 343–0001.
WEB SITE: www.brickpit.com

Mississippi

Hattiesburg

Leatha's Bar-B-Que Inn

If we were writing a guidebook for what a barbecue joint should be, we would use Miss Leatha's as our model. It's plain—that means they aren't spending a lot of money on "decorating." It's off the main road, on "Leatha Lane," for goodness sake—that means they aren't spending a lot of money on leases. And it employs the entire family—that means Leatha's will be here long after Leatha is gone. And that's good, since Leatha was eighty-three in 2006.

At her age, Leatha has earned her retirement from the kitchen. But she still presides over the dining room, welcoming visitors and passing out rib plates and hugs. Her three daughters, Bonnie Jackson, Myrtis Richardson, and Caroline Stephney, run the place with assistance from the grandchildren, as well as assorted nieces, nephews, aunts, uncles, even cousins.

But Leatha hangs around to make sure everything is done her way, the way she's been doing things since she opened up in 1974 after twenty years of working in other restaurant kitchens. She decided to open her own restaurant because she noticed, "Colonel Sanders got rich off another man's cooking, and Aunt Jemima still has a rag on her head."

Leatha's is definitely Leatha's. To begin with there's NO ALCOHOL, which is painted on the building. She credits her success to her faith, and she won't allow it to be mocked by unruly customers. Her other credo is trumpeted in a sign on the screen door: LET'S EAT.

The sauce is her own creation, thin and sweet and, Miss Leatha proudly proclaims, without a lot of vinegar.

Since our visit Leatha's special son Larry has passed away. While Leatha ran the dining room, Larry provided the entertainment, singing and offering homemade CDs of his greatest hits. Or hit. Often the CD would contain multiple versions of the same song. He serenaded us with his favorite song, "Thriller." When we approved with our applause, he sang it for us again.

Leatha also sells wood-grilled steaks, which we hear are real good. We wouldn't know.

RATING: As good as we've ever had.
LOCATION: 6374 U.S. Highway 98 West; (601) 271-6003.
WEB SITE: www.leathas.com

Clarksdale

Abe's Bar-B-Q Drive-In

Raymond Gibson Jr. remembers growing up in Clarksdale, Mississippi, and padding down to Abe's Bar-B-Que just to watch Abe slice the meat. "He sliced the barbecue so thin you could read the paper through it." Pat Davis, Abe's son, says that wasn't unusual. "Daddy kept the knives sharp, and he could slice the meat so fast people came to watch him. A man came in one time and asked him if he wanted to buy a slaw machine. Daddy said, 'What's that?' The man said, 'It'll cut up your slaw for you in five minutes.' Daddy said, 'I don't need it.' 'Why's that?' the man wanted to know, and daddy showed him. He could cut that cabbage right at the tip of his fingernails and he could do it quickly. The man watched for a minute and then turned around and said, 'No, you don't need it.'"

Abe was Abe Davis, an immigrant from Lebanon who opened his first barbecue stand in 1924. He quickly developed a reputation around north Mississippi for top-notch barbecue, and over the years the reputation has only grown. In fact, when the rock group ZZ Top stopped off at Abe's, it was the band's Billy Gibbons who asked for an autograph, instead of the other way around.

When Abe died, sons Pat and Abe Jr. took over the operation, and they've been running the place since 1960. About the only difference that we could see is that there's no one in the kitchen now who can handle a knife with quite the artistry that Abe could. Pat recalls, "It used to be the bus had a one-minute stop out here. The bus driver would run in and order a sandwich. Daddy would cut it and have it ready in twenty seconds."

We could go on at length about Abe's magic knife. Instead, let's talk about Abe's barbecue. The meat is flaky tender. Abe's prepares it a little differently than many barbecue stands. "We cook Boston butts over hickory from ten in the morning to four in the afternoon," says Pat. "That gets most of the grease out. Then we refrigerate it, slice it cold, heat it on the grill, and chop it." They squirt the meat with a tangy sauce made from ketchup,

Worcestershire sauce, and vinegar; top it with a rough slaw; and serve it on a grilled bun. How does it taste? The best recommendation we can offer for Abe's is an unsolicited one that we happened to observe. One of Abe's carhops was scraping the grill and came up with a tear of meat. He scooped it onto the chopping board, squirted it with sauce, and devoured it.

Abe's has another claim to fame besides Abe's slicing skills. The restaurant is located at the intersection of Highways 61 and 49, the legendary "Crossroads," where famed bluesman Robert Johnson supposedly sold his soul to the Devil in exchange for the ability to play the blues like no one else. Actually the roads converge at Abe's and then diverge again several miles north, meaning there are two possible "Crossroads." Or maybe, just maybe, it was just a metaphor.

RATING: Real good.
LOCATION: 616 State Street; (662) 624–9947.
WEB SITE: www.abesbbq.com

Gulfport

An-Jac's Famous Bar-B-Que

Talk about twice visited. Hurricane Camille tore through Gulfport in 1969, wrecking the town. Then thirty-six years later the town was visited again by Hurricane Katrina.

It was Camille that made An-Jac's reputation, so it was no surprise that in the wake of Katrina locals once again sought solace in their favorite local barbecue joint.

Jack Meeks, the "Jac" of An-Jac's, told us about Camille's effect for the first edition: "People that haven't seen a hurricane can't imagine. It's like a tornado times a hundred, plus it's 5 or 10 miles wide instead of 60 yards, and it lasts four or five hours." Anne, the "An," and Jack Meeks and their son Michael had been living in Gulfport on Mississippi's Gulf Coast only six years when Camille crash-landed in 1969. Jack recalled, "I drove in toward town the next morning, and there were three oceangoing vessels 250 yards inland. There was not a bird, not a sound. For two days after that all you heard was the buzzing of chainsaws. The birds didn't come back for a year and a half." Camille's 172-mile-per-hour winds killed 256 people, caused $1.4 billion in damages, and left scars that were years in healing, but her black cloud had a silver lining. It made An-Jac's Bar-B-Que famous. "We fed all the clean-up workers," recalled Michael. "I went all up and down the beach that week giving free barbecue poor boys to the highway patrolmen who were here to prevent looting."

An-Jac's was one of the few businesses to remain open during those tumultuous days. And people remembered. An-Jac's went from a home-town place to a barbecue stand that lived up to its middle name, "Famous." "Little did we know when I had the sign painted," said Jack. "I had the guy paint AN-JAC'S FAMOUS BAR-B-QUE, and he said, 'What do you mean, famous? You haven't even got outside Gulfport.' And I said, 'But we will.'"

Jack knew it because he knew how hard his family was willing to work. When they lived in north Mississippi in the early sixties, the Meeks gave new meaning to the term "moonlighting." During the day Jack worked a snack-food route and Anne ran a nursery. When Michael got home from school in the afternoon, he and his mother would begin making sandwiches. Meanwhile his father was out driving a paper route. When Jack got home, they would pile in the car and begin delivering their ready-made sandwiches to little stores all over the area. "My supper would be a Chocolate Soldier [soft drink] and a day-old sandwich at midnight," remembered Michael.

So when they took over the Gulfport grocery store, Jack began working on a new item to add to the menu, a barbecue sandwich. He knew how to cook the meat, so he set to work on the sauce. "I kept adding and taking away till I got it like I wanted it." The way he wanted it was sweet and hot, a lot of both. He got it right. It's especially potent on an "An-Jac stack," a pile of thick juicy chunks of hickory-smoked barbecue, swimming in a sea of An-Jac's sauce.

Katrina proved to be more fierce than Camille, and after this hurricane struck, An-Jac's was forced to close for two weeks for repairs. But then they were back open and back serving.

When we first visited An-Jac's two decades ago, Jack took us aside. He was getting tired, he said. Did we want to buy him out? We demurred, but we also worried. No need to worry: Jack found a buyer, David and Lacy Vickers, who have honored the past while bringing An-Jac's into the twenty-first century.

They now sell the famous sauce on the Internet. That's a plus for An-Jac's many far-flung fans. We remember on our first visit, a woman who had driven over from Shreveport, Louisiana, six hours away, to buy a case of sauce. "I'm down to one bottle in my old case." Now she can just turn on her computer and watch for the UPS man.

RATING: Real good.
LOCATION: 34 Twenty-ninth Street; (228) 868–6560.
WEB SITE: www.anjacsbbq.com

Vicksburg

Goldie's Trail Bar-B-Que

How's this for the name of a barbecue place: Goldie's Trail Bar-B-Que? You can almost see Gene Autry galloping up on Champion, the palomino rearing up, Gene waving his ten-gallon hat, the grizzled trail cook clanging the triangle, ranch hands lining up with their dinner plates.

But Goldie's Trail Bar-B-Que is on the greenhorn side of the Mississippi, on a bluff overlooking the mighty river. There is no hitching post, no bunkhouse, not even a souvenir saddle next to the cash register. It's a simple cafe decorated with framed pen-and-ink drawings from Vicksburg's Civil War past. And Goldie wasn't a grizzled cook straight out of a scene from *Wagon Train*. He was Gola Marshall, a Missouri native who learned to cook barbecue in Arkansas. "The sauce recipe was passed down in his family," says his nephew, Randy Wright, who has run Goldie's since Marshall's death in 1982. "Goldie's father gave it to him in 1949. Goldie refined it and went into the barbecue business in 1953 in Waveland, Arkansas." Goldie opened the Mountain View Inn, a little liquor store and restaurant. "Then the county went dry on him," laughs Wright. So in 1960 he moved to Vicksburg, the hometown of his wife, Wright's aunt.

And Goldie's has been there ever since. "In the sixties and seventies this was like Arnold's on *Happy Days,* the teen hangout. Now those kids are grown up, and they bring their kids in here." They want their kids to learn to love the barbecue they grew up on, and Wright tries to comply. "We do things the same way Goldie did. We peel our own potatoes for the potato salad. We still use Goldie's pits." They slow-cook pork shoulders, Boston butts, ribs, chicken, beef brisket, and sausage over hickory. The brisket and sausage are a nod to Goldie's barbecue training west of the Mississippi, as is the sauce, a thick, rich Texas-style accent that tastes as good as it looks, and it looks good. A serving of Goldie's thin-sliced pork barbecue is as beautiful as a Mississippi spring. When it is spread out on a plate, it looks like country ham covered with a thick brown gravy, waiting for a serving spoon full of grits and a *Better Homes and Gardens* photographer.

RATING: Real good.
LOCATION: 4127 Washington Street; (601) 636–9839.

Arkansas

Hot Springs

McClard's Bar-B-Q

It must have been during Burt Reynolds's third comeback—no later than his fourth comeback, for sure—that he starred in a television sitcom that brought more recognition to barbecue joints than anything before or since. The show was called *Evening Shade,* and it ran on CBS Monday nights at 8:00 P.M. for four seasons, from 1990 to 1994. One of the primary sets on the show was Ponder Blue's Barbecue Villa. (Ponder Blue was a character played by the late, great Ossie Davis.) That in itself gave barbecue joints a lot of good publicity and exposure: *Evening Shade* sometimes had as many as forty million viewers. But even better, during the show's opening credits, the producers—which included native Arkansan Harry Thomason—used photos of the real-life McClard's in Hot Springs.

In fact, McClard's was drowning in exposure in the nineties. In addition to being featured each week in the opening of *Evening Shade,* it was touted in political stories as Bill Clinton's favorite barbecue place. (That may have changed after the former president's heart bypass surgery.)

McClard's deserved all that publicity and more. It's been an Arkansas institution since 1928. That was when a roomer at Alex McClard's tourist court couldn't come up with the ten bucks to pay his month's rent. The dead-broke boarder cut a deal with the McClards: He would trade the recipe for "the best barbecue hot sauce in the world" if they would cancel his debt. It was a tempting offer (not to mention a tempting sauce). The deal was closed, and soon the little motel sported a barbecue pit.

The McClard family started out smoking goat. Legend has it that Public Enemy Number One Alvin Karpis would route his travels while on the lam through Hot Springs to satisfy his barbecued-goat cravings at McClard's. J. D. McClard, Alex's son, often told of getting a 50-cent tip from the gangster.

McClard's soon added pork to the menu and now serves up more than three tons of pork barbecue a week.

The sauce is still basically the same, a flavorful and sizzling creation that captures a pleasant freshness by building on tomato puree instead of a ketchup base. There's vinegar and lemon in there, too, for an aggressive tartness, and enough pepper of various varieties to make your lips feel like Mick Jagger's. It's a masterfully balanced amalgam of flavor and fire, the sort of thing that could lead people to pack a place out into the parking lot at lunchtime, which is exactly where customers willingly stand, waiting for a booth or a stool at the long counter.

And McClard's doesn't quit with a great sauce. Or even great barbecue. The chile-accented beans are Great Northerns, washed and cooked from scratch. The long, crisp french fries are cut from real potatoes. And the place even makes its own hand-rolled hot tamales fresh daily, which are meaty, crumbly, and close to addictive.

The barbecue itself is at least that good. The ribs are cooked over hickory wood, like the rest of the meat, but their flavor isn't overpowered by too much smoke. And the beef is fall-apart tender, after languishing in the two big brick pits on double-decker grills. All this stuff comes in typical combinations, from a beef or pork sandwich to an order of ribs with fries. But there also are meals only McClard's offers, like the Hot Tamale Spread, which includes Fritos, two hot tamales, beans, chopped meat, and barbecue sauce. It's the kind of order that can make you glad that beer's available, along with the milk shakes and pop.

The official McClard's motto is "Best in the State Since '28," a rhyme obviously composed by someone who hadn't gotten around much. It's an okay motto as far as it goes, but it aims a little low. McClard's is one of the best in the nation.

RATING: As good as we've ever had.
LOCATION: 505 Albert Pike; (501) 624-9586.
WEB SITE: www.mcclards.com

De Vall's Bluff

Craig Brothers Café

Name us another town of 783 with three—three!—world-class food joints. Got ya! There is none. Just De Vall's Bluff. This tiny town, on the bluff, of course, overlooking the White River, has Murry's Catfish, Craig's barbecue, and Mary's Family Pie Shop. We have to admit we are accepting on faith from other fellow travelers that Murry's is world-class. Whenever we visit De Vall's Bluff, we just can't seem to get out of the Craig's-Mary's nexus.

It was Pine Bluff native Bob Moody who first introduced us to Craig's. "The most unique thing about them is the sauce," he touted. And he was right. Craig's sauce is a peppery concoction, a long shot from the stuff they use just 100 miles up the road in Memphis. They generously douse your pork sandwich—you can get sliced or chopped; we prefer the latter, just because we always prefer the latter if given a choice—with this kicky concoction. Bob believes the barbecue is great, and it's not even the best thing about Craig's. That comes after the barbecue at Miss Mary's homemade pie shop. "Some days you can still buy them from her kitchen across the road, but when she's not feeling well they are on sale at Craig's. The chocolate pie is the world's best. I know people who used to drive from Memphis just to get them. The routine is for me to walk in and ask politely, 'Miss Mary, do you have a chocolate pie ready?' She'll say, 'I have a chocolate pie for one person, and I have a chocolate pie for many persons.' 'Miss Mary, I'll have a "many persons" to go, please.'"

RATING: Real good.
LOCATION: Highway 70; (870) 998-2616.

P.S. Murry's burned down recently and rebuilt in Hazen, 7 miles away. So De Vall's Bluff is down to two world-class eateries.

Little Rock

Lindsey's

"We only have one peach pie left," the counter girl said with a sly look. "And I was sort of saving that for myself." It's true: The only problem with Lindsey's selling first-rate barbecue is that it gets in the way of a headlong rush to dessert—one of those mystically flaky fried pies with its waves of intense peach and cinnamon. The peach pies (and the apple ones, which are almost as good) are part of a half-century tradition at Lindsey's. They are made from dried fruit, which gives them a concentrated dose of flavor, and the fruit is packed inside a crust as crisp and light as the breath of an angel.

Begun in 1956 by Church of God in Christ Bishop D. L. Lindsey, this downtown barbecue joint has been specializing in the heavenly ever since. Other Little Rock barbecue legends, like Fisher's, for instance, have changed owners and given up consistency, but Lindsey's (owned since 1972 by the founder's nephew, Richard Lindsey) still produces barbecue that's practically preordained delicious. "It's not easy mixing religion and barbecue," says Lindsey, "because religion is a twenty-four-hour-a-day job, and so is barbecue."

With its orange walls, the eat-in half of the restaurant is clean and neat, down to the forks that arrive in fork-size plastic bags. A fork sinks easily into the restaurant's rich, thin-sliced beef, which is cooked for fourteen to sixteen hours. It's complemented nicely by a distinctive, watery sauce that combines a sharp tomato tanginess with meaty undertones. The pork ribs are even better with the sauce; they are at that state of tenderness where a sharp look is sufficient to make them slide off the bone. Small ribs that have been specially trimmed, they are pushed into the pit about 8:00 A.M. After six hours or so, they are dunked in a thin dipping sauce and cooked for a couple more hours. "I remember the first bite of barbecue I ever put in my mouth," Richard says, "and I want to be the one to put that first bite in somebody else's mouth."

RATING: Good.

LOCATION: 203 East Fourteenth Street in North Little Rock; (501) 374-5901.

Blytheville

The Dixie Pig

There's no sense dwelling on looks. The Dixie Pig looks numbingly ordinary, like any of an army of little family restaurants stamped out of bricks and paneling and muted floral carpeting. But the sandwich, well, that's something else—a mountain of pork with a volcano of sauce. It proves, among other things, that you can walk into a place about as exotic as a Travelodge lobby and still end up with a tantalizing bunful of barbecue.

Actually, the Dixie Pig and its cookie-cutter decor started out in 1923 as the Rustic Inn, a log cabin that had to stretch to earn the word *rustic*. Buddy Halsell's dad, Ernest, started it, and, as Buddy says, "It if it wasn't the oldest place in Arkansas, it was close to." They figure it was up and running before Memphis's legendary Pig & Whistle, for instance. Ernest moved it to a rock building for a while, and then sold it in 1946 to try farming. In 1950, he came to his senses and opened the Dixie Pig at its present location. "We used to have a curb business," Buddy says, "but we stopped that when people got crazy." Besides not selling to crazy people in cars, Buddy also doesn't sell ribs. "People eat ribs about one night a week," he figures, "but if you try to serve 'em a second or third night, you just messed up your business." Instead he serves 'em sandwiches, great heaping sandwiches of pork flecked with bits so singed they taste like bacon, all nestled beneath a layer of mild vinegar slaw. It's the sort of sandwich where your second bite is apt to be bigger than your first, and so on, until you can begin to appreciate the motto: "Feeling Piggish? See Buddy." The sandwich also serves as a perfect canvas for some artistic splashes of the spicy vinegar sauce that reposes in converted Heinz ketchup bottles at each table.

The credit for the sandwich's crunchy come-on goes to Buddy's hickory-pit technique: Cook it hot and cook it fast. "I don't believe in smoking the meat," he says. "I don't understand people who put their meat on a rack and leave it until the next day; I don't see how they keep from making people sick." Credit for another of Buddy's specialties, the Pig Salad, goes to Miss Lucy Q., Lucille Quellmalz, a teacher at Blytheville High School, who ordered barbecue piled on her tossed salad so often that other customers began wanting it, too. A Pig Salad in its full glory, with lettuce and tomatoes and crunchy pork underneath a glob of oddball "blue cheese" dressing, is the sort of life experience one is not likely to find outside of Blytheville.

RATING: Good.
LOCATION: 701 North Sixth Street; (870) 763-4636.

Louisiana

Lafayette

The A & B Henderson Bar-B-Q Lodge (and Gator Cove)

Barbecue has a seafood soul brother—a dish with origins almost as humble and a following almost as fanatic, a dish so delightfully spicy and so satisfyingly sloppy that any stuffed shirt in the vicinity is sure to catch a drip. The nice thing is, at A & B Henderson's you can eat them both: smoky barbecue and steaming crawfish.

The barbecue came first, a pit with a tiny dining room built more than twenty-five years ago. And then the offshore drilling boom hit the Gulf, bringing hordes of hungry oil workers into the area. When the dust settled, the original pit had acquired a big new dining room, plus a second pit with its own dining room, a landscaped courtyard, offices, party rooms, and a catering service that still will cook crawfish for your party in a giant pot.

On the sunny summer afternoon we first visited, the huge complex was almost deserted. Inside the lodge (which looks like a lodge should, with A-frame timber ceilings and a big stone fireplace), the hats outnumbered the heads. This was due to the A & B "gimme cap" collection, scores of baseball caps with commercial messages nailed to the walls and rafters. There were caps from Hawaii, from the Melmar Tools Co., the NRA, and, of course, the A & B Henderson Bar-B-Q Lodge. Those hats are gone now, but you can still order a cold beer and an A & B Special, that tasty sandwich on a toasted bun that is loaded with bits of barbecue, many nicely burnt, and a splash of molasses-dark, tart tomato sauce. They won't say what's in the sandwich, but it tasted like a mixture of beef and pork, and it tasted real good, especially with the "dirty rice" that had more barbecue bits mixed in. Get there between eleven and two for the 'que. Add on an order of crawfish for an enjoyable, earthy surf-and-turf combination, the crawfish painfully hot and powerfully spicy. This may be the only place on Earth to try it, and try it you should.

RATING: Good.
LOCATION: 2601 Southeast Evangeline; (337) 264-1373.

Baton Rouge

Jay's Barbecue

There was a sandy-haired guy at the counter in Jay's, sitting on one of the five metal stools next to his sweet, shy bride-to-be. He had brought her to the little barbecue joint where his mother had always taken him—not as a test, perhaps, but just the same, he had ordered her some ribs and was watching her eat with more than casual interest. Marriages can survive many things, but a serious disagreement about good barbecue may not be one of them.

It would be hard to break up at Jay's, however. Jay's has real good barbecue. Jay's pitmaster of more than six decades, Floyd J. LeBlanc Sr., has passed on. He was a thoroughly entertaining pitmaster who started cooking at age fourteen. In a profession full of slow-talking characters, Floyd was permanently stuck on fast-forward. He would chat with customers, customers' little children, salesgirls from down the street, and someone just looking for change. He joked and joshed, sometimes carrying on a phone conversation at the same time. "Hey! Don't you go talkin' to me that way!" he laughed into the phone. "I'm bad! I drink barbecue sauce every day for a living, so you know I'm bad!"

Floyd LeBlanc was a big deal in Baton Rouge. Awards have been presented; film crews have filmed. But all that was almost incidental to a man who genuinely and completely loved barbecue, who said, "Barbecuing is like getting up and going to school every day; you are always learning something new." For Floyd that included smoked alligator tail, which was not featured on the menu, as well as beef, ham, pork, turkey, ribs, and chicken, which are.

There are barbecue cooks who understand barbecuing but don't eat it much; "It's like working in a candy store," they'll tell you. But Floyd LeBlanc was not one of those people: "How could you ever get tired of barbecue?" he wondered aloud. "I eat it every day. I eat it for breakfast every day. There are so many ways to fix it, so many kinds of meat. I eat it dry, I eat it on toast—this morning, I mixed it with potato salad and ate it that way."

One recommended way to eat it is in one of his Barbecue Po'boys. Floyd's son Milton runs the place now and still offers this hefty sandwich, built on a French-style loaf with handfuls of delicately pecan-smoked beef or pork (or both), sliced thin and tender and dressed with anything from lettuce and tomato and cheese to a simple slosh of Floyd's tonsil-tweaking, tangy sauce. It's an excellent sandwich and just one of the things at Jay's that has attracted attention.

"A fellow tried to talk me into opening up a place in California," Floyd said. "He said just to tell him how I cook the meat and do that sauce, and he'd set things up out there." It wasn't that Floyd had anything against California, but he turned the man down. "Some of this stuff is written down," he explained, "but a lot of it's just up in my head. And telling a man all your secrets on cooking is like letting him borrow your wife. It just doesn't work that way."

RATING: Real good.
LOCATION: 4215 Government Street; (225) 343–5082.

Ville Platte

The Pig Stand

The salty, smoky spare ribs were coated with a bright orange, homemade baste. They were served at an aging table with three brands of hot sauce, plus a bottle of peppers and onions—in a spare brick building with only a Coca-Cola sign announcing its presence. A classic barbecue joint, right? Well . . . no.

The Pig Stand Restaurant is a classic Cajun barbecue joint, and there's a difference. It's not just that the cooks and friendly waitresses chatter in French, either. A Cajun rib dinner is a wonderful experience full of surprises, and the ribs themselves are just part of the fun. Take the first course: It's true that most barbecue dinners don't include (or even allow) a first course, but the Pig Stand's oyster gumbo is reason enough to reconsider that tradition. Available a la carte, the gumbo arrives in an immense flat bowl, savory with the flavors of a buttery, mellow roux and studded with plump oysters. It manages to seem sinful and satisfying and vaguely healthful all at the same time. It's the perfect setup for a Bar-B-Q Spare Rib lunch—available on Sunday. The strip of pork spare ribs is cooked just short of chewy, smoked pink, and very salty, with a cumulative spicy heat. But the ribs aren't the hottest thing on the plate; that honor goes to the smothered potatoes, a luscious casserole of potatoes and cheese with stingingly hot greens cooked all through it. For six bucks, ribs and a superlative side dish may seem sufficient, but go ahead and add on some rich "rice stuffing" dense with crumbs of liver. And some meltingly soft and sweet butter beans (baby limas). And a heap of white rice with a dark roux gravy. It's generous and genuinely delicious.

While patting one's protruding tummy, a short after-dinner promenade may be in order, and just a few hundred feet down the street, at 434 East Main Street, is Floyd's "Nationally Advertised" Record Shop, jammed with Cajun music, blues, oldies, and scenic postcards of Martian Klansmen wearing what appears to be aluminum foil on their heads. You could do worse than walk out of there with Rockin' Sidney's *My Zydeco Shoes Got the Zydeco Blues*. And if you walk briskly in the hot Louisiana sun, you may make room for more oyster gumbo. For dessert.

RATING: Pretty good.
LOCATION: 318 East Main Street; (337) 363–2883.

Florida

Florida is the only state that has "Native" novelty license plates. Or needs to. Maybe that's why Sonny's and Fat Boy's, two barbecue chains, have done so well there. Too few natives to build up a strong barbecue tradition. That's why some of the best barbecue places in the state have names like Big John's Alabama Bar-B-Que and Georgia Boy's and Georgia Pig.

That doesn't mean you can't find good barbecue in the Sunshine State. We did. It just means we had to try a little harder.

Tampa

Big John's Alabama Bar-B-Que

Big John was a big man, and not just in stature. He had a big, big heart. His children tell about growing up with hobos at the dinner table, about drug addicts in the living room being counseled by Dad, and about family friends sitting in the living room while Big John wrote a check to help them catch up on their rent. In fact, if you listen to the story of Big John, you wonder how he had time to run a barbecue joint. He was a preacher with two churches and a father with ten kids and a philanthropist without portfolio.

And he had a barbecue joint, a great barbecue joint, that paid his bills and the bills of quite a few others.

Big John learned his craft growing up poor in Eufaula, Alabama—that's where the Alabama part of the restaurant's name came from. Barbecue was a family tradition, and he learned his lessons well; lessons that he preached—he was a Baptist minister, after all—to his children and his employees and, shoot, just about anybody who came in the restaurant and showed the least interest in the cooking art.

His guidelines were simple. Don't baste first; keep the fleshy side of the meat up until the end; and never take your eyes off the fire.

And when he died in 1994 he left his kids his barbecue joint, his barbecue traditions, and his secret sauce recipe. And they have carried on in a way that would make Dad proud. Big John had turned Big John's into a Florida institution. The kids have kept it there.

Big John's chopped-pork sandwich, saturated in an ochre made of tomato, Tabasco, vinegar, and God-only-knows is divine.

The family has kept Big John's in the same plain brick building that you might mistake for a used-clothing store if it weren't for the smoke. It's not much to look at, but you can't eat atmosphere.

RATING: Real good.
LOCATION: 5707 North Fortieth Street; (813) 626–9800.

Fort Lauderdale

Tom Jenkins' Bar-B-Q

There is a saying in Florida that the farther south you go, the farther north you are. What Floridians are trying to tell you is that South Florida is the home of many transplanted Northerners. Not fertile ground for a barbecue pilgrim? To the contrary. The best barbecue joints in Florida are located a bone's throw from each other on the so-called Gold Coast, the ritzy strip from Palm Beach to Miami. Okay, you'd have to have a mighty strong arm to throw a bone from West Palm Beach to Fort Lauderdale. But they are close in the scope of things in Florida: It is 813 miles from the tip of Key West to Pensacola. From Tom's to Tom's it's only 48 miles.

Oh, did we mention that both are named Tom's?

But therein the similarities stop. Tom's Place in West Palm has been around since the seventies. Tom Jenkins' in Fort Lauderdale dates to the mid-nineties, although it, too, has a connection that goes back to the seventies. That's when Harry Harrell and Gary Torrence met as freshmen at Florida A&M in Tallahassee. Twelve years later in 1990 they both found themselves in South Florida. Harry was a computer systems engineer, Gary a middle school math teacher. They decided to do something about a mutual love of cooking barbecue and opened up a weekend barbecue trailer in the parking lot of a quickie-lube shop, using family recipes they begged from relatives in Georgia, Alabama, and South Carolina. They named their modest little enterprise after Harry's Uncle Tom because Harry & Gary's just didn't sound like a grown-up name for a business. Their little trailer spewed smoke and looked for all the world like a hobby that would eventually disappear as its owners moved on with their lives. Then in 1996 Harry lost his job. So the two dug into their own pockets, tapped friends and relatives and credit cards, and opened up a real restaurant in a failed country music bar across the street from their trailer.

And true to the adage "if you smoke it, they will come," their little weekend hobby was soon a full-fledged business with payroll and withholding taxes and heavenly ribs, the sensuous, smoky kind that draw folks from what is usually called "the greater metropolitan area."

Today Tom Jenkins' is only a couple of steps above that old trailer, a homely little place with a mere forty picnic-table seats. But that's okay, because the food is also the same: wonderful.

RATING: Real good.

LOCATION: 1236 South Federal Highway; (954) 522–5046.

West Palm Beach

Tom's Place

The other Tom's has a longer but no less rich history. Tom Wright had cooked for the rich folks in Boca for twenty years when he decided he wanted to go out on his own. In '79 he opened up a soul food shack in some lend-lease-leftover Army barracks that he got for $30-a-month rent. To call it a barbecue "joint" would have been charitable. It was located in Pearl City, one of Boca's poorest neighborhoods. Wright says it was a full year before he had his first white customer, a newspaper reporter who ate some ribs, went back to the office, and drooled in print. That's how the rich people rediscovered Wright. It wasn't long before his lunch lines were longer than a New York block. He made enough money to buy the barracks, tear it down, and erect a large modern place.

But success didn't spoil Tom Wright. He still came in bright and early each morning, overseeing all the kitchen work and insisting that his employees start each day with a prayer. Tom hadn't forgotten where he came from. So many days he would stand by the cash register at lunch time and randomly pull checks and rip them up, giving the customer a free lunch. Matt Toth, a regular customer who lives in nearby Coral Springs, said, "I've been there when he's torn up one in every twenty checks."

But it wasn't Wright's philanthropy that kept those lines long. Heck, those customers came in intending to pay. It was his barbecue: baby back ribs spooned with a delicately sweet sauce. David Pinter, a fellow from Tappan, New York, was so taken with Wright's sauce that he offered $100,000 for the recipe. When Wright declined, Pinter tried paying a chemist $10,000 to duplicate it. He took the cloned sauce and opened a barbecue restaurant in Tappan. It closed soon. There's a moral there, and we don't think we have to enunciate it.

Tom died in February 2006, and the family moved his place to nearby West Palm Beach. But it's still Tom's Place, run Tom's way, by Tom's family.

RATING: Real good.

LOCATION: 1225 Palm Beach Lakes Boulevard; (561) 832–8774.

Mid-Atlantic and Northeast States

The North—that's what folks in the South call it.
Folks in the North break it down into niches like New
England and the Mid-Atlantic and New York. But
in the South it's a giant monolith, a barbecue wilderness.
Well, we are here to tell you: not anymore.

Washington, D.C.

The last time we surveyed D.C. barbecue twenty years ago, we found the best place was an hour south of the White House in the Maryland town of LaPlata. But in the intervening two decades, that same White House has been occupied most of the time by southerners. The result is a renaissance in capital barbecue.

That barbecue renaissance began with the invasion of southerners who followed Republican operative—and Georgia native—Lee Atwater to Washington with Reagan and Bush I. One of those was Don Sundquist, a newly elected congressman, who missed the west Tennessee-style barbecue of his home district. Sundquist, along with three friends, opened Red Hot & Blue in the suburb of Arlington in 1988 (the year our first edition was published). The publicity they engendered attracted a large crowd; the barbecue they served kept that crowd returning. And suddenly barbecue was back in D.C. For that reason alone Red Hot & Blue deserves a big Hee Haw-style salute!

So this time we didn't have to close our eyes and pretend that a southern diner was a barbecue joint. Barbecue places have sprouted all over town and spilled over into the suburbs. And God looked down and smiled.

Washington, D.C.

Rocklands Barbeque and Grilling Co.

The door was open, but Rocklands was closed. And our hearts sunk, for Rocklands had the strongest recommendations of any D.C. joint from our barbecue buddies.

"Can you just sell us a sandwich?" we pleaded.

"No electricity," the cook shrugged. "We might open up later if we get our lights back on."

Rocklands Barbeque and Grilling Co.

"You don't even have enough meat for one sandwich?" we beseeched.

"No man, we sent all our meat to the other store."

Bingo! We headed for the other store. As it turns out, there are three other Rocklands joints in the greater D.C. area. The powerless place had the funkiest decor. But all cook their 'que over real hardwood, chop it up, and baptize it with a spicy ointment—there's lemon juice, molasses, and brown sugar in there somewhere—that commands your palate to pay attention.

So in this edition we can proudly say that the best barbecue in D.C. is actually cooked, served, and sold in D.C. The flagship of the Rocklands fledgling empire is in the city proper, a mere 3 miles from the seat of government.

Rocklands opened in 1990 in the wake of Red Hot & Blue and in the intervening years has overtaken its elder for barbecue supremacy in the capital.

RATING: Real good.

LOCATION: 2418 Wisconsin Avenue Northwest (the original spot); (202) 333-2558. There are additional locations at 25 South Quaker Lane, Alexandria, Virginia (703-778-9663), and Wintergreen Plaza, 891A Rockville Pike, Rockville, Maryland (240-268-1120).

WEB SITE: www.rocklands.com.

P.S. We thought we were giving inner-city spot Kenny's a second chance to get in this book. The last time we visited, Vince was ordering his sandwich when a large fellow in a suit sidled up and tried to fence some stolen jewelry off on the counterman. That would have made a great Barbecue Rule: If they're fencing stolen jewelry at the counter, you can count on good barbecue. But alas, it wasn't good barbecue, just a good story. This time Kenny's was a bit more uptown. A jewelry fence would be turned away at the door at this neighborhood joint in Stanton Park. As it turns out, it is a different Kenny's. Apparently there is more than one Kenny in Washington who can cook barbecue. And this Kenny can cook. Douse the pulled pork with eastern North Carolina–style vinegar sauce, and you'll think

Kenny's BBQ Smokehouse

you're on your way to the beach. Kenny's BBQ Smokehouse is at 732 Maryland Avenue Northeast; (202) 547–4553.

P.S.S. If you like Blue-Ribbon Bar-B-Q in the Boston area, you'll like Willard's in Chantilly, Virginia, near Dulles Airport. North Carolina native Chris Janowski, who founded Blue-Ribbon, moved down to D.C., and in 2003 he opened Willard's. The name even sounds southern, but it is actually derived from nearby Willard Road. Both Willard's and Blue-Ribbon claim to be "inspired by the classic roadside barbecue joints that dot the American south." They even look alike. And the barbecue tastes alike. And that's good, real good.

Maryland

LaPlata

Johnny Boy's Ribs

If Johnny Boy's had bad barbecue, it might create a new credibility gap. People wouldn't trust their eyes anymore. For if ever we saw a place that screamed barbecue, it was Johnny Boy's. Johnny Katsouros and his mother, Sophie, opened their place in an open-air take-out shack edged up against busy Highway 301 in the tobacco country south of LaPlata, Maryland. There's a tumble-down stack of wood scattered to the side. Paint is peeling off the plank sign. But Johnny Boy doesn't care. "People don't have to read the sign to know it's a barbecue. If I built a fancy place out of cinderblocks and make it so people can come and sit down, well, you lose something."

Johnny Boy's Ribs

Katsouros cooks on an iron grate balanced on cement blocks, an open pit, the kind of barbecue cooker that is prohibited or regulated in some places but not in rural Charles County. The ribs and sandwiches are take-out only, but there are convenient picnic tables. You even have to get your drink from a machine. But if it's a hot summer day and you're cruising the open road with the windows down and the radio up, it would be impossible to speed through those billows of Johnny Boy's hickory smoke without stopping to sample the barbecue.

If you stop, your reward is a multitextured minced-pork sandwich with crunchies from the crust and delicate morsels from the middle. Or you could choose a generous slab of auburn-colored ribs, reeking of hickory and oak smoke, so good they don't even need sauce, although Johnny Boy has a strong peppery-hot one with an up-front pop; no surprises later.

RATING: Real good.
LOCATION: 7540 Crain Highway; (301) 392–9313.

Baltimore

Andy Nelson's Southern Pit Barbecue

This is the kind of barbecue town Baltimore was twenty years ago: The same month that *Baltimore* magazine picked the Wharf Rat as the Best Barbecued Rib Restaurant in the city, new owners dropped the item from the menu.

This is the kind of barbecue town Baltimore is now: Folks actually talk about barbecue, debating the relative merits of Boog's at the ballpark versus Andy Nelson's up north in Cockeysville.

It's great to have a barbecue debate again.

Last trip through the debate centered on the venerable Woody's, which has now been in business for fifty years, the rib joint of preference for the late professional wrestler Haystack Calhoun; Oprah Winfrey's favorite joint, the Dixie Pig, since closed; and Leon's Pig Pit, which is now, uh, Lake Trout.

Each had its fans, but the partisanship was wishy-washy; no one really claimed either of the three was destination barbecue.

Then came Andy Nelson.

If you're familiar with the movie *Diner,* then you know that it's only right that the best barbecue in Baltimore is served up by an old Baltimore Colt. The movie, which we are told brilliantly captures 1959 Baltimore (neither of us were in Baltimore that year), is about a guy who can't marry his girlfriend unless she can pass a prenup, a 140-question quiz about the Baltimore Colts football team. If she doesn't score at least sixty-five, well, the wedding is off. We won't spoil the ending of the movie, but we will tell you if you want great barbecue in Baltimore, you can have a happy ending. Just head north to Cockeysville and Andy's place.

Andy actually played for the Colts in that *Diner* season of 1959. He also played in '57, '58, and '60 through '64. Andy was a defensive back, and in 1959 he was only a year away from the Pro Bowl.

He came out of Alabama via Memphis State, and you can see his barbecue pedigree right there.

We arrived at his place shortly before noon, and already they were lined out the door. It's honor-system barbecue: You give them your order and wait around till they call out what you ordered. And it's an honor to get to eat it. Others agree. We were surrounded by grandmas and young blue-collars. It's a funky place, the interior of an old house that has been chopped up into rooms, and each was filled. The overflow spilled out onto picnic tables outside.

Andy's crew cooks over hickory in a pit next door in an old filling station. Andy says his dad was a cooker of "serious barbecue" back in Limestone, Alabama. For his restaurant Andy has combined the Memphis traditions he learned while playing at Memphis State with the family heritage. And doused it in an heirloom sauce.

Despite his Deep South roots, Andy also sells an indigenous Maryland style of barbecue, pit beef. It's top round, crispy on the outside, juicy on the inside, sliced thin, smothered in horseradish sauce, and served on a Kaiser roll. Andy proves he's a Marylander now because his pit beef is more than just top round, it's top-notch.

RATING (PORK BARBECUE): Real good.

LOCATION: 11007 York Road, Cockeysville (a Baltimore suburb); (410) 527–1226.

WEB SITE: www.andynelsonsbbq.com

P.S. We regret the closing of Baltimore's late, great Cafe Tattoo—or the Tattoo Café—depending on how you entered. "If you go in the front, you are in the barbecue joint; if you go in the back, you are in the tattoo parlor, which is run by the barbecue guy's wife," our barbecue connoisseur friend, Bob Moody, told us twenty years ago. The Tattoo was run by Rick Catalano and his wife, tattoo artist Elayne. Elayne was a dead ringer, no pun intended, for Morticia Addams of TV's *The Addams Family.* Elayne was the brains behind the business according to Rick. "If it weren't for her, I'd be sleeping in a cardboard box over some steam grate." It was Elayne who concocted the sauces. She had the gustatory equivalent of perfect pitch. "A friend went to Arthur Bryant's and brought back his sauce," Rick told us. "She went in the kitchen and came back later and said, 'Here it is.' She had duplicated it exactly."

What happened to that Tattoo? It had a similar fate to Rick and Elayne's honeymoon back in 1969. "Elayne and I were going to go to Woodstock for our honeymoon. But by the time we got out of the reception, they were saying on the radio that all the roads were blocked, so we didn't go. It was just as well. Everybody we knew who went came back with walking pneumonia."

The Tattoo was at 4825 Belair Road. It's now the Mojo Room and Lounge. R.I.P. to the only barbecue joint where you could chow down on great 'que and get *Mother* stitched onto your bicep in one stop.

Pennsylvania

Philadelphia

Zeke's Mainline Bar-B-Que

If the name makes you think that perhaps the barbecue at Zeke's must be eaten in white tails and ball gowns with pinky raised, never fear. It may have *Mainline* in its name, but this isn't a fancy joint. For one thing, the Mainline isn't what it once was, at least in Zeke's neighborhood. Affluence has moved the Mainline farther out. Zeke's is just working folks. You won't run into any of Grace Kelly's descendants in Zeke's.

First off, let's be honest; this is a cheesesteak town. But man cannot live by cheesesteak alone. There's plenty of room in the Philly diet for the occasional visit out to Zeke's.

Zeke's is southern style—his pit is a Southern Pride that he dragged up from Chattanooga. He serves his pulled pork on white bread with candied sweet potatoes on the side. Zeke's prices aren't southern style. A sandwich is $8.00. But it is huge. We couldn't finish ours, not and still get a healthy sampling of the yams.

While we were eating, Zeke asked if we were from New York. The question puzzled us until Zeke—real name Prentice Cole—pointed to the paper we were reading. It was a copy of the *New York Daily News* we bought when we stopped to get gas outside town. We thought it was the *Philadelphia Daily News,* but Zeke spotted the difference immediately. You see, Zeke is a reformed newspaperman, ten years as a photographer at the *Philadelphia Daily News*. Zeke is a bit of a renaissance man to be running a barbecue joint. He's a graduate of the prestigious Wharton Business School and worked for fourteen years as a wine merchant before opening his 'que spot.

He's done it right, cooking dry-rubbed meats with hardwood and smoke (the Southern Pride also burns gas for a consistent temperature), then finishing the meat off on a direct hardwood grill.

If it can be barbecued, Zeke barbecues it: pork, beef brisket, baby back pork ribs, pork spare ribs, beef long ribs, even chicken and wings.

RATING: Real good.
LOCATION: 6001 Lancaster Avenue; (215) 871–RIBS (7427).

New York

New York City

Big Apple Que

John Stage and Andrew Fishel and Adam Perry Lang and Danny Meyer should thank their lucky pigs every day for Barry Farber, whether they know it or not. Stage and Fishel and Lang and Meyer are the proprietors of four of Manhattan's newest, hottest, and best barbecue joints (respectively Dinosaur, R.U.B., Daisy Mae, and Blue Smoke). But without the groundwork laid by Barry, they might be in other lines of work.

It was Barry, the Godfather of New York City Barbecue, who paved the way for the current explosion of barbecue joints in Manhattan—and it is an explosion.

In 1977 Farber first introduced the city that never sleeps to the food that takes all night to cook. At the time Farber, a popular New York radio talk-show host and North Carolina native, decided that his adopted city should become acquainted with the cuisine of his native state. He thought he could satisfy his hunger for authentic North Carolina barbecue and maybe even make some money. "I have a theory—never believe a fact unless it's supported by a theory—that foods have blister power to reach beyond their boundaries and make friends," says Farber. "The food with the greatest blister power is pizza. Pizza broke out of Italy and conquered the world.

The lowest blister power is Philadelphia scrapple. It's not sold one yard outside the city limits. It's just bad. Estonian codfish heads have low blister power. Second to pizza, North Carolina barbecue has the greatest blister power on Earth. If properly presented, it will conquer the world."

He took his theory to his friend Alex Parker, who owned a building on Times Square. "I told him, 'I've got a product that is the next pizza.'" Farber explained his blister theory to Parker, and the next day the two were flying down to North Carolina to let Parker taste the theory. "Alex didn't want to eat the barbecue. It was so good, he just wanted to put his head down in it." With Parker convinced, Farber arranged to have Fuzzy's Bar-B-Que in Madison, North Carolina, package chopped pork in Dixie Cups and send it to New York every night by air express.

Parker had already rented his Times Square space to a Greek restaurant, but as luck would have it, the man was behind in his rent. "So Alex goes to the guy and says, 'Tony, I want you to put this [barbecue] in your restaurant for me. We want to see how it goes.'" Farber went on the radio and advertised this great place on Times Square that had authentic North Carolina barbecue. And sat back and waited for the fame and adulation, and also money, that should naturally accrue to someone who had brought the Real Thing to the Big Apple. But it didn't happen. "I began getting hate mail from North Carolinians. They would hear me say it's authentic North Carolina barbecue on the radio, and they would drive down from Yonkers and White Plains, and then the guy would serve it to them on a cold bun with no slaw. The Greek seemed to be going along like a Viet Cong who knew his rights by the Geneva Convention. Every day it was no rolls or old rolls or cold rolls or 'We forgot to make slaw.'"

The Great North-Carolina-Barbecue-in-New-York-City Experiment ended when Farber took a prominent North Carolinian to try out the place. "And the Greek served him authentic North Carolina barbecue on a bagel. Authentic pork barbecue on a bagel! If Moses had seen that, there would have been another commandment."

Things have changed dramatically since Farber's Folly. Barbecue is no longer an alien dish in New York City. Clueless deli owners don't plop it on a bagel. In fact, it's hot; it's cool; it's what's happening now. In the new century it seems a new "authentic" barbecue joint is being opened every week. Oh, the menu-writers still have to explain the pink smoke ring, to hold down all the orders being sent back to the kitchen, but New Yorkers are picking up on the difference between Memphis style, North Carolina style, and Texas style. They understand that "pulled" and "rubbed" have nothing to do with the Manhattan massage parlors.

Now when the words *authentic* and *barbecue* are printed side by side in a restaurant opening notice, locals flock. And we think that is de-lovely.

Not all the new barbecue places get it. Some might best be described as "barbecue theme" restaurants, where the rustic decor is more important than the food. But a handful are doing it right, or as right as you can in a city with strict pollution laws and even stricter neighborhood watchdog groups.

It's expensive to do it right. Smoke-scrubbing technology can cost thousands of dollars. But a one-bedroom apartment with a view of a brick wall is also expensive. It's the nature of New York.

R.U.B.

Isn't it ironic that in the city that invented irony, the New York barbecue joint with the worst name—R.U.B. stands for (ick) Righteous Urban Barbecue—serves the best barbecue?

You could say, "Well they should serve the best, their guru is the king of the competition circuit, Kansas City's Paul Kirk, who at last count had won 425 barbecue cook-offs." But cooking competitively and cooking commercially are not the same thing, as many a Memphis in May winner can attest (see John Willingham and John Wills, both winners who opened restaurants that are now closed). A restaurant may cook more pork on an off day than a competition team cooks in a summer season.

The road from barbecue cook-offs to barbecue cafes is littered with broken dreams and dry bones. But if there is any justice, R.U.B. is in for a long run. This open-air cafe—at least in nice weather it's open-air—serves up tender pulled pork; flavorful, moist sliced beef; and scrumptious ribs that the menu calls the Barbecue Standard. We agree. We were most taken with the brisket sandwich. Beef brisket is the toughest barbecue meat. It takes a long time to smoke but a short time to lose its moisture. And beef is a less forgiving meat than pork. But at R.U.B., they've got it right.

We're not really sure what a BBQ Reuben is or even want to know. But it's on the menu along with an item that demonstrates the place has a New York sense of humor: a smoked mushroom sandwich is called a Pulled Portobello.

RATING: Real good.

LOCATION: 208 West Twenty-third (between Seventh and Eighth Avenues); (212) 524-4300.

WEB SITE: www.rubbbq.net

Dinosaur

All we asked was, "How did this place get started?" We didn't say, "We're world-famous barbecue authors here to evaluate your food and see if you deserve a spot in the next edition of our definitive guide to American barbecue joints." We just casually asked our server how Dinosaur came to be.

And in less time than it takes to pull your pork, John Stage was standing at our table, introducing himself and telling us the story of Dinosaur Bar-B-Que. That's the kind of place Dinosaur is: friendly, personal, and serious about the barbecue.

Stage laughed as he told us how he got into the business. He was living in upstate New York, mostly involved with motorcycles, when he bought a barrel cooker and began selling grilled steak sandwiches at various festivals around. "I was calling it barbecue. Then I did a festival below the Mason Dixon line."

Whoa. His southern customers were quick to tell John that what he

A sample of the real barbecue served at Dinosaur in New York City

was cooking was not barbecue and even quicker to show him how to cook barbecue, real barbecue.

The next thing he knew, he was opening Dinosaur in Syracuse, along with two partners. That was in 1988. He kept perfecting his technique and opened a second upstate place in Rochester in 1998. And then in 2004 he decided he was ready to take on the Big Apple. He knew where he wanted to set up shop. Not in downtown. Not in uptown. Nowhere fancy. He wanted it in the heart of Harlem.

And that's where he is, just about as far west on 131st Street as you can get without operating a floating restaurant in the Hudson River. He converted a former meatpacking house into a jumping joint, with windows that open out, inviting in the cool river breeze and also any cars that happen to be driving up Twelfth Avenue.

It is the friendliest barbecue joint we've ever been in, right down to the waiter who insisted on finding the owner to tell us his story. We suspect that attitude filters on down to the pigs, who are happy to serve on your sandwich.

RATING: Real good.
LOCATION: 646 West 131st Street, West Harlem (at Twelfth Avenue); (212) 694–1777.
WEB SITE: www.dinosaurbarbque.com

Daisy May's

A barbecue joint in North Carolina can be open for fifty years and accumulate only a handful of newspaper clippings. But open a new barbecue joint in Manhattan, and you can plaster an entire wall with the press from just the first month.

And that's how we came to be reading what seemed like a book-length accumulation of newspaper stories about Daisy May's on the West Side while waiting for our order to be prepared. We didn't have to ask the staff any questions. Anything we could possibly want to know was already answered on the Wall of Fame.

And one thing we didn't want to know: We didn't want to know that the pitmaster was called executive chef. That term popped up all over New York when referring to what we call the "cook." At Dinosaur our waiter insisted we should meet the executive chef, whom he identified as a former biker who was covered with tattoos. We met him, and he met none of our preconceptions about an executive chef. He wasn't wearing one of those froufrou hats; he wasn't fussing around with some delightful sauce. He was wearing a T-shirt, and he was covered with tattoos. He was a cook, titles notwithstanding.

We think the term "chef" keeps popping up in connection with New York barbecue cooks because it's in the culture. When the restaurant critorati write about eateries, those eateries have kitchens run by chefs.

Adam Perry Lang, the executive chef/pitmaster at Daisy May's, built

Daisy May's

up quite a little reputation in New York's cafe (literally) society, working in the kitchens of such snooty eateries as Le Cirque and Daniel (we've never been to either). But when we met him, he was wearing a ball cap and apologizing for the tardiness of our order (we were incognito).

What you get with a trained chef at the helm is more complex sauces. This isn't doctored-up Open Pit. There are enough notes in Daisy May's sauce to send a wine critic heading to the thesaurus.

Of the four top NYC 'que joints, Daisy May's looks the least like a barbecue theme restaurant. It is an example of an age-old barbecue practice, where the joint adapts to the architecture rather than vice versa. You enter the door—if the line isn't already out it—make a sharp left, where you order at the beginning of a long counter; pick up your food at the far end; and then head into a tiny dining area where you eat boardinghouse style, elbow to elbow with total strangers. It's the Automat with smoke.

But our choice, the pulled-pork sandwich, served Carolina style, slaw on top, might make you think you were back in the South, if not for the taxis whistling up and down Eleventh Avenue. They are not whistlin' "Dixie."

RATING: Real good.
LOCATION: 623 Eleventh Avenue (at Forty-sixth Street); (212) 971-1500.
WEB SITE: www.DaisyMaysBBQ.com

Blue Smoke

Give Blue Smoke credit. At least they didn't try to create a faux southern roadhouse just off Park Avenue. They went for a fancy-pants jazz club that happens to serve exceptional barbecue. This is the East Coast's answer to Beverly Hills's RJ's the Rib Joint, only the food is a lot better. Other barbecue restaurateurs in New York credit Blue Smoke with solving the smoke problem. It requires a fourteen-story-high smokestack, but you don't hear a peep from the neighbors.

This place is Classy with a capital C (oh yeah, we already gave it a capital C) from the high ceilings to the plush booths to the tasteful bar. Most self-respecting barbecue connoisseurs wouldn't be caught dead in a place like this. But they should.

In the town that gave us "You're the Top," Blue Smoke is near the top.

Back-home barbecue in New York City? You bet, at Blue Smoke.

You might criticize the place's Rand McNally approach to barbecue: St. Louis spare ribs, Kansas City spare ribs, Memphis baby back ribs, and Texas salt and pepper beef ribs. But New York is not a town with an indigenous style, and eight million residents, many of whom came from elsewhere, want that back-home barbecue.

We sampled it all—you don't want to know how much the bill came to; this is New York—and came out raving about the pulled pork, which was tender and moist if a little light in the smoke loafers.

Blue Smoke is a little too designed for our tastes. But what would we know. Someone once told us all our taste is in our mouth.

RATING: Good.

LOCATION: 116 East Twenty-seventh Street (between Park Avenue South and Lexington Avenue); (212) 447-7733.

WEB SITE: www.bluesmoke.com

Vermont

Putney

Curtis's All American Ninth Wonder of the World Bar-B-Q

When we first set out to document America's great barbecue joints back in 1986, we intended to bypass New England. We were afraid they might do something like put blueberries in the sauce. Or barbecue beavers. It turns out they do. Put blueberries in the sauce. But that's in Maine, and on the whole it seems appropriate. We didn't find any barbecued beaver.

But we found something just as strange sounding: Curtis's All-American Ninth Wonder of the World Bar-B-Q. We figured we should make the trip to Vermont just to find out what the eighth wonder was. On that trip we found not one but two great barbecue joints in New England. The past twenty years have been good to New England barbecue. This time we found two more worthy barbecue places as well as a host of other folks who are making the effort and may make the next update of this volume.

Curtis's still has great barbecue written all over it. Curtis hand-lettered it himself: GREAT BAR-B-Q. Curtis operates his barbecue restaurant out of a refurbished school bus. Actually, it hasn't been refurbished, just sort of painted and outfitted with a 275-gallon oil-drum cooker. "It's comfortable," Curtis says. "And you can drive along and cook at the same time."

Curtis is Curtis Tuff, a Buffalo native who just fell into barbecuing back in the sixties. "I was working around here, doing odd jobs, when some of the students at Windham School asked me if I knew anything about barbecuing a pig." Curtis didn't, but that didn't stop him from volunteering. He taught himself, and pretty soon his skills were in demand at parties and school functions all around southern Vermont. It was just a small step from that to opening up his pit on a vacant lot beside a Mobil gas station. He says it wasn't easy at first, teaching Vermonters to eat barbecue. "They didn't have no idea what it was. But they're getting here."

Curtis cooks his ribs over a mixture of hardwoods, primarily oak, rock maple, and ash. He doesn't use any of the traditional barbecue wood, hickory, though. "That's out. I can't get it. I used to clean off mountains for big apple growers. I did that for twenty-four years, and in twenty-four years I found one hickory tree." All he sells is takeout. No seats in the bus. But you can hang around and watch Curtis cook and eat on one of the many picnic tables he has strewn all around the lot. His ribs are chewy but not tough. You enjoy chewing them. And he adds a lip-smacking sweet sauce that he invented himself. It's an award-winning sauce. Curtis has the award proudly displayed in one of the bus windows: CURTIS'S SAUCE, BEST IN VERMONT.

Before we left, we had one last question for Curtis. We told him we knew about the seven wonders of the world, and now we knew where to find the ninth wonder of the world. But we wondered: What is the eighth wonder? Curtis turned his head sideways, squinted his eyes, and got this thoughtful grin on his face. "I can't remember the name of it," he said, "but I know it's somewhere down in New York."

RATING: Real good.

LOCATIONS: Route 5, Putney; (802) 387–5474. Route 103, Chester; (802) 380–8104.

WEB SITE (believe it or not, Curtis has a web site): www.curtisbbqvt.com

Massachusetts

West Newton (Boston)

Blue-Ribbon Bar-B-Q

When we walked into Blue-Ribbon, we felt like we'd been there before: the screen door, the order counter in back, the counters and stools seemingly arranged haphazardly around the cramped room, all creating the look of a genuine southern barbecue joint.

Then we realized we had been there before, six weeks earlier in Chantilly, Virginia, when we visited Willard's Real Pit BBQ, a place that feels like a barbecue joint even though it's in a shopping center and frequented by computer-tech-looking guys.

It turns out that Willard's was opened by North Carolinian Chris Janowski, who opened this barbecue place, and a sister joint 7 miles away in Arlington, before heading south to the D.C. area to found Willard's.

Blue-Ribbon doesn't pretend to be an authentic joint. It says plainly on the menu that it was "inspired by the classic roadside barbecue joints that dot the American south."

It may be faux authentic, but it's up-front faux authentic, which makes it even more appealing. And the food helps. The pulled pork will stand up to just about any "authentic" place of our acquaintance, and it far outshines the chain joints that are trying to invade the North.

Blue-Ribbon Bar-B-Q

Blue-Ribbon does what any nonindigenous barbecue place has to do: It offers a variety of barbecue styles. There's a pulled-pork sandwich— we approve!—with North Carolina styling; a Texas beef brisket sandwich, sliced, of course; Memphis dry ribs; and burnt ends a la Kansas City.

RATING: Real good.

LOCATIONS: 1375 Washington Street, West Newton; (617) 332–2583. Massachusetts Avenue, Arlington; (781) 648–7427.

WEB SITE: www.blueribbonbbq.com

Sunderland

Bub's Bar-B-Que

Howard "Bub" Tiley opened his roadhouse in 1977, shortly after he returned from a vacation in Florida, a twelve-year vacation. It had started as a two-week tour, but he enjoyed it so much, he stayed and stayed. Bub's began as your basic barbecue stand, with waitresses and all. But soon Bub converted it to a cafeteria with a self-serve line. "Getting rid of waitresses, you get rid of a lot of trouble." The cafeteria line begins in front of the pit, where Bub his own self takes your order, and then winds around to the drink bar (yes, they do have beer), stops at the cashier, and then circles back to the steam table, which Bub keeps overloaded with slaw, beans, fries, and rice.

You carry your own tray to one of the varnished-pine picnic tables, plop down, and then dig into Bub's piquant pork sandwich. Bub chunks his meat, then lathers it in an apple red tomato-based sauce that is flavorful without overwhelming the smoked meat. If you are of the slaw-on-top persuasion, Bub has white slaw on the self-serve bar.

Bub got his sauce recipe when he was managing a golf course in Plant City, Florida. He used convict labor to maintain the greens and fairways, and one of the convicts gave Bub his mother's recipe.

Bub's is a popular hangout for Amherst students. That explains the free jukebox. It doesn't explain the odd mixture of hard country and hard-core rock, from Crystal Gayle to Jody Watley, from Little Richard to Little Jimmy Dickens. Bub's its own self has been celebrated in song, although it's not on the jukebox. In 1983 Jeff Holmes, a professor of music at nearby University of Massachusetts, composed "Bubs," a jazz piece, and it was performed in concert locally.

Like many of your new-generation barbecue men, Bub cooks on gas. If you are opposed for religious reasons, we suggest you not make the trip. Bub's not one to argue with. Remember, this is a man who got a convict to give him his recipe.

RATING: Real good.
LOCATION: Route 116; (413) 548–9630.
WEB SITE: www.bubsbbq.com

PORKLORE

Barbecue Insults

After being told that Bub, of Bub's Bar-B-Q in Sunderland, Massachusetts, had acquired his sauce recipe from a convict in Florida, Arkansas native Bob Moody opined, "That just goes to prove that any convict in Florida knows how to cook barbecue better than anybody in Massachusetts."

Maine

Freeport

Buck's Naked BBQ

We'd heard rumors of barbecue in Maine, so Vince checked with his old high school classmate Frankie Plymale, who lives in Portland. "There used to be one right here in Portland," she reported back. "Uncle Billy's. It was a funky place. You'd go in, and the TV sets would all be set on static. It closed. But I heard there's a new place in Freeport if you make it up this far."

All we need is an invitation.

And surprisingly—to us, anyway—you can get good barbecue in New England, right in the shadow of L. L. Bean. That's figuratively, of course. L. L. Bean would have to be about 4,000 feet tall for its shadow to reach all the way to the south side of town and Buck's Naked BBQ.

Buck's is what you would get if your barbecue man wore Gore-Tex hiking boots: part barbecue joint, part Maine tavern.

And to maintain its Maine credentials, there's even a sauce with genuine Maine blueberries. And it's good, real good. Don't pass it up just because blueberries belong on the top of pancakes and not on the top of barbecue. Remember, tomato is a fruit, too.

RATING: Good.

LOCATION: 132 Route 1; (207) 865-0600. Locals will tell you it's right across from the Indian.

Buck's Naked BBQ

The Midwest

*The Midwest would become the melting pot of barbecue,
where the various styles of the Carolinas, the Deep South,
and Texas met and formed a perfect union.*

Illinois

When you fly into O'Hare International over the city of Chicago, you may be excused for believing for a moment that you see a soft, romantic fog like the one usually associated with San Francisco. It's probably just your imagination, sparked by the knowledge that Chicago's South Side is a concentrated urban barbecue mecca, smoldering in soulful versions of ribs and hot links, basking in deserved fame and sending its seductive, distinctive signature upwards into the summer air.

Then again, it may actually be Lem's, which puts out more smoke than a runaway choo-choo train from its tiny spot in the 300 block of East Seventy-fifth Street.

Chicago

Lem's

It's possible that Lem's may not single-handedly be able to fog in the entire city of Chicago, but the place certainly can do a number on a slab of ribs, producing barbecue that is as surprisingly tender as it is distinctively smoky. Lem's ribs are not something a visitor quickly forgets. Wrapped in slick paper and nestled into a cardboard carton on a mattress of greasy fries, these are not just another batch of not-too-bad carryout ribs. These are the sort of ribs that will lure a man back from Kansas City just to see if his memory is playing tricks on him. These are ribs that make a Statement— about daring to be different, about not compromising. But mostly about smoke.

Smoke doesn't just boil from Lem's tall, battered smokestack, which has towered over the shopworn sidewalks of Seventy-fifth Street for forty years. It also seems to seep in huge, lazy billows through the building's circular roof itself, giving the whole thing the look of a recently crashed flying saucer. Inside the tiny kitchen, seen from the even tinier carryout area, the smoke caresses racks of ribs in an aquarium of a cooker with glass on all sides. It's a contraption that would afford a tempting view of the meat inside—if it weren't completely obscured by hickory clouds. That's the way Lem's has been doing it since Miles Lemons started the whole she-bang in 1952.

The object of the incendiary attention, the ribs, are an edible master-piece. They are among the smokiest served anywhere, but they never flirt with the caked-on char that can ruin oversmoked ribs with a chimney-sweep flavor. The smokiness of the ribs stops short of stealing the show from the pork, and the pork itself is that agonizingly perfect match of textures that makes good ribs almost impossible to stop eating. The sat-isfyingly tough exterior is cushioned by a tender, meaty middle that is juicy without any grease. One food-loving female compared them to the complementary textures of good French bread—slightly crisp and chewy on the outside, pleasantly soft underneath. They really don't require sauce, but Lem's will slap it on or serve it on the side in two varieties—a sledgehammer Hot too much like straight Tabasco sauce, and a milder version that leaves at least a couple of taste buds alive for appreciating the meat.

RATING: As good as we've ever had.
LOCATION: 311 East Seventy-fifth Street; (773) 994-2428.

Leon's

Although its ribs are one of the best reasons for going there, Lem's is far from alone in Chicago's South Side barbecue scene. In fact, one of the best barbecue sauces in the country comes from a place not far from Lem's—Leon's, over on South Cottage Grove Avenue. Both places are locally famous, and both have their ardent followers, but the ribs at Leon's, while tasty and respectable, aren't the distinctive work of art on display at Lem's.

Leon's sauce, on the other hand, is one of the best tomato-based types served on planet Earth. Tell your wine-loving friends that it comes at you in stages, like a fine chardonnay (if chardonnay were hot enough to make you sweat and sigh at the same time). First the sweetness hits, a discreet shot of tomatoey, molasses-rich flavor on the tip of your tongue. Then the barest hints of smokiness begin to creep up on you, and just as you're starting to think you've got the sauce pegged, it whips a roundhouse right to the back of your throat with a delayed-action time bomb that's somewhere between a pleasant, warm feeling and a free tonsillectomy. Get the hot, not the mild. Get it on Leon's ribs if you like. A gallon is barely enough. After you're done eating ribs, you will find yourself dipping french fries in it, and after you finish wolfing down your fries, heaven help your fingers.

Leon's offers an appropriate occasion to deal with the fact that the South Side can be intimidating to tourists and Chicagoans who see it only as they flash by on the Dan Ryan Expressway. This is a shame, and it's a good example of how skittishness can screw up a good meal.

It's true that the takeout at both Lem's and Leon's takes place behind thick protective glass, with the goodies passed out through tiny windows. But you won't find two friendlier places. At Lem's and Leon's there's no such thing as sitting down (they are both carryout only). If venturing the few blocks east of the expressway seems daring at midnight, think of South Side barbecue as a summer-afternoon sort of thing, born of parks and cookouts—and sample it then.

Actually, Lem's and Leon's are simply two of the best of a whole barbecue colony that stretches roughly from downtown on through the University of Chicago area, often bounded by industry or railroad tracks but filled with pleasant, tree-lined residential streets. In this part of town, on streets like State and Cottage Grove and Halstead and the many cross streets between them, there is a concentration of storefront barbecue shops that rivals those found in any city anywhere. They pop up every 2 or 3 blocks in all directions. It is possible to get mediocre barbecue from some of them, barbecue that has been warming too long until it's more like tree bark than pork. But at the best of these South Side eateries, like Lem's, you'll find ribs made by a maestro for a knowledgeable audience. Visit Lem's and Leon's and find out what real city barbecue is all about.

RATING: As good as we've ever had.
LOCATION: 8251 South Cottage Grove Avenue; (773) 488–4556.

Mt. Vernon

King Barbacoa

Angelo's is more exciting, and Arthur Bryant's is more famous, but you'd have to go a ways before you'd find a place that is just plain nicer than King Barbacoa, especially on a lazy summer afternoon. There's a picnic table in the side yard of this former doughnut shop, shaded by a big oak tree that has so far escaped the two big barbecue pits out back. And there's a sandbox near the picnic table, making for a parklike setting in a quiet residential area of this southern Illinois city.

Warm July breezes bring the buzzing of distant lawn mowers, and they blow a lovely counterpoint to the delicious barbecue sauce created by Ernest D. Bowman, the king of King Barbacoa. His sauce is a deep brown, with the rich sweetness of molasses and the steady-state burn of cayenne—great on the crusty beef sandwich that's sliced thin and served crisp on an oblong bun. But if it's good on the sandwich, it's even better on the ribs. They are cooked so long, you'd think they'd taste like one of Charlie Chaplin's shoes, but the dark, ruddy brown crust is meaty and chewy without being at all tough. "They're not tough," the late Mr. Bowman once told us. "You can eat them without any trouble. I'm proud of that."

Bowman took pride in a lot about King Barbacoa, from the name (suggested by his daughter at college and harking back to barbecue's origins) to the history of the place. "I was working at the foundry," Bowman said. "I wasn't making $3.00 an hour. I had six kids and just couldn't make ends meet. Something was telling me, 'Try it. Try it.' I told my wife, and she didn't believe we could do it, but I went on. I worked at the foundry and at the barbecue, and my daughter helped. One day I went to the restaurant, and my eyes got big: I had such a crowd! But I couldn't cook nothing! I didn't know nothing about barbecue! But I was determined that I was going to make that thing work. I quit my job." He allowed himself a little chuckle: "It's taken me a long time to learn how to cook meat." But the lessons stuck: The crown that towers over the parking lot isn't just for looks. Bowman earned it.

RATING: Real good.
LOCATION: 918 Gilbert Street; (618) 242-2264.

Cairo

Shemwell's

It's not exactly the Hatfields and McCoys, but once upon a time in little Cairo, there was a genuine family feud over barbecue. There was Darrell Shemwell and his "Shemwell's Barbecue"—and a short ⁰⁄₁₀ of a mile down the street his step-nephew Skip Shemwell's "Shemwell's Barbecue," sitting in defiant opposition. They weren't battling to the death. Not quite. "When you teach a child to do something, it doesn't mean he's going to follow it," said Darrell of Skip's sauce. "It's the same recipe," replied Skip. "The difference is in the people that make it. I like the taste of mine better."

It all started in Cairo (pronounced KAY-row) with Luther Cashman Shemwell, who ran a barbecue place in what was then a bustling river town where the Mississippi and Ohio Rivers met. Luther had arrived with quite a barbecue reputation: Up at his first place in Murphysboro, Illinois, he had rolled two big fuel tanks together and cut the insides out with a blowtorch for seating. Luther's place in Cairo started doing so well that his son Howard opened up another restaurant. After that, it got a little confusing. Somewhere in there, Luther retired and then reopened in a former Chinese laundry. Luther's other son, Darrell, Howard's half-brother, took over

Luther's new place; and Howard's son Skip, Luther's step-nephew, took over Howard's business, building a new place of his own in 1961. By the late eighties it was Darrell's versus Skip's. "It's not a family feud," Skip said at the time. "We just don't do business together." But Darrell's pointedly used as its slogan: "The Best in Town."

And, appropriately enough, it was. The barbecued pork at Darrell's classic lunch counter is smoky and tender, served on bread or a bun in a sandwich that's squashed flat on the grill into a dense, delightful, compressed collection of barbecue. And Darrell's sauce is delicious, too—a tantalizing tan with flakes of red pepper and grainy spices suspended in a vinegary mixture. It's pleasantly hot, served in squeeze bottles in a very pleasant place, with metal stools along the counter and tables and booths scattered elsewhere. The palm tree planted in a white Sliced Dill Pickle bucket sort of sets off the decor.

These days the Shemwell's Barbecue Battle is but a distant memory. Skip's place is now a hamburger joint named Nonny's. And Darrell's Shemwell's Barbecue is the only Shemwell's Barbecue in Cairo.

RATING: Good.
LOCATION: 1102 Washington Street; (618) 734-0165.

Indiana

Corydon

Jimbo's Barbecue

Sometimes a good road and a top-down day are the only two reasons you need to eat barbecue. It's a simple mathematical principle: convertible + hickory smoke = heaven. You couldn't find a better combination to complete this equation than Highway 62 and Jimbo's Barbecue. The old highway winds from just outside of New Albany on through Indiana's original capital city, Corydon, and in between is Bob Berringer's cozy little spot. Grab a couple of cans of Pepsi, some pulled-pork sandwiches or a rack of ribs, and wander Indiana.

RATING: Pretty good.

DIRECTIONS: 3845 Highway 62 Northwest; (812) 738–1771. Jimbo's is closed from late December until April, but it's too chilly to have the top down most of those days anyway.

Ohio

Cincinnati

Burbank's Real Barbecue

In western North Carolina it's the pork shoulder. In Texas it's the beef brisket. In Cincinnati ribs are king, thanks in large part to longtime rib purveyor the Montgomery Inn. The Montgomery Inn, which sells more pork than any other restaurant in America, has been serving ribs in Cincinnati since 1951, when Ted Gregory, the self-proclaimed Rib King, bought the old McCabe Inn and renamed it the Montgomery Inn. No rib joint in America has been so successful. The Montgomery Inn has served princes and paupers and every American president since Jimmy Carter.

It didn't make the first edition of this book for one simple reason: Our title is *Real Barbecue*. And the Montgomery Inn doesn't serve real barbecue. It serves tasty ribs slathered with an incredible sauce. This is a good place to correct a misconception about ribs that is floating around out there. And it usually begins with this phrase: "The ribs are so good, they fall off the bone when you pick them up."

As barbecue connoisseurs know, just because the rib meat falls off the

PORKLORE

Rib Rah

How's this for confusion: Cleveland girls dressed as Hawaiian hula dancers to promote a Michigan company? That makes mixed metaphors seem okay.

But that was the Rotisserie Girls from Rotisserie Grills of Auburn Hills, Michigan, one of the competitors at the National Rib Cook-Off in Cleveland. The Girls, four Cleveland high school students hired for the festival, were decked out in Hawaiian hula girl outfits. They invited passersby to try their ribs with this synchronized cheer:

Ours are better,
You better believe,
Because ours
Are guaranteed . . .
Juicy, juicy juicy.

bone doesn't mean the ribs are good. It means they are tender, yes, but maybe too tender. When the ribs are so tender they fall off the bone, it is a good sign that the ribs were boiled before they were cooked.

Nothing stirs more debate in rib-eating circles than the debate over "parboiling," the process of boiling the ribs before placing them on the grill. Let's get this straight at the outset: There is nothing illegal or immoral about parboiling ribs. Home cooks have been doing it for decades. Parboiled ribs cook faster on the grill. They come out moist and tender in a third of the time. In fact, we have only one complaint about parboiled ribs: They don't have as much taste as barbecued ribs. In the process of parboiling, much of the flavor is boiled off.

To illustrate, we often tell a story about our late, beloved barbecue friend Lucious "The King" Newsom, who learned his craft at Memphis's famed Pig 'n' Whistle. We were talking barbecue when a young woman came up and asked Lucious if it was okay to parboil ribs before you barbecued them. Lucious's reply went like this. "Yes ma'am, it is. But if you are going to parboil your ribs, let me tell you what to do. When you go to the grocery store to get your ribs, also get you a little pack of noodles. And when you get through boiling the ribs, drop in the noodles. And that way you'll have something to eat, because you just boiled the best part off the ribs."

Which brings us back to Cincinnati barbecue. We first met Lucious in the Queen City where he was training the man who now serves up the best barbecue in that town, Gary Burbank. Gary grew up in Memphis, Tennessee, and he was raised right. "Daddy would bring barbecue home in an eight-pack. Momma nursed me on a sauce called Bottled Inferno. I cut my teeth on a rib bone."

When he moved to Cincinnati in the eighties, he couldn't find any real barbecue, not the kind that he grew up on. "Some of the people I worked with took me to this place that they said had great barbecue. They brought it out, and it was covered in what looked like grape jelly. I took one taste, and I told them to take it out and give it to the poor."

So he decided he had a new purpose in life. "I had to become a missionary of sorts and bring barbecue to the North."

So he opened Burbank's Real Barbecue in Sharonville, one of Cincinnati's northern suburbs, and serves up Memphis-style—and Memphis quality—pulled pork and ribs.

The formula is simple: slow cooking, good meat, and a creed that is emblazoned on his menu, "Give us real Bar-B-Q or give us Spam."

RATING: Real good.
LOCATION: 11167 Dowlin Drive; (513) 771–1440.
WEB SITE: www.burbanksbbq.com

P.S. Just across the Ohio River in north Kentucky is a worthy little barbecue place, Walt's Hitching Post, 3300 Madison Pike, Covington; (859) 331-0494. It's unique in that the pit is right out in the parking lot. In fact, if you aren't paying attention, you may think it's the valet parking shack and toss your keys in the window. Walt's serves a nice rib with a nice sauce and a nice slaw that adds up to a Real Good rating.

Missouri

St. Louis

Charlotte's Rib

His nom de barbecue is Dr. Rollin River. "Herb Schwarz just doesn't sound right in this line of work sometimes," he said. So it was Dr. Rollin River who ventured into the foreign territory of Kansas City and came away with the American Royal Barbecue Cookoff prize for the best commercial barbecue—a plum that doesn't often go to out-of-towners. Such an award is only to be expected, however, because the good doctor could cook up barbecue that was better than good. Herb Schwarz is now retired, and his daughter Lisa Schwarz serves the pork sandwich here that is one of the best in the country. Barbecue sandwiches may be ordered a multitude of ways, but consider this: thinly sliced pork piled on a big, oblong seeded bun—the meat so perfectly smoked that it is luxuriously tender inside and seared crisp on its edges, which twist like smoky threads through the maze of thin slices in the sandwich, offering an unexpected cache of crunch in every bite. The sauce lathered on the meat is a tomato-rich homemade concoction, with tiny bits of meat floating in it, just spicy enough to make your hair stand up without straightening out your new perm. The bun is so fresh that the FBI could lift your fingerprints from it.

The restaurant that sells such a superlative sandwich is a modest place, outfitted in saloon drag with western knickknacks and murals. The decor is in character with Dr. Herb's mother-in-law, the late Charlotte Peters, pictured in complete "Annie Get Your Gun" cowgirl regalia on the front wall. The restaurant's namesake, she was the "First Lady of Television" in St. Louis for twenty-three years, beginning in 1947. In fact, it was Charlotte who, in a burst of investigative journalism, wheedled the basic recipe for the restaurant's barbecue seasoning from a Roman chef who was a guest on her talk show. This dry rub, used to flavor the meat during its long cooking period, was further modified by Herb's father, Armand Schwarz, a career chef.

Brisket is the trickiest meat to cook, Schwarz said, and the restaurant boasts a swell beef sandwich, too, along with the C. B. Joe, a combination sandwich of chopped pork and beef. All sandwiches are available on rye, whole wheat, or bun; chopped or sliced; without sauce or with regular or hot. There's also a full range of chicken, rib, beef, pork, and even shrimp dinners. There is fresh-brewed iced tea or cold beer, and anything on the menu is available for carryout.

The pork shoulder is the meat that won the prize for Schwarz, but he was prouder of his "charbroiled huge pork steak," an eighteen-ouncer trimmed to sixteen or so. It's still offered on the menu, and it sounded good; it really did. But what with ordering two more of those scrumptious sandwiches to go, there was hardly time to try it.

RATING: As good as we've ever had.

LOCATION: 15467 Clayton Road, Ballwin (a St. Louis suburb); (636) 394–3332.

C & K Barbecue

First we'd better deal with "snoots."

Snoots are a part of the soul-food barbecue scene in St. Louis that will stare you in the face at the C & K, as well as any number of other places in town and across the river in East St. Louis. Snoots are deep-fried pigs' noses. You can request an order of "barbecued snoots," and what you'll get is a heap of crunchy fried nubbins, roughly half a snout per snoot, all of them crisp like cracklin's and suitable for snacking, if you're the sort who snacks on snoots. If you're not that sort, you may skip the snoot part of the menu and go on to the ribs, which are distinctive and delicious at the C & K. And you may also thank your lucky stars that you haven't been offered the other regional specialty associated with St. Louis: brain sandwiches.

Anyway, on to the ribs. These are the reason that Ozzie Carr's homely C & K Barbecue fills to overflowing on weekend evenings, with people lined up onto the asphalt parking lot.

A small-end rib sandwich arrives in a butcher-paper package bulging with goodies. There's the requisite couple of slices of white bread, with saucy ribs sticking out of either end, but there's also a C & K bonus— potato salad, slapped in a heap all over the ribs. If it sounds messy, it is; if it sounds weird, it's not. It's very, very good. The potato salad is creamy and cool, a sweet respite from the smoky ribs. The ribs themselves are smoked long and hard, stopping just short of chewy, and are served in an unusual dark orange sauce that is packed with pepper—not red pepper, either, but a blizzard of big flecks of good, old black pepper. It's delicious and different. But even with the five napkins provided, it's also hopelessly messy. The C & K sells only carryout, but restrain yourself from eating an order like this in the car. Go home, or to your motel room, and sit in the shower stall. Then stop worrying and enjoy yourself.

RATING: Real good.
LOCATION: 4390 Jennings Station Road; (314) 385–8100.

Kansas City

Every argument about Kansas City barbecue begins with the name Arthur Bryant. Quite a few of those arguments end with it, too.

Arthur Bryant's Barbeque Restaurant is the single most famous barbecue joint on the planet, thanks to Calvin Trillin, who famously called it the "single best restaurant in the world" in a 1985 *New Yorker* article. But there are those in Kansas City who argue it isn't even the best barbecue joint in town.

And that is the single most important thing you need to know about Arthur Bryant's, that more than two decades after founder Bryant departed to tend that Eternal Pit, folks are still debating his joint's place, not in history, but in current affairs.

Bryant had been dead three years when that *New Yorker* article celebrated his joint. Despite Calvin Trillin's certitude, there were those in Kansas City who had already downgraded the place. They were of the opinion that when a barbecue restaurant's founder dies, the joint slips back into the pack. On the other side were those who contended it wasn't the owner, it was the pitmaster who mattered. And at Bryant's, while Arthur was gone, his longtime pit chief, the aptly named Woodrow Bacon, was still in charge of the cooking.

And so the argument has gone for the last two decades, back and forth: Arthur Bryant's is back; Arthur Bryant's is back into the pack.

We guess that's what research is for. We're here to tell you that while Arthur may be gone, and Woodrow Bacon is retired, Bryant's barbecue is still in the first rank in a town that knows how to rank barbecue joints.

Kansas City knows barbecue because it is Ground Zero, America's premier melting pot of smoke and sauce, the headquarters of hickory, Cow Town Central, the Capital of 'Que. Where else but in Kansas City could you have the most famous barbecue joint in the world—and it's not necessarily the best in town?

Other cities can claim to be the Barbecue Center of the Universe: Lexington, North Carolina, has more restaurants per square citizen. Lockhart, Texas, has a turn-of-the-twentieth-century pedigree. Memphis, Tennessee, has better ribs; Owensboro, Kentucky, has better mutton; Chicago has more sizzling sauce. But no place puts it all together like K.C., a one-city crash course in American barbecue. Choosing one joint in Kansas City as the "best" is a pointless exercise, like looking down a row of Rockettes and worrying about who has the best knee dimples. The thing about Kansas City is that you don't have to choose: It's all there for the sampling. Lots of places have their strong points, and it's hard to find a loser. But here are the best of the best:

The Best Legend: Arthur Bryant's

The barbecue boom of the eighties can be traced in part to old Calvin Trillin, who enlisted several score of his better adjectives in praising a dumpy little place in his old hometown as "the single best restaurant in the world." Calvin Trillin brought a writer's sensibilities to Arthur Bryant's, but the legend was there waiting for him at Eighteenth and Brooklyn.

Arthur Bryant, born poor in East Texas, moved to Kansas City in 1931 and began tending pit. He eventually took over his brother Charlie's restaurant in 1946, and he remained so dedicated to his ribs and brisket that he cooked them on his smoke-stained white-tile pits almost daily until his death in 1982. He served them to Jimmy Carter and Emperor Haile Selassie and shipped them to a New York gathering of French chefs. He served them with a sauce that went beyond inventive to flat-out strange—a fascinating mixture grainy with paprika and a little cayenne that would cling to the dark, chewy ribs chopped by cleaver-wielding countermen. He served them with beer that was tooth-cracking cold, and with rich handfuls of unskinned french fries cooked in sizzling-hot lard. And he served them without pretension, in a place that had tile floors, linoleum tables, and huge jugs of sauce in the window that had separated into countless layers of oil, tomato, spice, and vinegar. Such is the stuff of legends, and Bryant's became the place to send hungry tourists for barbecue.

Bryant's is a holdover from the era of the downtown lunchroom. It still fills up when the noon whistle blows. The place is plain, but the charm at Bryant's isn't in the decor; it's in the design. You can watch your meal being prepared—if behind plate glass. You can watch as the cook snags a smoked brisket off the pit and piles it on other steaming hunks of beef. You can watch the meat sliced, slapped onto Wonder bread, and then painted with a claret-colored elixir that mere mortals call sauce. Yes, painted; they use a paintbrush to apply the sauce.

It still is a mandatory stop on any Kansas City barbecue pilgrimage. But it has become ever so slightly . . . cleaner. And the beef seems a bit less burned and more lightly smoked. And there are T-shirts, too, somewhat of a self-conscious flourish. But the basics of cared-for food and cold beer that made Arthur Bryant's a legend are still in evidence, ready to jog the memories of native sons and capture the hearts of travelers.

RATING: Real good.
LOCATION: 1727 Brooklyn; (816) 231-1123.
WEB SITE: www.arthurbryantsbbq.com

(Best fries: Forgotten in the debate over Arthur's barbecue are the fries. Former Kansas City resident Chris Wohlwend recalls how he could fill up on Arthur's oleaginous french fries: "I'd just pour the sauce over them.")

The Best Brisket: L.C.'s Barbecue

While L.C.'s Barbecue doesn't come close to Bryant's or Rosedale in longevity, it is our pick as heir to the Arthur Bryant legacy. The good news is that L. C. Richardson is still with us. He comes in every day, overseeing the cooking in his custom-made steel pit. The cooker is right behind the counter, so when L. C. opens the pit door, smoke seeps out into the dining room. And that's a good thing. It's a wonderful smoke, aromatic and enticing.

L. C.'s sauce is piquant and profound. As is the experience of eating his barbecue.

The dining room is decorated in what can only be described as Early Taxidermist, with an assortment of mounted fauna, from deer to goose to quail. L. C. doesn't serve all these meats—he doesn't serve any of them—but he makes up for the false advertising with some of the finest barbecued beef this side of . . . well, Arthur Bryant's.

RATING: As good as we've ever had.
LOCATION: 5800 Blue Parkway; (816) 923-4484.

The Best Barbecue Sandwich: Rosedale

Anthony Rieke opened Rosedale Barbecue in 1934, when he was just a pup of about thirty. He kept improving his barbecue pit, and finally, in 1949, he designed and built his masterpiece, a motor-driven rotisserie rib smoker. It was sitting out in his barn untested, and he needed to try some ribs on it. So he did—his own. "I got in the pan. It's like a Ferris wheel," he said. "I rode around in it to see how it would operate." It did just fine, and it still does. Rieke (pronounced "Ricky') is now tending with Arthur Bryant, but his place still sells some of the best barbecue in town, using that same oven—and a couple of newer ones. Close to downtown, the Rosedale sells a lot of wax-paper-wrapped lunches over its plain sheet-metal counter. The tender, tattered beef and pork sandwiches are moist and meaty, served on bread with a substantial sauce that's sweet enough to inspire seconds and sharp enough to inspire doubt.

Rosedale serves an eclectic crowd, which proves that not only does great barbecue cross state lines (Rosedale is just across the border in Kansas), it crosses cultural lines. The place rivals Bryant's for longevity, for plainness, and for flavor. The low-slung brick building looks like a lunchroom from the thirties, which is what it is. Nothing much has changed since founder Rieke started selling smoked meats, except maybe the bar part of the joint. Did we mention that it's not real fancy?

RATING: Real good.
LOCATION: 630 Southwest Boulevard, Kansas City, Kansas; (913) 262-0343.

The Best Ribs: Gates & Son's Bar-B-Q

Gates & Son's is what every barbecue purist is afraid will happen to a good place: It branches out, goes fast-food, moves to the suburbs, and starts hollering a rehearsed "Hi! May I help you?" at people who just have one shoelace inside the door. Well, Gates did it all and still sells wonderful barbecue. "Barbecue doesn't have to be dirty, greasy, and ugly," Ollie Gates is on record as saying. And since a big part of Gates's business comes from people who are grabbing carryout, the slick "chain" approach is hardly out of place. Besides, Gates is building on a tradition that can go up against any in the city, stretching back to his father, George, who got started in 1946 and ran a place called Gates Ole Kentuck Bar-B-Q.

Piled on a trademark red and yellow paper plate, with a bunch of "Struttin' With Gates" yellow napkins lying around, Gates's ribs are the best way to redecorate a living room—or a motel room. The ribs are chewy and meaty, cooked long enough to have gained character but short of requiring an epitaph. The fries that invariably accompany them are greasy and good, suitable for dunking in the little cups of sauce. The sauce, by the way, is a zingy, chili-esque number with oodles of cumin and a nice, rosy glow to it—another idiosyncratic style in a city with more styles than anywhere else.

RATING: Real good.

DIRECTIONS: There are six locations; ask around for the one nearest you. Or call headquarters: (816) 923–0900.

The Best Burnt Ends: Hayward's Pit Bar-B-Que

The Betty Ford Institute has no cure for burnt ends. The craving for crusty, burned nubbins chopped off the end of a brisket can strike without warning, and as close as you can come to effective treatment is to head out into the night to a place like Hayward's Pit Bar-B-Que. Burnt ends are a particular affliction of Kansas Citians; they're not sold in most parts of the country, and barbecue lovers elsewhere seldom seem to realize what they're missing. But enough are eaten here to make beef cattle an endangered species. Hayward's sleek suburban restaurant serves the best in town, each little chunk charred and chewy on the outside, with a juicy and tender interior. They're so flavorful that sauce is served on the side—and best ignored.

In fact, the best way to get them is to go. They are the perfect barbecue munch food, not sloppy like ribs or bulky like brisket, and a sack on the seat makes driving a pleasure. Besides, if you get them to go, you don't have to reconcile dining at Hayward's, a slick brick palace of a restaurant that sports a Chemlawn lawn and etched-glass panels between the tables. There's a ten-lane intersection out front, and vacuum-formed office buildings and country clubs for company. Overland Park is such a chichi suburb that they complained when a White Castle hamburger stand wanted to move in. It wasn't that the city council was opposed to hamburgers; they wanted the White Castle to be beige. It's quite a place for Hayward Spears, a guy from Hope, Arkansas, "a little old town about the size of my restaurant." He built three pits in his backyard and ran a place down the street before he built this rib-tip Taj Mahal. And there's no doubt that his custom-made rotating hickory pit turns out luscious meat.

But it's better you should stand in the take-out area and stare at the autographed pictures from people like Walter Cronkite ("With toothsome memories") and sneak out of there with a paper sack. Burnt ends are a phenomenon somewhere between addiction and perfection, and they shouldn't be eaten in front of ferns.

RATING: Real, real good.

LOCATION: 11051 Antioch, in Overland Park, Kansas (southwest of Kansas City); (913) 451-8080.

The Best Rib Sandwich:
Danny Edwards' Famous Kansas City Barbecue

Formerly known as Lil' Jake's Eat It and Beat It Barbecue—and we wish that were still its name—this downtown joint has its roots in Georgia, where Lil' Jake was born. He got his first job in Detroit, and then worked in his cousin's barbecue establishment in Texas before arriving in Kansas City in 1938 to open his own place. The restaurant came by its name honestly. There are only eighteen seats, so Lil' Jake was happy if you would eat and get out so he could seat someone else at your table. Lil' Jake is helping Arthur Bryant tend the Eternal Pit now, so it's Lil' Danny, Lil' Jake's son, who runs the place and runs you out. But not before filling you up.

The rib sandwich is especially fine here. For the uninitiated, a rib sandwich is a slab surrounded by sandwich bread, but it isn't eaten like a sandwich. You eat the ribs the old-fashioned way, like a Popsicle. The bread on your plate is for sopping up the sauce. So don't embarrass yourself, and us, by trying to eat a rib sandwich like you would eat a Big Mac.

RATING: Real good.

LOCATION: 1227 Grand Boulevard; (816) 283–0880.

The Best Barbecue Beans:
Winslow's City Market Smokehouse

Downtown in what was once the city's open-air Haymarket, Winslow's cooks on a truly unique pit. Owner Dave Winslow said the cooker was designed by an "engineering genius who had never done a pit before." The result is a twenty-five-gallon water tank between the fire and the meat; the steam ensures that the meat is moist and that the flame never touches the meat. Winslow explained that he evaporates fifty gallons of water a day. Evidence that the process is working is the smoke being pushed out the bottom of the cooker door. Further evidence that the process works is on your plate, tender, moist barbecue, available in all the variations: sliced beef, sliced ham, dry-rub ribs, and sausage, all coated with a healthy helping of house sauce, an orange nectar whose secret ingredients include ancho peppers and blackstrap molasses. Best of all are Winslow's barbecue beans, which are flavored with meat and onions and smoked for three days.

RATING (BARBECUE DIVISION): Good.

RATING (BARBECUE BEANS DIVISION): Real good.

LOCATION: 20 East Fifth Street; (816) 471–7427.

The Best Contradictory Name and Contradictory Location: Oklahoma Joe's

Oklahoma Joe's name doesn't make much sense in a town that straddles Missouri and Kansas. Its location is even kookier: It's inside a gas station with all the ambience that implies, giving credence to the old joke, "Eat Here and Get Gas." But Joe's 'que won't give you gas, just a smile. It's tender and moist and doesn't last long on your plate, even a Jumbo sandwich. It's that good. There's an assortment of different sauces at a self-serve table so you can mix or match.

RATING: Real good.

LOCATION: 3002 West Forty-seventh Avenue; (913) 722–3366.

WEB SITE: www.oklahomajoesbbq.com

Kansas

Topeka

The Pizza Parlor

As one travels across America in search of great barbecue, a serious problem soon becomes evident: Sure, it's possible to have barbecue for lunch and dinner, but what about breakfast? With most barbecue joints opening midmorning at the earliest, one can easily find oneself faced with nothing except healthful fruit and cereal, a disturbing prospect for anyone who hasn't had ribs since late the night before.

Thank heavens for the late John Ingenthorpe and the Pizza Parlor. He just might have invented the best barbecue breakfast in the nation.

From the beginning, things didn't always go smoothly for John. When he first started out, in the mid-sixties, he just wanted to open a little neighborhood beer joint, but the neighbors "fought me tooth and toenail." After a couple of failed attempts at getting a license to sell beer, he tried a different tack. What if, he inquired discreetly of the licensing board, he just opened up a little pizza place and sold beer on the side? That'd be different, he was told; that'd be fine. But just getting the nod for his license wasn't enough for Ingenthorpe, who never did things halfway. So he backed a big truck up to his place and pretended to haul out all the equipment. But actually he was moving most of it downstairs into the basement. "You beat me," he told curious neighborhood residents who peeked into his apparently empty building. "You beat me fair and square." The truck drove away, and the neighbors went to sleep. The next morning, with equipment hauled up from downstairs, Ingenthorpe was in business as the Pizza Parlor. By comparison, the story of why a place named after pizza started selling barbecue seems almost commonplace.

But sell it the Pizza Parlor does, and for breakfast, too, starting at 9:00 A.M. Bill Domme, who "grew up with the Ingenthorpe family," decided to "bring the place back to the way it used to be." After John died, the Pizza Parlor went through several owners, and it took Bill to return the place to its glory days. And he'll let you start out the morning with that breakfast. Here's how to make early-morning barbecue part of a nutritious meal: Order a rib dinner with beans and slaw. Lots of food groups. Since it's breakfast, you may feel shy about ordering a beer, which is the absolute best thirst-quencher to drink with spicy food. Okay. Order a "red draught" instead. It's draft beer mixed with tomato juice, served in a mug like a blue-collar Bloody Mary. Perfect for beginning a wonderful day.

The ribs at the Pizza Parlor are wonderful, too, meaty and smoky and sloppy and abundant. The slaw is a standout, as well—crisp, fresh, and long-cut with a peppery vinegar taste. But the barbecue sauce is where Ingenthorpe lavished most of his attention, and Bill made sure he "got it right." The sauce is tomatoey and tangy at first bite, and it has a cumulative kick that heats up gradually like an August afternoon.

Ingenthorpe was passionate about sauce. He once told us, "We were on vacation down in North Carolina. I ordered some barbecue, and they brought it, and I said, 'Where's the sauce?' They pointed to a bottle on the table with a hole punched in the top. Now, you could tell that was just vinegar with some red peppers in it. I went ahead and ate those ribs, but as we left, I said to my wife, 'I don't think I'm going to order any more barbecue on this trip.'"

Back at home in Kansas, he found people trying to copy his pride-and-joy sauce recipe. "One good old boy took some out to Goodyear to have it analyzed," he once told a reporter. "But they couldn't figure it out." So Ingenthorpe pressed on, sending various of his nine kids through college and selling barbecue in his spare, rectangular beer joint. He talked about getting out of the business when the gang graduated: "I didn't send 'em to college to run a place like this. Any dummy can run a place like this."

But even though Ingenthorpe seemed crusty at times, like his ribs, he was a little soft underneath. Take the time in October 1985 when a Topeka charity called Let's Help needed some holiday dinners for the elderly. They asked John how much he'd charge them to cook some turkeys, and he said, "Oh, for you folks I won't charge a thing." He opened up the kitchen on a Sunday to smoke four or five turkeys. He set his place on fire. He pretty much burned it down. It took him six months to reopen.

There's just one problem with having barbecue for breakfast: After you eat it, nothing better is likely to happen to you for the rest of the day. You might as well go back to bed.

RATING: Real good.
DIRECTIONS: 1919 Seward Avenue; (785) 232-5190.

Williamsburg

Guy & Mae's Tavern

"Guy always wanted to try barbecue," Mae said. "We started as a beer joint, and Guy said, 'If we're gonna stay up here all this time, we might as well build a barbecue.'" That one "might as well" changed history for the G&M Tavern, transforming it from a back-roads beer bar to a Certified Barbecue Mecca. It opened in 1975, when Guy got out of the service-station business, but now the little brick hole-in-the-wall serves some of the tastiest, tenderest ribs in the Midwest, ribs laden with blushing pink meat so eager to please that it leaps to the lips from a distance of half a foot.

Such delightful dining has not gone unnoticed: Students road-trip for Guy & Mae's ribs from Kansas University, and big wheels roll in from the state capital. The rest of the booths and stools and picnic tables fill up with blue collars, farmers, and famished tourists. And this all happens in Williamsburg, Kansas, an eye-blink of a town that you could call "sleepy" if you thought it might ever wake up. Kansas doesn't have tumbleweeds; otherwise, they'd be blowing down the main street of town. In fact, if it weren't for the G&M Tavern, it seems likely the whole main street would blow away.

But inside the paneled walls of the G&M, things are warm and lively, especially warm by the big pit where they lay out those luscious planks of pork. "We started doing one box of ribs a day," said Mae Kesner. "Then we did twelve to fifteen boxes." And what they do to them is downright inspiring, cooking them for four hours over a hickory fire, and then letting them sizzle in foil in a special warming oven. "It's the stuff we put on 'em," Mae explained. "The spices and basting with vinegar and painting with marinade. Then we wrap 'em in foil, and that makes 'em tender." How tender? You can't pick them up too fast, or all the meat stays on the table. Of course, it tastes just as smoky and succulent down there—on top of the foil and old newspapers that serve as plates. The ribs are joined by some sauce at the table, an idiosyncratic broth that shares a lot with vegetable-beef soup. Frankly, the ribs don't need it. They are pushing perfection pretty hard in their natural state. The only liquid they require is a bottle of the tavern's supernaturally cold beer.

Guy & Mae's looks like what it is: an appropriately dim little bar where wives wouldn't come unless they planned on staying. It does contain the following objects: a pool table, a collection of framed clippings, and a gushing letter from a Philadelphia attorney tacked to one wall. It also contains a staff that's all-family and all-friendly—Guy's and Mae's daughters Diane and Judy; daughter Christina's husband, Steve; and Judy's daughter Lori. They're running the place now; Mae is retired, and Guy passed on in 1985. But the openness and good cheer of the place—and its unforgettable food—are a fitting testament to a man who once explained barbecue to *KS* magazine like this: "Eggs ain't worth a damn without bacon. Barbecue ain't worth a damn without washing it down with beer. And barbecue ain't worth a damn unless the juice rolls down your elbow."

RATING: Real good.

LOCATION: 119 West William Street (trust us, you'll see it); (785) 746–8830.

Hutchinson

Roy's

There are barbecue joints with no tables and barbecue joints with seating for 425, but there is only one barbecue joint with exactly one table, and that's Roy's. Of course, that one table seats fourteen in a big circle that fills up most of Roy's tiny dining room, but it's still one table, with all the elbow-knocking and napkin-passing you'd expect when a bunch of hungry people crowd in close with plates of ribs and sausage.

If you order a lot, which it's almost impossible to avoid doing considering how good the food is, you have to arrange your stuff out toward the center of the table, or else you start crowding into neighboring territory. As it is, a certain amount of the conversation tends to be along the lines of "Is this your coleslaw, or is it mine?" Still, for true singleness of purpose and devotion to the barbecue code of camaraderie, you can't beat it.

Dining at one big table eliminates whatever pretensions might be left among barbecue lovers. You can't try to look cool, because the telephone repairmen across the way will see the sauce dribble down your chin before you have a prayer of catching it. You can't pretend to stick to your diet, because all those bones pile up in plain view. You can't even hope to come off as a sophisticated barbecue connoisseur, because your slurping and sighs will inevitably join the general chorus. You might as well loosen up and enjoy yourself; everybody's there for the same reason.

The truth is, two tables would be one too many.

What you eat at this one big table are some of the smokiest, most fetching ribs in Kansas. They are slow cooked and meaty, with the same sort of balance between tough and tender that you get from, say, George Clooney. They have enough hickory flavor to attract beavers, but they aren't overcooked. And the sausage is just as smoky, with chunks of plainly visible hot pepper that do some definite hoo-doo to the unprotected tongue. However, the best bite in the place may belong to the beef sandwich, served on big slices of thick toast hot off the griddle, piled with tender chunks of brisket and doused with a no-comment secret sauce that's molasses-dark and tangy.

The homestyle beans are good, too, and there's the world's smallest salad bar off to one side with some salad-bar stuff. But watch yourself: If you get the ribs and the sausage and the beef sandwich and the beans and the salad bar—and a beer—you'd better have the approval of the guy next to you. Or else bring your own table.

RATING: As good as we've ever had.
LOCATION: 1018 West Fifth; (620) 663–7421.
WEB SITE: www.roysbbq.com

The West

Barbecue was a perfect fit for the wild, wild West.
Lots of open range, lots of cattle, lots of the scrub brush they
called mesquite, and lots of hungry cowboys.

California

Los Angeles

Twenty years ago we had a simple recommendation for finding great barbecue in Los Angeles: Simply listen for the sound of the surf, then head the other way. We noted that good barbecue wasn't to be found where the yachts dock in Marina Del Rey and where the statuesque roller-skaters cruise Venice Beach. Instead, we said, barbecue joints are scattered throughout the vast interior of the city—from Hungry Al's and its Louisiana hot sauce to Benny's Bar-B-Que and its homemade sausage.

That advice still holds. In fact, it applies to most of the country. The closer you get to the ocean, the worse the barbecue. Seafood takes over by the sea. Barbecue is an inland ecstasy.

Our strongest California recommendation in the first edition of this book was a run-down section of Slauson Avenue in the Hyde Park district, a short drive rich with good barbecue that we called "Barbecue Alley."

PORKLORE

Barbecue Insults

"In California they think putting a steak on the grill and flipping it over is barbecue."

> —Paul Skolnik, a California native, who learned about barbecue at the Memphis International Barbecue Festival

It's still worth getting off at the Slauson Cut-Off and cutting off your Slauson, as Johnny Carson quipped. But Barbecue Alley is a much shorter drive today. Only Woody's Bar-B-Q survived into the twenty-first century. Mr. Jim's and The Pit are both shuttered.

That's too bad, both for barbecue lovers and barbecue chroniclers. That means we don't get to type Mr. Jim's pithy slogan: "You don't need teeth to eat Mr. Jim's beef." Or wouldn't have if we hadn't figured out that sneaky way to slip it in to this paragraph.

R.I.P. Mr. Jim. R.I.P. The Pit.

But long live Woody's.

Woody's Bar-B-Q

The luscious hot links at Woody's give you a neon grin when the spice kicks in, no matter which kind you get—the kind they make themselves or the kind they import from Louisiana Pete's, back in owner Woody Phillips's home state.

Woody's Bar-B-Q

Dipped in some of Woody's deep, dark, and mysterious hot sauce, the coarse-chopped chunks of sausage crank up the temperature gradually until it's hissing-radiator hot. It's a subtle and satisfying effect; the work of a man who has been a pro since 1972. "I always had a feel for cooking," he told us. "I been playing around with sauces since I was twelve years old." And it's not just the sauce, either. The ribs, beef, and links are slow-smoked over oak with care. "I designed my own pit," Phillips said, "and it's similar to an old-time pit." In fact, it's so authentic that it's built 2 feet below the concrete floor of this carry-out operation. Phillips is proud of California's barbecue, calling it "better than most of the states' I've visited." And he's proud of his staff, which works two shifts seven days a week. "We are in demand," is how he puts it. And, to be fair, it's hard to drive past a place with a snarling cartoon bulldog that grins threateningly and says, "I think y'all ought to buy some BAR-B-Q!"

RATING: Real good.
LOCATION: 3446 West Slauson Avenue; (323) 294–9443.

Van Nuys

Dr. Hogly-Wogly's Tyler, Texas, BBQ

While researching the first edition of this book, we met George Larrimore, a member of the Hollywood Hogs Barbecue Experience, a team of fanatics who had been as far as Memphis, Tennessee, to enter cooking competitions. "Here in L.A.," he said at the time, "it takes a half-hour just to get to the mailbox." But he had left his backyard pit and headed across the Los Angeles basin on a mission. Which is why the Mercedes sedans and blacked-out BMWs in the parking lot at Dr. Hogly-Wogly's really mean something: This is barbecue that people are willing to drive for. Since they're coming on freeways full of metal-to-metal madmen, it's high praise indeed.

This Valley barbecue joint is the real thing, silly name or not. And if you need convincing, consider this: They frost their beer mugs. And they

Dr. Hogly-Wogly's Tyler, Texas, BBQ

light the dark-paneled restaurant with bare fluorescent tubes. And there is nothing on the menu except barbecue (as long as you consider chicken to be barbecue). Oh, a little fried shrimp snuck in there, but it gets lost in the stampede of smoked meat.

The barbecue is very good for California, and it wouldn't be out of place back in its founder's hometown of Tyler, Texas. The late John Wideman started the place in 1970, in what had been a coffee shop. As a boy growing up in Tyler, Texas, Johnnie had worked as a bag boy at the local legendary grocery chain Piggly Wiggly. His friends nicknamed him Hogly Wogly. Years later when he opened his Southern California joint, he gave a shout out to his roots and named it Dr. Hogly Wogly's Tyler, Texas, BBQ. Of course, no one would have driven across town for Dr. Hogly Wogly's Van Nuys BBQ.

John is gone—he didn't sell out, he died—but they still cook his way, over wood in a brick pit, producing a brisket that is pillowy plush, the sort of soft you could fall asleep on. Tender and juicy, it's cut in big chunks and served with a Texas-style barbecue sauce that's authentically long on tomatoey tartness and short on peppery heat. The ribs are good, too, but (befitting a place named after the Lone Star State) the brisket is king. Unless you count the hot link, that is—the smokiest meat on the menu. It's a big-shouldered beef sausage, crammed with garlic and good juices, and cooked, like the rest of the meat, over a slow fire. A lot of barbecue joints slap *Texas* on their signs, but the Doctor's earns the right. Success hasn't spoiled the Doctor. He still hasn't moved his bathrooms inside. Just tell the waitress you need to wash up. She'll give you a token that will admit you to an outside john.

RATING: Real good.
LOCATION: 8136 Sepulveda Boulevard; (818) 782–2480.
WEB SITE: www.hoglywogly.com

Los Angeles

The Original Texas Barbecue King

We pulled out our little pocket camera to take a snapshot of the Original Texas Barbecue King's picturesque cooking area—five oversized barrel cookers in an array to the side of the restaurant—when the Enormous Tattooed Gentleman in the car next to us honked his horn. Uh oh, we thought. Did we offend the Tattoo King here at the Barbecue King? Our temperature shot up, and we broke out in a sweat. And it wasn't the heat from the rib sandwich we had just devoured. We smiled through our sauce-encrusted teeth as we acknowledged his toot. And yes, we were prepared to jump in the rental car and peel out, if a four-cylinder Pontiac Vibe with 126 horses will peel out. He put us at ease as he raised both hands in the classic thumbs up signal. "I love this place!" he testified. "I come here as often

The Original Texas Barbecue King's picturesque cooking area

as I can." It was an unsolicited testimonial from a man who outweighed us by a hundred pounds each. "Too often," he grinned and rubbed his belly as *he* peeled out and our temperature dropped back to normal.

There's nothing fancy about the Original Texas Barbecue King—the fanciest thing is its Web site. Rod Daniels opened this place in a converted filling station in downtown L.A. in 1994, and the cars haven't stopped jamming the parking lot since. It's strictly take-out, although you can take out to the convenient picnic tables under the King's shed.

Rod drew on his mother's Texas roots to create the place.

The Texas Ribs are king here, long and meaty and begging to be soaked by the King's sweet, pungent lotion. Which they are.

We hate to mention this, but the King also prepares a great hamburger—many say it's L.A.'s best. We can't testify to that. That's someone else's book.

RATING: Real good.
LOCATION: 867 West Sunset Boulevard; (213) 437–0885 or (213) 437–0881.
WEB SITE: www.texasbbqking.com

Venice

Baby Blues BBQ

We arrived at 11:00 A.M., hungry to begin our barbecue day. "We're not open yet," said co-owner Danny Fischer from behind the bar. We looked quizzically at our watches. "We don't open till 11:30," he noted. "Oh, what do you want?" When we suggested a pulled-pork sandwich, he told us to go ahead and sit down, he'd take care of us.

Baby Blues looks like an art gallery, but that's a concession to their city of location. It really is a barbecue joint, opened by a couple of old friends who'd cut their restaurant teeth in New York City. Danny was from Philadelphia; his longtime pal Jimmy Peterson from Fayetteville, North Carolina.

They'd often talked of opening a barbecue joint when they were slinging stew in the Big Apple, but it wasn't until Jimmy was visiting L.A. and saw a BUSINESS FOR SALE sign on an old rib restaurant in Venice that the idea came together.

Talk about destiny. They had lost touch over the years, but they hadn't lost phone numbers. James called Danny on his cell phone, thinking his old friend still lived in New York. When he asked if Danny knew where Venice was, Danny laughed. "That's where I live now," he answered. Two minutes later the two were reunited on the front step of the business for sale. And before you could say "serendipity," they were in the barbecue business.

They offer a varied menu with fun names like the "Memphis Queen" platter, with a half rack of baby backs and a half rack of Memphis dry rubbed ribs; the "Ace in the Sleeve" Ribs, Catfish, and Shrimp dinner; and the "Get Down Miss Brown" pulled-pork plate. Thanks to Jimmy's Carolina roots they offer an authentic Down East sauce, a real good, real vinegar sauce with real spices floating around. No California barbecue joint would be authentically California if it didn't offer its own spin on the fare, and Danny and Jimmy do that with their sandwich bun. It's ciabatta bread. Danny told us, "We tried a hamburger bun and a potato bread bun. Then this guy down the street who owns a bakery came in. He bought a sandwich, put it on his bun, cut it in half, and gave half to me and half to my partner. That settled it." The ciabatta bun has a nice chewy texture, unfamiliar in barbecue environs but a really nice change in a nonbarbecue town.

Baby Blues BBQ

Our favorite meat was the tender pulled pork. It's almost as good as Danny's business card, which reads, "Hey, if you're not supposed to eat animals, why are they made of meat? (Vegetarians welcome)."

RATING: Real good.
LOCATION: 444 Lincoln Boulevard; (310) 396-7675.
WEB SITE: www.babybluesbarbq.com

Long Beach

Lucille's Smokehouse Bar-B-Que

Holy cow, we exclaimed to our waitress. Did you realize you could eat a week's worth of barbecue in North Carolina for what one sandwich costs here? "I've never been to North Carolina," she demurred. Then she brightened. "But I've been to Mexico. And Hawaii." But east? Well, Fullerton was it.

We took the opportunity to explain to her the intricacies of fine barbecue. Then we bit the bullet and ordered the pulled-pork sandwich at $10.50, and that didn't include a drink or a tip for Miss World Traveler. That was three bucks more than a sandwich at Dr. Hogly's. (Just for comparison's sake: A sandwich at Wilber's, which is in North Carolina, is $2.50.)

But neither Dr. Hogly nor Wilber has to pay primo rent for a storefront in the swanky Long Beach Towne Center. One month in Towne Center probably costs the same as a year by the side of the road in Goldsboro, North Carolina.

Lucille's is an example of a barbecue trend that's taken off since our first edition: the barbecue theme restaurant. Lucille's didn't begin as the dream of a little woman named Lucille. It began as a concept: a barbecue restaurant that could be duplicated and perhaps, eventually, down the road, franchised. And that's certainly as American as real barbecue; create a franchise and get rich doing it.

So let's give Lucille's its due. A concept can never be authentic. But that doesn't mean it can't offer up great food. And in that respect, Lucille's

Lucille's Smokehouse Bar-B-Que

has a lot to recommend it: huge portions, a nifty outdoor patio to take advantage of Southern California weather, lots of good Southern-fried sides, a variety of tasty smoked dishes, an interesting peanut slaw, and warm towels to wipe up your indiscretions when you are done. But the wide-mouth, thirty-two-ounce Mason jar they use for drinks is not one of those good ideas. We've never seen that even in an authentic Southern barbecue joint. And, frankly, jar rims are unpleasant to the lips.

The barbecue is well cooked and well smoked with the flavor you choose yourself from three house sauces, including a mustardy "Memphis sauce" that had us scratching our heads, trying to remember where in Memphis we ever had a mustard sauce.

The place was "inspired" by Lucille Buchanan, who grew up working in her grandmother's barbecue place near Greenville, South Carolina. Craig Hofman, whose dad created the famous Southern California Hof's Huts franchise, took Lucille's story and built around it. Boy, did he build around it. The Lucille's we visited, in that mall parking lot, is a fabulous location with a menu that looks like it was created by a Hollywood set designer. In fact, *design* is a key word when discussing Lucille's. The place is nothing if not designed. Like the Dude's rug in *The Big Lebowski,* the barbecue holds the room together. And it does a pretty fair job at that.

RATING: Good.

LOCATION: By the time you read this, there may be a Lucille's in your backyard. Hofman has big plans for expansion. At this writing there are eight Lucille's, with more slated for Arizona and the World. We visited the Lucille's in Long Beach at 7411 Carson Boulevard; (562) 938–RIBS (7427).

WEB SITE: www.lucillesbbq.com

San Francisco

Memphis Minnie's

We'd heard the story before, many times, and it never seems to have a happy ending: guy from (fill in the blank with the name of a non-Southern state) gets the idea to open a barbecue joint, travels around the South checking out legendary joints, open his own place.

The next sentence usually has the word *closes* in it.

Well, Memphis Minnie's turns that cliché on its head. Yes, owner Bob Kantor is from Brooklyn, not exactly the heart of barbecue country, and, yes, he did tour the South and Texas hoping to learn the secrets from the masters. And, yes, he did open his place in the most unlikely of unlikely places, in the heart of Haight-Ashbury in the heart of hippie heaven.

And it still came out wonderful.

Memphis Minnie's

Memphis Minnie's was a hole-in-the-wall from day one. And proud of it. Because as all barbecue lovers know—and swear by—the best barbecue places aren't much to look at.

Minnie's isn't much to look at, but boy, the surrounding neighborhood sure is. The sixties never escaped from the Haight, and that's great. This may be the easiest place in the country to run over a pedestrian. They are totally oblivious.

Minnie's takes the "Memphis" part of its name seriously. And it also takes the "Barbecue" part of its name seriously. This is seriously good barbecue. Brooklyn Bob learned from the masters, and he learned well.

The pork sandwich reminded us of something else from the sixties, that commercial where the guy said, "I can't believe I ate the whole thing." We went into Minnie's for a tasting and came out full.

RATING: As good as we've ever had.
LOCATION: 576 Haight Street; (415) 864–PORK (7675).
WEB SITE: www.memphisminnies.com

Oakland

Everett & Jones

It's the sort of story presidents like to mention at news conferences: Why, here's a little ol' dollar-an-hour maid who had her hot sauce featured in the gourmet section at Macy's. It's also a story that helps to keep alive the Barbecue Dream, dreamed during long, smoky nights by owners and cooks across America, and even admitted to by some: One of these days, my family recipe is going to make me famous, and I'll be lighting my pit with hundred-dollar bills.

The difference is, Dorothy Turner Ellington didn't just dream it; she lived it.

In 1961, at the age of twenty-nine, Dorothy (then Dorothy Everett) broke up with the man she had been married to since she was fifteen. She found herself with a few problems: no job, no training, little money, and eight daughters. She worked as a maid, and she got an after-hours job tending a pit in a barbecue restaurant. "I thought I would never earn more than $2.00 an hour," Dorothy said. But she prayed and thought and eventually gathered her daughters together and told them that two things were going to save them: family togetherness and barbecue: They would open a restaurant. "At least we'd never starve," she thought. So in 1974, with a borrowed $700, credit from suppliers, and a pit built in a condemned East Oakland building, the first Everett & Jones barbecue restaurant became a reality. On the first day, they gave away free samples for publicity, and the place was packed. On the second day, nobody showed up.

There have been hard times and good times since—like the time the original location burnt down while the family was celebrating their third anniversary in the business. Everyone rushed from Dorothy's house in their party clothes, but all they could do was watch. Joined by her son Allan and James Jones (husband of her eldest daughter, the Jones in the name), Dorothy also watched her family pull together. They are still together now, partners in their celebrated barbecue restaurants—restaurants where you might see one of Dorothy's grandchildren (she is blessed with well over two dozen). The sauce recipe she brought with her from Alabama is available online and at retail stores all over California, and the daughters who were teased as "the Barbecue Babies" in school have helped Momma retire from the front lines. Daughter Shirley once told a reporter, "It was miserable watching other girls go dancing on weekends while we toiled over the barbecue pit. But she knew what she was doing, and she welded a wonderful family from what she had to work with. We all respect Momma's toughness now. She taught us everything."

The story has a happy ending for hungry visitors, too, because the food that made E&J famous still is on hand. The ribs, cooked in open kettles over oak for four or five hours, are a crusty burgundy on the outside, pulling off the bone with a tugging, satisfying resistance. The hot links are crude and chunky and wonderful, flecked with spices and begging for a bath in the E&J "Super Q" sauce, which is best in its medium and hot varieties. The sauce is very sweet, almost fruity, and very smoky, with a persistent perspiration factor that builds with each bite. Similarly hot are the tremendous baked beans, spicy with a blizzard of black-pepper flakes and studded with stray chunks of the links.

Various E&J locations (there are six) have their fans, but we prefer the one on Fruitvale in Oakland, a storefront operation that recalls the early days. The Chevron across the street is now a supermarket, but one thing that hasn't changed is the delightful conversation of Shirley Everett. She'll be happy to serve you great barbecue and share the stories of her remarkable family. With your feet up and a rib in your hand, it's easy to believe in legends.

RATING: Real good.

LOCATION: 2676 Fruitvale Avenue, an easy jaunt south from Interstate 580 in Oakland; (510) 533–0900.

WEB SITE: www.eandjbbq.com

Colorado

Boulder

Daddy Bruce's Bar-B-Q

From a homely little shack, Daddy Bruce's grew and grew in Denver until it was more than a barbecue joint. It was an institution, certified by the fact that the street in front of the place was renamed from Thirty-fourth Avenue to Bruce Randolph Avenue. Why would a city rename a street from an orderly number to honor a man who happened to have a restaurant on the avenue?

Because Daddy Bruce was more than just a barbecue man. He was a philanthropist. He didn't fund libraries or art museums. He fed the masses, thousands of them, a hundred thousand of them he told us for our first edition. Every Thanksgiving, Daddy Bruce would take care of the needy. "I feed the people all over the city," he told us. "They call me and tell me what they need, and Yellow Cab delivers the food." From small beginnings, his annual Thanksgiving food giveaway grew, attracting volunteers from all around Denver and donations from across the nation. Twenty years ago Daddy Bruce said, "They sent me 500 pounds of cheese from Chicago and a semi-freight of potatoes from Texas. Somebody, I can't remember who, sent me a freight-car load of rice. I'm still giving away rice." In preparation for his big giveaway, he would start cooking and freezing ribs in September.

Of course, Daddy Bruce served ribs hot, too, something he had been doing since '64. Daddy had come from a little Ozark town in Arkansas, and before making it to Denver, he cooked in Texas and Arizona. "Anywhere I cooks, they like it," he told us. The ribs were cooked over hardwood on a custom-built pit of his own design, and he was a little tight with any tricks of his trade: "I put the wood in there, put the meat on it, and it'll go." His Daddy Bruce Bar-B-Que Sauce came from a recipe handed down through three generations.

More than just a great pitmaster, Daddy Bruce had turned cooking into a calling. He put his philosophy on the trunk of his car: "God Loves You, And So Does Daddy Bruce."

Daddy Bruce's charity work continued for six years after our little nod of approval in our first edition. Then in 1994 Daddy Bruce died at age ninety-four.

Teeth were gnashed, garments were rent, and foundations were formed to make sure that his good work was continued. And it was. For a decade anyway. But in 2004 his family canceled the long-running Thanksgiving event, citing squabbling among the organizers. Church leaders picked up the tradition the next year, but the scale was smaller. And Daddy Bruce's family was no longer involved.

The official charity is gone. But the barbecue tradition lives on, 30 miles north of Denver. Daddy Bruce's namesake, Bruce Randolph Jr., has been running his own joint for the last twenty years, using his father's nickname, methods, and recipes and producing the same ribs, dark and full of smokiness and bite, and pouring on the same sauce, rich with the flavors of ketchup and Worcestershire sauce, taking the familiar and transforming it. There's the pointed perkiness of lemon and vinegar, with a hint of sweetness and a glowing, sunny warmth that shines on your tonsils long after you wash it off your hands. Daddy Bruce Jr. serves only pork, no beef. He told our friend Jeff Bradley that's because "Daddy never did."

Daddy Bruce Jr. shares something else with his father: his heart. He vows that no one who comes in his place hungry will leave until they are full, even if they don't have enough money to pay. Proving that he is his Daddy's son.

RATING: Real good.

LOCATION: 2000 Arapahoe Avenue; (303) 449–8890. Daddy Bruce's is just a block from Naropa University, which was the first Buddhist university in America, and home—honest—of the Jack Kerouac School of Disembodied Poetics. A wag at Daddy Bruce's counter said, "Did you hear what the Naropa student said to the hot dog vendor? Make me One with everything."

Oklahoma

Oklahoma City

Leo's Barbecue the Original and Leo's Bar-B-Q Inc.

When it's high noon in Oklahoma City, it's as dark as midnight in Leo's (the original). Well, maybe not midnight. But 10:00 P.M. anyway. With the windows covered up and the huge bright orange brick pits going full blast and the guys with meat cleavers whanging away along one side of the dim dining room, Leo's is the sort of barbecue joint that Central Casting would send over. It's a classic, and a look at the jammed parking lot tells you that's no secret, either.

In accordance with one of the Great Laws of Barbecue, Leo's is located in a former something-or-other, in this case a former gas station. The restaurant and pits now occupy the bays where mechanics used to work, and the carryout counter is where they used to stack the washer fluid and candy bars. The men's room is still the men's room. The gas pumps outside are gone, but the concrete islands remain, lying in wait for an unwary Mercedes.

Inside, the joint definitely jumps. Around lunchtime, between the busboys and businessmen, it's standing room only—without enough room to stand. TIPS ARE ENCOURAGED TO INSURE GOOD SERVICE a sign says, and it's something to think about. The pace is fast, egged on perhaps by the relentless staccato of blades hammering through juicy ribs.

All the hubbub could be a bit befuddling to a first-time visitor, but Leo's has solved one problem: what to order. Order the Leo's Special, which includes beef, ribs, hot links, bologna, baked beans, and potato salad. All you have to remember is to get your beer and your sugary, scrumptious Leo's Homemade Banana Strawberry Cake for dessert.

Nibble what you like from a Leo's Special; you absolutely cannot go wrong. The beans, for instance, are spectacular, among the very best in the nation, brimming with plump chunks of various smoked meats. And if the idea of barbecued bologna is a foreign one, Leo's funky, thick-sliced version makes a perfect introduction, nicely seared and sensuously soft. The ribs are smoky pink in the middle and crusty from the cooker. The beef brisket is tender and mellow. And Leo's flamboyant hot link is a fully armed torpedo with a candy apple red exterior surrounding chunky meat flecked with spices in red, orange, green, and black (there may have been other colors, too, but your correspondent's eyes were watering). Speaking of hot, Leo's hot sauce earns its moniker, a thick, vinegar-sour concoction grainy with enough spice to light up your lips like one of Leo's neon signs. A suggestion: Order the special with medium-hot sauce (it's sweeter and thinner, an altogether different affair), and get the hot sauce on the side for dipping and thrill seeking.

Owner Leo Smith has passed, but his son Charles is still using the recipe for that smoldering sauce his dad inherited from an uncle in Tulsa. Leo once told us that the secrets of good barbecue are simple: "Don't rush it. We get here on time—5:30 A.M. every morning. We cook our beef eighteen hours." Oh, and one more thing: "I don't have any microwave be in my business."

Leo's was apparently the first and only barbecue joint to sponsor a golf tournament, the annual Leo's Bar-B-Q Open, first held in August 1985. A mouthful of Leo's hot sauce should be good for an extra 10 yards off the tee.

RATING: As good as we've ever had.

LOCATIONS: Leo's Barbecue the Original is still at 3631 North Kelley; (405) 424–5367. Leo's Bar-B-Q Inc. is on 7 Harrison Avenue; (405) 236–5367.

PORKLORE

Wood You If You Could?

When the manufacturers of modern electric and gas cooking pits failed to win over barbecue purists, who consistently chided their product as "not barbecue," they tried a new tactic: They tried to get the definition of barbecue changed. In 1982 Smokaroma of Boley, Oklahoma, makers of pressure "barbecue" cookers, petitioned the U.S. Department of Agriculture to change the regulations for barbecue. The purists swamped the agency with opposing comments, the nicest of which said, "If they've got a new method, let 'em come up with a new name, too." Five years later the USDA ruled, "There is not sufficient justification to propose a change to the current barbecue standard." The purists won. Barbecue is still barbecue.

Texas

If you always thought they called it the Lone Star State because of the restaurants, then you haven't had any Texas barbecue. When it comes to 'que, it's the Four Star State.

Dallas

Sonny Bryan's Smokehouse

What would it take to make a Texan in a three-piece, custom-tailored suit sit on the hood of his black Lincoln and drip sauce on his silk socks? There's only one thing that could inspire such behavior: an order of some of the best barbecue in America, served at one of the best barbecue joints, Sonny Bryan's Smokehouse.

This tiny barbecue shack sits a bit outside Dallas's central business district, and its limited seating (a couple of long wooden benches with grade-school-armrest writing desks) falls so far behind its popularity that crowds of people in the big parking lot spread out lunches on the hoods of their cars, or even sit on the hoods themselves, eating fresh-from-the-fire beef brisket before it cools.

Sonny's became a genuine phenomenon, churning out about 800 pounds of beef every day in a cement-block building the size of a double-wide mobile home. Founder, head chef, and master theoretician R. L. "Sonny" Bryan once said, "I saw how happy my father was when he had a little barbecue place, and I saw how unhappy he was when he built a big place." So Sonny, who started out toasting bread in his dad's place when he was eight, kept his quarters cramped for three decades. Sonny passed on in 1989, and Walker Harmon owns the place now and proudly claims, "Only at this location do you get that good a-cookin'."

At lunchtime, it's a cross between a barn dance and the floor of the

Just Married

How do you cook barbecue? Joey Sutphen of Sutphen's Bar-B-Q in Amarillo, Texas, said, "First you stick your face in the smoke, and when all the hair's gone from your arm, that's how you know you're cooking good. When it's almost uninhabitable for human beings, that's when the smoke and the sauce get married to the rib."

New York stock exchange, with orders being hollered out, beer tabs popping, and the cement floor in front of the counter filling up with everything from ten-gallon hats to hundred-dollar hairpieces and designer dresses to "I'm With Stupid" T-shirts. "I got the most varied customers in the world," Sonny once bragged, "from bottom to top."

Waitresses cruise the crowd, taking orders and bringing the waiting legions cans of beer to help them bear up under the heat and hullabaloo. The cashier announces when the orders are ready by shouting the customers' initials over the general din. By 12:33 P.M. on a summertime Friday, the hungry crowd already had run the place out of ribs. But there was plenty of brisket left, and brisket is the star of the show. It is mouthwateringly moist, with a burnt crust and a haunting smokiness, chopped in chunks and piled high on a toasted bun. Scattered around the restaurant are square-sided glass bottles of sauce, some resting on a hot plate to keep them warm. The sauce inside is thin and tart, with tomatoey tang but no hot pepper at all. It's good sloshed on the beef sandwich, and it's even good on the monstrous onion rings.

A trip to Sonny's seems semi-mandatory for tourists in Dallas, judging by the cameras and out-of-state plates we saw. But it'd be worth making your way there for lunch if you're anywhere in the area, say within the confines of continental North America. For all of those whose dream of the perfect barbecue joint is delicious food served in a dump, Sonny Bryan's cheerfully fills the bill. As the late great pitman once said, "I guess my dinky, greasy barbecue place is what people expect Texas to be."

RATING: As good as we've ever had.
LOCATION: 2202 Inwood Road; (214) 357–7120.
WEB SITE: www.sonnybryans.com

Fort Worth

Angelo's

There are numerous barbecue joints in this great land that, for one reason or another, choose not to sell beer. Angelo's makes up for all of them. Angelo's sells beer in eighteen-ounce schooners the size of glass-bottom boats. Angelo's sells beer in "longnecks," chilled, old-fashioned bottles the very mention of which can make Texans all misty-eyed. It's hard to tell if the place is a beer joint selling barbecue or a barbecue joint selling beer. But after a round or two of either, the distinction ceases to matter. Besides, the barbecue is first-rate, the beer is cold, and the huge rooms are so ratty and raucous that you could howl like a coyote without being noticed. Especially by the people howling at the next table.

In fact, if you're going to argue about who makes the best barbecue in the nation, you really should come to Angelo's. It's not that the ribs and brisket are so good that they'd end all discussion of the matter. No, it's just that arguing at Angelo's is so much fun.

The first clue may be the stuffed bear in the camouflage Angelo's shirt that greets you when you enter. Then there's the crowd, waving and laughing and tearing into platters of meat, sort of like a huge pinball machine on full barbecue "tilt." The gangly dude in the "Ya-Hoo!" T-shirt and the stay-pressed slick wearing an Alfa Romeo hat look equally at home. And when the waitresses bellow, "Two large!" over all the other hollering, they're not criticizing your girth or your order. That's Angelo's code for "Two more horse troughs full of beer!"

But lest you think that Angelo's may not be a "family" place, consider this: Since Angelo passed away, his son Skeet runs the place, his sister keeps the books, and Angelo's grandson Jason is the pitmaster. The night we visited, Skeet was helping by sitting at the bar and joshing with some customers; if you feel like saying hi, Skeet's the fellow who looks like the stuffed bear in the entrance, only bigger.

And lest you think that all the frivolity blunts the focus of the place, rest assured: The barbecue at Angelo's is excellent, good even for Texas, with seriously smoky pork ribs—crusty, chewy, pink to the bone, and cooked so fresh they don't even go on sale until five in the afternoon. The beef brisket, chopped into hefty hunks, is shot with smoky perfume and tender as a kiss from a cowgirl. The sauce served with all this is typical Texan—not too thick, not at all hot, but lively with a tomato tang. Angelo wasn't much for giving away tricks of the trade. Asked what makes his barbecue so good, he said: "Buy the very best you can, and don't get in no hurry." Angelo also wasn't much on giving credit to his rivals. What other Texas barbecue did he like? "I don't eat nobody else's."

But if you could eat at Angelo's every night, why would you?

RATING: Real good.

LOCATION: 2533 White Settlement Road; (817) 332–0357.

Glen Rose

Hammond's Bar-B-Q

They say that if you run a barbecue joint long enough, it will eventually burn down. Well, pity poor Hammond's. It has burned not once, not twice, but three times since it opened in 1966. The first fire was in 1974 at the

Barbecue Insults

"Texans tend to talk louder with their mouth than with their meat . . . The meat itself is about as much real barbecue as an oak toilet seat."

—Jim Dodson

Coyote Strip location in the rolling hills of central Texas. Founders A. J. and Liz Hammond rebuilt that place and kept it running until 1989. By then their son Tom had opened a second Hammond's in town, so they retired and left the barbecuing to him. Tom's dining room burned in 1996, and by the time he rebuilt he decided it was time to sell. Enter Darrell Caldwell, who had owned the place for only four months when it burned again in June 1997.

You would think this would be enough to discourage anybody from barbecue. But fortunately it didn't. Hammond's is still in the Caldwell family—it's now owned by Darrell's sister and her husband, Judy and Larry Higgins.

But it's still Hammond's pit and Hammond's methods and Hammond's quality. And that quality springs from what A. J. Hammond told us twenty years ago: "Patience. You've got to have it. If you don't have it, you'd better get it." At Hammond's you better have the kind of patience that would have convinced Job to get out of the barbecue business. That patience—and a special cut of brisket that is not trimmed as lean as some other Texas pitmen order it—means slow-cooking beef in a closed pit for thirty-five hours. A. J. said, "Aw, you can't get the blood out in fourteen hours. Those people who brag on cooking it eighteen hours, that's noth-ing." What you get from that thirty-five-hour investment is some of the best pit-cooked brisket in the state of Texas, which pretty much means the best brisket anywhere. So much juice has percolated through that meat in its stay in the pit that it is absolutely supercharged with the opulent, but-tery flavor of fine steak, and despite its thick cut and substantial heft, it is tender as a sigh. A. J. had a rule for tenderness. "I look out over the tables. When I see somebody taking that first big bite, it should come away clean, not have pieces pulling out of the sandwich onto the plate." As a rule, the rule holds true. But one time, A. J. did spot a customer with bits of his brisket pulling out of his sandwich. A concerned chef, he checked on it. "It turned out the man had just had major dental work."

RATING: Still real good.
LOCATION: 1106 Northeast Big Bend Trail; (254) 897–3008.
WEB SITE: www.hammondsbbq.com

Taylor

Louie Mueller Barbeque

Louie Mueller's looks the way a small-town Texas barbecue joint should. Its weathered brick exterior is dusty, its windows are boarded up, and its screen doors slam with a bang against aging frames. There's no air-conditioning, just two big fans mounted at either end of a huge, barnlike room. The glass skylights high in the roof are stained with brown, and the peeling green walls show enough layers to interest archaeologists. The floor is made of worn wooden planks, and, two stories up, so is the ceiling.

Oh, they could have fixed it up; enough barbecue and beer have flowed out of the place. But they haven't, and they won't. "We'll keep it just like it is," said Bobby Mueller, Louie's son, who owns it now. The building was put up in 1907 and has done time as a grocery store, a typewriter-repair shop, and even a basketball gym ("It must have been a short court," said

Bobby). But now it's barbecue—brisket so tender that it's almost like pot roast and a loose, juicy sausage with a rosy ring of smoke surrounding a center of rich, beefy brown.

The brisket is different from most in Texas, having been smoked over oak for four to six hours and then wrapped in butcher paper to steep in its own juices. That's the way Louie did it when he started out in the mid-fifties in a little tin shed, and that's also the way Fred Fountaine did it for years at Mueller's as the chief cook. "When I started at Mueller's," Fred told us for the first edition, "they had two barbecue pits. One cook quit, and Mr. Mueller said I was the new cook. I didn't know how to build a fire; I thought I'd burn the place down." He didn't, and before he retired at Mueller's in 1987, he had accumulated nearly forty years of experience. "The most exciting day was in 1978, when the *New York Times* came in," Fred said. "There was four of 'em, and I gave 'em something to eat. They said, 'This is the best we found.'"

It is definitely good barbecue, especially the brisket, which is so tender it practically collapses from the effort of staying in one piece. It's served cafeteria-style on butcher paper on an ancient plastic tray, accompanied by a delicious homemade broth of a sauce that is watery but meaty, full of tomato flavor and dotted with pepper flakes and chunks of onion. It's a slow-to-anger sauce, but there's a big bottle of ill-tempered hot-pepper potion on each worn table, just in case.

At Mueller's you can lean back in your creaky chair, listen to the roar of the fans, and imagine what it must have been like to play basketball in boots and spurs.

On the other side of a big gravel parking lot from Mueller's is Rudy Mikeska's, a big red barn of a barbecue joint run by Tim, Rudy's son. Rudy senior was one of six brothers who operated barbecue restaurants in different Texas towns. Three of those brothers are in their eighties and still tending the fires of good Texas barbecue. Rudy's place has made a few concessions to the modern world. The lamb ribs aren't offered except on special occasions.

That forty-eight-gram fat content made health-conscious customers nervous, but if you ask nicely, you can still get them special-order. There seems to be enough business in this town of about 10,000 and in the small nearby towns to keep all of the family busy.

RATING: Real good.
LOCATION: Louie Mueller's: 206 West Second Street; (512) 352–6206.
WEB SITE: www.louiemuellerbarbeque.com
LOCATION: Rudy Mikeska's: 300 Second Street; (800) 962–5706.
WEB SITE: www.mikeska.com

Elgin

Southside Market

Some folks will tell you that the Southside really started going downhill in 1983, after the big fire. That's when the place began to put out forks. "I never had anything in here but knives," owner Ernest Bracewell Jr. told a reporter at the time. "But we had too many people coming in from the North who couldn't eat with their fingers."

For Bracewell, who took over the Southside in 1968, it was only one in a series of heresies affecting the specialty that had made the little meat market famous across much of Texas since 1882—its chunky sausage that old-timers called "Elgin hot guts." For instance, there was that business with the ladies' room. Bracewell put one in. And first thing you know, the ladies came, too, ruining what had been an otherwise fine place for a bunch of men to stand around and eat barbecue. There were other things. Bracewell cut back on the red pepper, again to go easy on the suffering Yankees he calls "imports." He took the pork out of the sausage and changed the recipe to all-beef. And to make matters worse, he pulled the switch in secret, and nobody noticed for three months, not even his staff.

But to be fair to Mr. Bracewell, he can't be doing everything wrong. He still sells as much as a ton of sausage a day, sometimes sending it out of

Southside Market

town on buses. His bright orange hot sauce still sits around on the tables in old whiskey bottles. And his sausage and sublime beef brisket still show up on brown butcher paper without a hint of a plate.

And what meals! The place may be famous for sausage, but the brisket is tender and flavorful, among the best in the state. The sausage itself is moist and meaty, no longer really all that hot, but it picks up some quick zing with a dash of the thin, vinegary sauce that's colored orange with cayenne and other spices.

The sausage here is made "straight," as Bracewell put it, in one continuous rope, not sectioned off in links (except for special orders). When you cook several hundred pounds of sausage a day, Bracewell decided, turning all those little links just took up too much time. The long tubes of sausage are stretched across the oak-fired grill and rotated for about a half an hour to cook evenly. "We do it with pride," he told us for the first edition. "We've still got quality to it."

Mr. Bracewell is now vice-president of the company, and the sawdust floor was left behind in the 1992 move from downtown to the intersection of U.S. Highway 290 and Texas Highway 95, but his newfangled notions still make sense. The results taste great—and if you get a little wistful for the good old days, well, you can still stand up to eat, you can leave the ladies out on the sidewalk, and you sure don't have to use a fork.

RATING: Real good.

LOCATION: West side of Elgin. That's Elgin with a hard *g*, as in "hot guts." (512) 285-3407 or (877) 487-8015.

WEB SITE: www.southsidemarket.com

Austin

Iron Works Official Texas B-B-Q

If everything you know about Texas came from old *Dallas* episodes—and that was pretty much our experience before this book—then Austin will surprise you. It's not flat and boring with an occasional tall building for variety. It's rolling countryside, what Texans have named Hill Country, and when you drive out toward Mansfield Dam at Lake Travis, you can look back over some breathtaking landscapes. The weather, however, is flat and boring. Austin has two seasons: summmmmmmmmmmmmer and winter and nothing in between. No glorious fall coats on the women or the trees. (You don't notice the trees since most of them are undersized, a result of root systems stunted from trying to burrow into the rock that rests just below the surface soil.)

Over the two decades Austin has grown faster than any city in America. You don't need a government report to tell you that. Traffic on the drive into town from the airport is all the convincing you'll need.

Austin isn't exactly a great barbecue town, maybe because you can easily drive a few miles out into the country and get some of the best barbecue in the world. But the city does have a pretty good version, sold right downtown in an atmospheric, corrugated-steel building that was built in 1935 as the Fortunat Weigl Iron Works and is now a for-sure Historic Place.

Owners Charlotte and Jerry Finch took over the building a couple of years after the iron works quit working in 1976. Jerry had been with the state health department before opening his own barbecue joint; in this business, that's sort of like joining the other side. But he made good barbecue for a health-department man, cooking it for about seventeen hours in a big, temperature-controlled brick pit. Now Charlotte Finch runs the place, and you can still get those smoky beef ribs. They are big, meaty, and delicious. The slightly dry brisket falls a bit short of true Texas Transcendental, and the sauce is a trifle ketchupy—but add a couple of complimentary "japs" (what the locals call jalapeño peppers), and they will more than make up for any sass lacking in the sauce.

There's a wooden deck out back where you can eat and watch the turtles cruise Waller Creek. With its scattered antiques and old photos, and its sometimes-Polo-shirted patrons, the Iron Works runs the risk of coming across as a theme restaurant, but it's too funky to be Friday's. There's no air-conditioning, just screen doors and big floor fans in the summer. There's no table service, just do-it-yourself. If you get thirsty, you can get up and get another dripping-cold bottle out of the antique ice coolers, one for beer and one for pop (the opener is mounted by the cash register, and the bottle caps fall into a coal bucket on the floor). There is better barbecue to be found in Texas, but while you're pouring back a Shiner Bock beer fresh from a pool of icy water and listening to the turtles gurgle, it's hard to get real fired up to go look for it.

RATING: Pretty good.

LOCATION: 100 Red River; (512) 478–4855.

P.S. Austin is a music town, if not always a barbecue one, and the two mix happily at Stubb's Bar-B-Q. Originally, this was a swell little spot tucked into one end of a discount motel next to Interstate 35. C. B. "Stubbs" Stubblefield, who made his delicious West Texas barbecue famous in Lubbock, moved to Austin in the eighties. His restaurant was plastered with auto-graphed posters and photos of musicians from B. B. King to Bobby Bare, from Los Lobos and the Fabulous Thunderbirds to Ponty Bone and the Squeezetones. The jukebox was a marvel, too, with songs by Little Milton, Joe Ely, John Lee Hooker, Big Mama Thornton, and "I'm Too Poor To Die" by Louisiana Red. There also was a small stage for performances at one end of Stubb's, but the barbecue was the sweetest song sung there. Cooked over oak and sometimes a little mesquite, it was the result of more than fifty years' experience, and you could taste every year in the tantalizing beef. Cooking real good barbecue came from a feeling, a God-given talent you're born with, Stubbs said. He gave out his recipe "to individuals, not competi-tors," and then they would call him on the phone and say, "Stubbs, I've got a mess over here." Stubbs would have to straighten them out. Well, Stubbs is not around now to get things straight, but you can still sample the same rub and spices on the barbecue at the new location. The manager, Channing Lewis, said that the team is trying to "create a new history" with the music, but they are staying true to the Stubbs legendary barbecue tradition. Accord-ing to Channing, you can still hear some of the old stories from the "sauce company guys," at (512) 480-0203. Just ask for Eddie Patterson, "the histo-rian," who can tell you great tales about C. B. "Stubbs" Stubblefield. Or, catch an act on one of the two stages (indoor/outdoor). On Sunday there is a gospel brunch. The restaurant is at 801 Red River Road; (512) 480-8341.

Lockhart

Kreuz Market

Smitty's Market

What kind of cowboy name is "Kreuz"? And why is a lot of the best barbe-cue in Texas to be found in the back rooms of butcher shops and meat markets? Well, there's a good reason: That's where it all began, at least on a commercial scale. Back in the late nineteenth century, a tide of German

Smitty's Market cooks its barbecue in an L-shaped pit with open fires at either end.

and Czechoslovakian immigrants washed across the New Braunfels area of Texas, in the south-central part near San Antonio. With them came a passel of butcher shops. Their owners had an old-world butcher's aversion to tossing out perfectly good meat—but a frontiersman's good sense to see what wasn't selling. So they took their scraps and turned them into sausage, and they took their tougher cuts and cooked them over slow wood fires to enhance their flavor and tenderness. It was a good idea then, and it's a good idea now. People are still lining up to eat it.

So when you spot the big brick smokestack with MARKET painted on it (it used to say KREUZ, but we'll get to that in a minute), you're not only looking at a slice of Texas history (it has been operating since 1900, in this building since 1924)—you're also looking at a slice of barbecued beef of the sort they'd

Kreuz Market

serve in Heaven (or maybe Hell, where the cooking's better). The shoulders favored here are a slightly more expensive cut of meat than the usual Texas brisket, and they're cooked a different way: hot and fast. Well, fast for barbecue—about four and a half or five hours. The towering, 35-foot brick chimney that rises from the corner of the L-shaped pit creates a strong draw that inhales heat and smoke from open fires set at each end, burning right out on the concrete floor of the two-story back room. It cooks by indirect heat, and a thermometer in front of the pit can measure as high as 600 degrees.

A bare counter runs in front of all this fiery activity, and that's where you order your barbecue. When you order, ask for lean—it's as tender as an old lady's heart. But don't ask for sauce. Not that you'll offend them. You just don't need it.

The tender strips are served on brown butcher paper crumpled at each end to make a tray. Actually, there is no tray, as well as no plate and no fork. A plastic knife is included (they used to bolt knives to the tables), and you have your choice of bread or crackers. Choose crackers (everybody else does); to serve them, a pitman pulls a plastic-wrapped stack of Saltines out of a box and cleaves them neatly with a very large, very sharp knife. Half the pack is yours.

The eating gets done away from the pit, in a two-story, tin-roofed room that's air-conditioned enough to take the edge off the 600-degree fires, but completely ineffective against the jalapeño peppers. There are bottles of Louisiana hot sauce sitting on the long tables, and little cardboard trays of a salt-and-pepper mixture—but both are absolutely unnecessary. The shoulder is perfect as it sits, cooked just shy of dry, startlingly full of flavor and too tender for even a plastic knife. And the smoked sausage, tied with string into U-shaped links, may be the best in Texas. It's

City Market

spicy and peppery and spilling with chunky meat that's moist and precisely cooked. The spice lives on in your mouth for minutes, and the memory should last for months.

That's the way barbecue is served at Smitty's, and it's the way it used to be served at Kreuz, back a decade ago when Smitty's was known as Kreuz. But in 1999, just a year shy of the place's centennial, a dispute between Kreuz owners Rick Schmidt and his sister Nina Sells came to a head. Or more specifically, to the door. She owned the building that had housed the barbecue joint since 1900, and she showed him the door. Not to be outdone, he built a huge new 23,000-square-foot restaurant with 30-foot ceilings, a virtual palace, out on the main road, christening it Kreuz Market because he owned the name. She kept the old space, and the old pits, and renamed her place Smitty's Market. After their dad!

The winners in all this are the barbecue lovers. Where before they had one, now they have two great barbecue joints in Lockhart.

RATING FOR BOTH: As good as we've ever had.
LOCATION: Smitty's: 208 South Commerce; (512) 398-9344.
WEB SITE: www.smittysmarket.com
LOCATION: Kreuz: 619 North Colorado Street; (512) 398-2361.
WEB SITE: www.kreuzmarket.com

P.S. Another nearby market with barbecue in back is the City Market Restaurant, 633 Davis Street, in Luling, Texas (830-875-9019). It's near Interstate 10 on U.S. Highway 183. This market is smaller and more seemly than Kreuz, without all the pyrotechnics. But the barbecue is real good, and it makes an interesting comparison. Get there before closing at 6:00 P.M., and remember, it's all pick-up after 5:30. Don't confuse this place with the Luling City Market in Houston. That's the place in the Galleria area, and that's a different story entirely.

La Grange

Prause's Market

"The Best Damn Butcher Shop in Texas" this market has been known to call itself, though the claim is open to more or less endless argument. But some poetic license should be allowed since Prause's is located in the hometown of the former Chicken Ranch, popularized on stage and screen as "The Best Little Whorehouse in Texas." For a lot of folks in La Grange, the Chicken Ranch isn't exactly what they'd like to go down in history for, no matter how good a whorehouse it was. Finding it out east of town is kind of tricky these days; there's no monument or anything, although a promoter supposedly sold off so much Chicken Ranch property mail-order (at $8.00 per square inch) that he can no longer get to the place without trespassing.

Still, the city fathers are doubtless glad to have a butcher shop making a claim for the spotlight instead of those more sprightly heifers, and Prause's makes a good claim indeed. In the back-room tradition of Texas butcher-shop barbecue, it features an excellent back room. It's tucked right behind the meat counter itself, where you also can order fresh cuts of meat. In back where the barbecue's sold, there's brisket and sausage.

It's served on long, red Formica tables with scuffed wooden benches on a cement floor. Along one wall is a clothesline for holding announcements. Every now and then along the tables there used to be corked whiskey bottles full of indeterminate and intimidating ingredients. Now there's only one bottle, and it's chained down to the back table, because somebody kept taking off with the others. As with all Texas butcher-block barbecue, the meat in Prause's Market is served without benefit of the runny, tomatoey sauce that holds sway over so much of the state. Instead, you have these bottles of . . . stuff. The management is tight-lipped about their contents, but the one they call "green-pepper sauce" seems to consist of big chunks of onion and tiny green peppers floating in vinegar. It is sour and tart and mildly hot—and delicious on the brisket, which percolates with beef flavor and is served with a strip of fat along one edge. The other sort of bottle, the kind they call "Louisiana sauce," is a similar composition using larger red peppers. It was a touch hotter, but possessed of a gentle simmer that went fetchingly with the coarse-ground sausage. Juicy and flecked with pepper, the sausage wasn't really hot, and a shot of Louisiana sauce made the ideal complement. Could a mere whorehouse ever be this satisfying?

RATING: Real good.
LOCATION: 253 West Travis Street; (979) 968-3259.

Houston

Otto's

There's an old barbecue-hunter's axiom that holds: "If it says 'burgers' on the sign, don't waste your time." But what is such wisdom to do in the face of Otto's? Otto's sells hamburgers all right, but in an entirely separate building! The Hamburger Otto's faces the parking lot on Memorial Drive, out by the main BARBEQUE AND HAMBURGERS sign. It's what you see first, and if you were hungry for some of Houston's traditional favorite barbecue, you might walk right in. You wouldn't find any. But what you should have noticed was a big arrow painted above the windows that points around back; BAR-B-Q DINING ROOM, the lettering says. But let's get this straight: It's not a "dining room." There's an entirely different building back there, different architecture, different street, different parking lot, different menu. It's the Barbecue Otto's, and it's good.

"We started in front," said Miss Annie Sofka, "then we added on another building. A lot of people were asking for barbecue." Miss Annie, the wife of the late founder, Otto Sofka, was the life and soul of the place, greeting and chatting with customers at the cafeteria-style serving bar with an unforced friendliness that once led the city to declare a "Miss Annie Day." She dished up some delicious barbecue, so it was easy to smile back.

"People come from New York with briefcases," she told us. "Then they fill them with ribs and take them back to New York." Miss Annie has passed away, but the out-of-towners keep coming for the barbecue prepared by her son and daughter-in-law. The brisket in the beef sandwich is fall-apart tender, spouting with juice, seared along the edges, and simply begging for an application of the tart, apple-butter-brown tomato sauce. To capture the maximum flavor, the meat isn't trimmed until after it's cooked. Ribs, hot links, and ham round out the menu.

The interior is pleasant and paneled, with a blizzard of witticisms plastered all over the place. There's the funny-monkey section, with photos of chimps in human clothing. A discreet distance away, in the back dining room, there's the George H. W. Bush section, with photos of George in human clothing, and a nice letter from the fellow.

Before any barbecue hunters get too distraught at seeing a perfectly fine rule about hamburgers go down the tubes at Otto's, let us reassure them: Otto's does confirm another Prime Theorum of good barbecue, the parking-lot test. Simply stated, it's this: Look at the cars in the lot; the greater the range, the better the eating. And Otto's tested out with the best parking lot we visited. It didn't just go from a primered Pinto to a Jaguar and a Jeep Wagoneer; there also was a black stretch limousine that was idling at the curb while its driver waited for his charges to finish dinner and lick the sauce off their manicured fingers.

RATING: Good.

LOCATION: 5502 Memorial Drive; (713) 864–2573.

Goode Company

Fear of yuppies and dishonest "theme" barbecue has prejudiced some purists against Goode Company, which was created in the 1970s to look like it was created in the 1870s. Its location, on one of Houston's prime restaurant rows, near "Armadillo Palace," puts detractors off, too. They'll tell you that, despite its outdoor benches and its old-barn exterior, it's a "concept" restaurant, as planned out as Disneyland and just as authentic. But you can't eat concepts, and the food served at Goode Company would shut up such critics in a hurry if they'd consent to shove some in their mouths. It's better than Goode; it's almost Greate.

One reason is the beer: It floats in deep, icy water in a row of coolers that lets you pop one open before you even hit the cafeteria line. Another reason is the side dishes. At most barbecue joints, side dishes are straightforward, slap-together stuff, but not here. The beans are jazzy jalapeño pintos; served with pieces of bacon and pepper bits, they are toes-to-the-fireplace hot and luscious. The Jambalaya Texana is a vivacious version of rice, with an avalanche of ham and pepper chunks. And then there's the Jalapeño Cheese Bread. In sandwiches or separately, it's dangerous. Cut thick and swirled with seductive, golden bands of cheese, it's plush and inviting—until Mr. Jalapeño jumps on your tongue with sharpened cleats. You may expect the sauce to be hot, but here you get blindsided by the bread.

The basic barbecue is straightforward and respectable, with tender brisket and chewy, smoky pork ribs that are blushing pink and accompanied by a sauce as unusual, in its own way, as the Attack Bread. The sauce is not hot, and not made from ketchup, either. It is filled with hunks of meat and onion, tomatoey and rich and homemade; dieters could eat it from the cup like soup. There's also another barbecue oddity: barbecued duck.

All this is evidence of an active imagination in the kitchen, and some of it belongs to owner Jim Goode, a commercial artist who retired and went into barbecue, opening the place in 1977. "We bought a former fast-food barbecue restaurant," he said. "We got in here and tried to do things right." There's an active imagination in the design, too, with a mounted buffalo head, an antique jukebox, and display cases of memorabilia from his great-grandfather's tenure in the Texas Cavalry during the Civil War, along with cornball old signs that say things like WHAT THE—ARE YOU LOOKING UP HERE FOR. We decided not to mention the $37.50 "bull bags" for sale at the cash register. Not in a book about eating.

RATING: Real good.
LOCATION: 5109 Kirby Drive; (713) 522-2530.
WEB SITE: www.goodecompany.com

The
Final Course

The Name Game

We have eaten barbecue at Mom's in Los Angeles, Pop's in Nashville, and Unkie's in St. Louis. In Cleveland we checked out Baby Sister's and Mama's Boy. In Knoxville we sampled the fare at Brother Jack's. San Francisco offered us Bro-In-Law's, and Columbia, Missouri, Cousin Bob's. In Indianapolis we ate at Pa and Ma's. In Jackson, Mississippi, we chowed down at Pappy's.

That is one of the best things about barbecue joints: their names. Because barbecue is one of the last bastions of individual enterprise, the naming process hasn't been taken over by ad agencies and public-relations firms. Barbecue joints are named by their owners. They don't try to reflect the national mood or cash in on a craze. They don't commission market-research studies to determine optimum name recognition and consumer preferences. They just try to give their places good names. And they do.

The favored name for a barbecue joint over the years has been Old Hickory. We've visited twenty-two towns from West Palm Beach, Florida, to El Dorado, Arkansas, and from Dayton, Ohio, to Clinton, Mississippi. Adding in all the variations on *hickory*—Fred's Hickory Inn (Bentonville, Arkansas), the Hickory House (Atlanta, Georgia), the Hickory Smoke-house (Hopkinsville, Kentucky), Luchenbach's Hickory Hut (Birmingham, Alabama), Stubby's Hik'Ry Pit (Hot Springs, Arkansas)—it is the runaway winner for most popular.

But "Bubba" is coming up fast. You could eat your way across the country if you knew Bubba. At this writing there are twenty-one barbecue joints operating under Bubba's moniker or a variation, including Bubber's in New Orleans and Big Bubba's in Louisville. In addition, Sikes Bar-B-Q in Eastover, South Carolina, is run by Bubber Sikes, and Sweatman's Bar-B-Que in Holly Hill, South Carolina, is owned by H. O. "Bub" Sweatman. And in the Orlando area there are four joints run by the female Bubba, Bubbalou!

A good name is a good name, even if it doesn't seem to fit. Some good names are just in the wrong place. We've been to the Tennessee Pit in Jackson, Mississippi, the Tennessee Mountain in New York City, and Tennessee Andy's in Pompano Beach, Florida. We've visited the Texas Smokehouse in Dayton, Ohio, the Texas Cattle Co. in Baltimore, Bull's Texas Cafe in San Francisco, and the Texas State Line in Atlanta.

Other names are more suited to a different cuisine. At one time Miami had the Swiss Chalet Barbecue. ("Oh, Hans, I love your sauce.") Philadelphia had Mama Rosa's (barbecued spaghetti?). New York City still has the Pink Teacup, which sounds like a Fire Island tearoom but is a soul-food place.

Some names are just plain bassackwards. Lamb's in Memphis cooks pig, but Chicken Comer's in Phenix City, Alabama, doesn't serve chicken. If you're in west Tennessee, you can head over to Goat City Bar-B-Que in Milan, Tennessee. Just don't go expecting to eat goat.

A good name is a good name, even if it no longer applies. Big John's in Marble Falls, Texas, was bought by a fellow named Henry. Brady and Lil's in Memphis was sold to Frank and Hazelteen. Jay's in Baton Rouge was run by Floyd LeBlanc. Mr. Allman has been dead for years, but his name lives on in Allman's Barbecue in Fredericksburg.

In Lexington, North Carolina, John Wayne's Barbecue is not owned by John Wayne but by Mike Eller and Vaughn Miller. The same barbecue place has had a long and confused history. It was originally Stamey's, run by Warner Stamey. When Harold Craver and Paul Cope bought it in the fifties, they changed it to Old Hickory, the name of a restaurant they owned in

Great Barbecue-Joint Slogans

"We barbecue everything but the baby. We boil him."
—Big Shoe's, Terre Haute, Indiana

"Hogs smell better barbecued."
—Andy Nelson's Southern Pit
Barbecue, Baltimore, Maryland

"You don't need teeth to eat Mr. Jim's beef."
—Mr. Jim's Barbecue, Los Angeles

Winston-Salem. It became Stamey's again in 1979, when Dan Stamey, no relation to original owner Warner Stamey, bought it. Dan was the son of Smiley Stamey, who owned Smiley's Barbecue, which is now Southern Barbecue. In 1981 Dan Stamey sold it to John Wayne Little, who changed it to John Wayne's before selling it to Eller and Miller. There is now a new Stamey's in town, owned by the same Dan Stamey, who had bought John Wayne's back when it was Old Hickory. Whew.

Big Bubba's in Middletown, Kentucky, is run by H. P. Stainback, who admits no one ever called him Big Bubba before he applied the name to his barbecue stand. "It could be Billy Bob's or something like that, but you've got to have a name . . . I'm 295 and six-four, and that's a pretty big Bubba, isn't it?"

Sometimes the name is better than a good name—it is a great name. Anyone who has seen the hard work required in cooking barbecue knows that there couldn't be a more appropriate name for a barbecue pit than Sweatman's Bar-B-Que in Holly Hill, South Carolina, or Sweat's in Soperton, Georgia.

At some barbecue joints you can kill two birds with one stone: The Hickory Pit and Gift Shop in Dawson Springs, Kentucky. Ace Cab and Barbecue Barn in Atlanta. The Bar-B-Que Inn and Donut Shop in Hopkinsville, Kentucky. Chavous Pit in Beech Island, South Carolina, was a barbecue joint and auto-repair shop. At Paul's Place in Cave City, Kentucky, you could kill three birds with one bone: barbecue, country music, and square dancing. Our favorite in this category is the late House of Prayer Bar-B-Q, Fort Lauderdale.

References to "pigs" are popular in barbecue-joint names. A few of the best we've collected over the years: Dr. Hogly-Wogly's Tyler, Texas, Bar-B-Que, Los Angeles, California; the Pink Pig, Frankfort, Kentucky; the Red Pig, Fort Thomas, Kentucky; the White Pig Inn, North Little Rock, Arkansas; the Flying Pig, Hapeville, Georgia; the Whistlin' Pig, Fulton, Kentucky; the Pig Squeal, Waverly, Alabama; Hog Heaven, San Francisco; Fat Willy's Hawg House, Rock Hill, South Carolina; and Maurice's Piggy Park, West Columbia, South Carolina.

Only Los Angeles would have a Flying Saucer Barbecue.

Here are a few other of our favorite names: Bangkok Bar-B-Que, Claremont, California; Barbecutie, Nashville, Tennessee; Bar-B-Cuisine, Oakland, California; Big Shoe, Terre Haute, Indiana; Bozo's, Mason, Tennessee; Bubbalou's Bodacious Bar-B-Que, Orlando, Florida; Choo Choo Bar-B-Q, Waverly, Georgia; Curtis' All-American Ninth Wonder of the World Bar-B-Q, Putney, Vermont; Do-City, San Francisco; Hoo Doo Barbecue, Boston; Mr. Boo Boo's Bar-B-Que, Vero Beach, Florida; Beasy's Back Porch Barbecue, Ashland, Oregon; the Pits Barbecue, Edmonton, Kentucky; Radd Dew's Bar-B-Q, Conway, South Carolina; and Wrinkle Belly's, Atlanta.

Our favorite barbecue name comes from Corbin, Kentucky: the Moo Moo Hut.

And finally there was Jehan's in Sanford, Florida. At least that's what the sign on top of the building said. The awning said SKIP'S. And it was listed in the phone book as Joe's.

Barbecue Festivals

There is no more serious gathering of serious barbecue cooks than at the Memphis in May World Championship Barbecue Cooking Contest, held each spring on the third weekend in May. These serious cooks come to win, and they come from as far away as California and Massachusetts, even Ireland and Estonia.

Because the teams are so serious about their cooking, they are very carefree about everything else. They treat the contest as a two-day party that gives grown men and women a chance to act juvenile again. The craziness starts months ahead when the teams pick their names. They use every imaginable play on pork nomenclature: The Best Little Boarhouse in Texas. Swine Lake Ballet. Capitalist Pigs. Dr. Smoke and the Professors of BBQ. ZZ Chop. Rib Ticklers.

The fun even extends to the barbecue cookers. These aren't your garden-variety Weber kettles. Many of the grills have personalities of their own. Ray Green of Euless, Texas, had a whole table full of trophies he had won at festivals around the country using Bubba, his 5-foot-high armadillo-shaped cooker. Joe Amyx, another Texan out of water, brought along his 6-foot-high rabbit-shaped cooker, complete with brass genitalia. The Diesel Powered Porkers, a Memphis cooking team, converted a Detroit Diesel motor into a cooker. The Federal Express team cooked in a 4-foot-long, plane-shaped cooker that was so sharp and spiffy you might think it was the model the company used during corporate rallies. You might think this if you didn't see that eerie smoke pouring out of the fuselage. There may be a locomotive-shaped cooker and a pig-shaped cooker and, in memory of Elvis, a guitar-shaped cooker.

Our favorite all-time team, now retired, was the Leisure Brothers, five guys from Nashville who never put aside their leisure suits. Some years they employed a card table covered with pig parts and a handmade sign reading SOLAR BAR-B-Q COOKER. They usually finished near the bottom, attributing their poor showings to their rather, uh, leisurely approach to the judging process. When the judges arrived at their tent for the taste testing, they were too involved in partying. They served the judges on paper plates, and when one judge asked about sauce, the brightest of the Leisures snapped his fingers, mumbled, "Oh, yeah," and raced over to the Heinz tent to fetch a sample bottle. "We're here one part for the cooking and ninety-nine parts for the partying," Larry B. Leisure, occasional spokesperson for the Leisures, told us at one festival. The Leisures only spoke occasionally. They preferred to turn up their hi-fi and boogie. They made their cooking area as leisurely as possible, installing a waterbed and a portable bar and an Elvis-on-black-velvet tapestry on the wall. It sure seemed like home.

The Memphis in May Annual World Championship Barbecue Cooking Contest is but one of hundreds of barbecue cooking contests held each year. Barbecue festivals can make for a lively weekend outing. We've also found them to be great places for tasting great barbecue. At most festivals, once the judging is over, the contestants start passing out free meat. All you have to do is stand in line. At others you may need to make friends. But that's easy enough. One thing about barbecue cooks: They love to talk about their barbecue. Just pick out a contestant who looks interesting (or who has a large number of trophies displayed out front) and start talking to him (usually) or her. Next thing you know, you'll be gnawing away on barbecue that is as good as you've ever had.

Here is a list of some of the top barbecue festivals held each year. Call or check the Web site to make sure the event hasn't been rescheduled. The big barbecue societies have Web sites, such as www.kcbs.us.com (Kansas City) and www.ctbahome.com (Central Texas), and they have renamed and are sponsoring a lot of local festivals. Some of these contests are sanctioned by the societies and are preliminaries for events like Memphis in May. Some are traditional local fests open to the backyard cook.

February

Smokin' on the Rio Texas State Championship Barbeque Cook-Off

Mercedes, Texas; www.smokinontherio.com
Raises money for youth agricultural products in the Rio Grande Valley.

End of March

Newport Pig Cooking Contest

Newport, North Carolina; www.newportpigcooking.com

April

Southaven Spring Festival Barbecue Cooking Contest

Southaven, Mississippi; www.southavenspringfest.com

May

Grain Valley Daze Cook Off

Grain Valley, Missouri; (816) 847–2627; www.grainvalleychamber.org

Pigs in the Park

Danville, Virginia; www.visitdanville.com

Second weekend in May

International Bar-B-Q Festival

Owensboro, Kentucky; www.bbqfest.com

Third weekend in May

Memphis in May Annual World Championship Barbecue Cooking Contest

Memphis, Tennessee; (901) 525-4611; www.memphisinmay.org

Late May

Inaugural D'Arbonne BBQ Fest and Louisiana State Championship BBQ Cookoff

Farmerville, Louisiana; (318) 368-8935; www.darbonnebbqfest.com

Tops Great American Rib Cook-Off

Tower City Amphitheater, Cleveland, Ohio; www.cleveland.com

June

Mississippi State Barbecue Championship

Clarksdale, Mississippi; www.clarksdale.com

Ribfest

Chicago, Illinois; www.northcenterchamber.com

Show Me State Cook-Off

Kennett, Missouri; www.showmemissouri.net

Late June

Great Lenexa Barbeque Battle

Lenexa, Kansas; www.ci.lenexa.ks.us

August

Fiddlin', Brewin', Bar-B-Q'n Festival

Nashville, Tennessee; www.nashville.about.com

Taylor International Barbecue Cook-Off

Taylor, Texas; www.taylorjaycees.org/cookoff/

September

Best in the West Nugget Rib Cook-Off

Reno/Sparks, Nevada; www.nuggetribcookoff.com

Blue Springs Barbeque Blaze Off

Blue Springs, Missouri; www.bluespringsgov.com

Carolina Pig Jig Barbecue Cook-Off

Raleigh, North Carolina, at the State Fairgrounds;
www.carolinapigjig.com

Sponsored by the Masonic Lodge barbecue teams
and benefiting orphanages and a rescue mission.

Do Dat Barbecue

Nacogdoches, Texas; (888) OLDEST-TOWN;
www.ci.nacogdoches.tx.us

Smoke on the Water Arkansas State Championship Barbecue Cook-Off

Pine Bluff, Arkansas; www.smokeonthewaterbbq.com

October

American Royal Barbecue Contest

Kansas City, Missouri; www.americanroyal.com

BBQ Championship Cook-Off, Traders Village

Grand Prairie, Texas; www.gptexas.com

Big Pig Jig

Vienna, Georgia; www.bigpigjig.com/forms.htm

Jack Daniel's World Championship Invitational Barbecue Contest

Lynchburg, Tennessee; www.jackdaniels.com

Lexington Barbecue Festival

Lexington, North Carolina; www.barbecuefestival.com

Roast N' Boast Barbeque Contest

Columbus, Mississippi; www.columbus-ms.org

Teams from the mid-South compete to represent Columbus at Memphis in May. Local teams compete to be the Back-yard Grand Champion.

The Sheriff's Posse Championship B-B-Que Cook Off

Pecos, Texas; www.pecostx.com

Second weekend in October

Possum Fest and Great Outdoors Barbecue & Chili Cook-Off

Graford, Texas; www.possumkingdomlake.com

You're Only as Good as Your Grill

Hey, you there.

Yes, you in the backyard with the apron and the funny hat. The time has come to face an awful Truth about Life: Maybe you can't judge a book by its cover, but you can tell a heck of a lot about a cook by his barbecue grill.

A dedication to the never-ending quest for perfect barbecue means searching for the ultimate apparatus. So a tricked-out grill is a sure measure of madness—and method.

Yes, it is possible to cook barbecue on the most rudimentary of grills, darned good barbecue, and we'll even tell you how—but that is missing the point. Barbecue may be the melding of meat and hot air, but all of the latter doesn't come from the coals. Boasting and basting go hand in hand, and the war of words over the best backyard barbecue has its own arms race of barrels, dials, drip pans, and smokestacks.

A novice needn't worry unduly about such matters, however. Barbecue fanaticism isn't something one needs to cultivate; it simply takes over. One day a guy may be perfectly happy with his hibachi, and then, in an instant, he'll find himself eyeing the specs for something different, something imposing, perhaps even something intimidating, like a runaway freight train screaming full throttle down on quivering tablefuls of innocent diners— something like . . . Big Baby.

But we'll get to that soon enough.

Basic-Grill Basics

There's no shame in using a simple hardware-store grill to cook barbecue. Well, maybe there's a little shame. But there's no reason you can't go ahead and do it anyway. The fact is, you can produce delicious meat using such a grill; it's just that some recipes will be out of your grasp, due to space limitations or the difficulty of maintaining the right sort of slow fire. The price of admission to the backyard-barbecue world, however, is a grill with a lid that closes.

The whole idea behind barbecue is to cook meat slowly in hot air and smoke. With a basic grill, you use charcoal for heat and a few wood chunks for smokiness; that's why you can't get by with an uncovered design. Leaving the top open would be a waste of that precious wood smoke. Also, a covered grill takes advantage of convection cooking (hot air blowing around the food), and that keeps meat much more moist and evenly cooked. The air vents in a covered grill allow a chef to control the coals better, too, damping them down to make for longer cooking times. It's theoretically possible to simulate a covered grill by making a tent of aluminum foil over a hibachi or open grill, but such a jury-rigged contraption, especially in a bit of a breeze, is a lot better way to learn new curse words than to cook food.

Step one in barbecuing on a hardware-store special is to grab yourself by the throat (you may use either hand for this) and shake until you have sufficiently reminded yourself: "I am barbecuing; I am not grilling. I am barbecuing; I am not grilling." Grilling is what takes place when your neighbor's backyard burgers nuke themselves to cinders in a burst of flame: It's quick cooking over hot coals, designed to sear the meat to hold in juices that would otherwise be boiled out by the heat. It's fine for hamburgers, hot dogs, and chicken. It is not barbecuing.

Barbecuing is a different proposition, gentle by comparison, that uses lower temperatures and no direct flames. Hot smoke does the cooking, gradually adding its own flavors to the meat, which remains naturally moist.

When starting a basic charcoal fire, remember that all charcoal is not created equal. The holy grail of the grill is charcoal *au natural,* with all the twigs and uneven chunks that come from the real wood used to produce it; that's good stuff.

Acceptable stuff, available in both national and local brands, is made by smoldering hardwoods or mesquite into charcoal and then pressing the crumbs together into briquettes. It is quite likely that some sort of binder will be used to hold the briquettes together, and in "off brands" this can be something as unappetizing as recycled petroleum products. You usually can spot these by sniffing, however, and avoid them. Instant-light briquettes, which are preimpregnated with starting fluid, are okay for grilling or fire-starting, but not genuine, long-haul barbecuing—because they are consumed too fast, and adding new ones supplies new chemical fumes.

Wood chips and chunks of various varieties, available in stores and by mail order, are not intended to be burned like charcoal. Instead, they are usually soaked in water for at least an hour (to keep them from incinerating immediately) and then added to hot coals to provide true wood smoke.

There are a multitude of theories on the best way to light charcoal, from arranging the briquettes individually over tight twists of newspaper to just tossing on some lighter fluid and standing back. The best system, for our money, is the chimney, in which a bunch of charcoal is suspended in a ventilated cylinder over a recently ignited, crumpled copy of the op-ed page. It's fast, efficient, and sort of environmentally friendly, and you can always fire up a new one and add hot coals to your grill when they're needed.

Nonetheless, feel free to argue about these techniques, as well as everything else that has to do with barbecue. The fact is, almost any method will work, as long as you allow enough time for the coals to mature. Remember: A stopwatch isn't a good guide for charcoal. The right time to start cooking is when the hot coals are almost all spotted with gray ash, with an occasional flicker of blue flame.

However you did it, short of using a tactical nuclear device, let's figure you got your charcoal going. For most basic-grill barbecuing, you're going to want to shove the coals off toward the sides and stick a drip pan (cake pan, iron skillet, whatever fits) in the middle. As the meat cooks over this pan, the drippings are caught; they help to preserve the moisture inside the closed grill and send their sizzling flavor wafting back up to the meat.

Fancier Grills

The popularity of backyard barbecuing has brought a boom in all sorts of charcoal grills better suited to serving up the gen-you-wine article. Once available only by mail order, these also turn up now in hardware stores and woodstove outlets.

The water smoker. These are the cookers that look like R2D2, squatty cylinders with rounded tops. They first became popular with outdoor types who used them to smoke game, but they work pretty well for barbecue, too. A pan to hold liquids is mounted inside the closed smoker between the coals (or electric coils) below and the meat above. When making barbecue (as opposed to smoking a turkey), it's good to go easy on the liquid in the pan, as it tends to keep the meat soft instead of letting it get crispy. Some barbecuers complain that the temptation to dump anything from the rest of your beer to Aunt Olive's rosewater in the pan means you're likely to end up with meat that tastes like anything but what the Good Lord intended. And it's also true that you add at least fifteen minutes to your cooking time every time you peek at the meat, because raising the lid lets out a considerable amount of heat, and the relatively small charcoal fire takes a while to build it back up. Soaked wood chips can be used with water smokers, tossed in among the coals, just as with a standard closed grill. Some water smokers even have little doors in the side to make adding chips, or more charcoal, easier to do without letting heat escape. Most water smokers have simple, semi-useful thermometer dials mounted in the lid.

The Chinese kettle or Japanese Kamado. These smoking ovens look a bit like decorative vases, the Chinese version being more barrel shaped and the Japanese vaguely egg shaped. In fact, one popular American variation is called the "Big, Green Egg." They are made of ceramic, which is rugged and a good insulator. The coals rest in a firebox at the bottom, which can be pulled out to add more charcoal and includes an adjustable air vent. Meanwhile, the meat sits in the middle. With the lid off, these Oriental cookers can work like a grill for burgers; closed up, they will contain the smoke for good barbecue. Owners sometimes like to brag about how hot they can get their Kamado grills—4,000 degrees or something. That may be ideal for reprocessing spent fuel rods, but it's no way to cook barbecue. Low and slow does it, and, again, wood chips may be added for extra smoky flavor.

The gas grill. Gas grills are easy to light, compact, portable, and nice to roll around the deck. They also are kind of a prissy way to make barbecue. It is possible to buy accessories to convert such a grill, which was basically designed to cook steaks and burgers, into something that will sort of cook barbecue. For twenty bucks or so, you can buy a ventilated metal box in which to put wood chips for smoking (it sits directly on the fire bricks). There even are variations that include a water pan for moist heat. But let's face facts: A gas grill is good for a spur-of-the-moment sirloin, but it makes a lot less sense when you're talking about cooking beef brisket for five hours or so. Gas grills can maintain an even heat for long periods of time, but their compact size makes it difficult to fit drip pans in there anywhere or to keep the meat away from the fire bricks. Plus, gas grills are seriously short on soul.

The gas or electric smoker. This isn't the same thing as the more familiar backyard-patio grill; these often look like little metal shacks with doors on them. Inside, these smokers use a heating element at the bottom, then a pan or tray for wood chunks, and finally some racks for the meat to recline upon. Like water smokers, these were originally used mainly by hunters to smoke game. But they come with a thermostat and can be cranked up to produce barbecue, too. In many ways, they are like miniature versions of the commercial gas or electric equipment used by Brave New Barbecue restaurants that seem to be in too much of a rush to mess with a traditional pit.

The backyard brick barbecue grill. Across America, suburban houses of the proper post-war vintage are possessed of a giant brick edifice in the backyard, a Sphinx of a grill, a superstructure suitable for feeding the masses at a state park. Unfortunately, it is entirely unsuitable for cooking barbecue. Burgers, yes; barbecue, no. To put this in a more optimistic light, just think of what wonderful planters these brick grills would make! Or fountains! Why, with a little plumbing and some water lilies, it could be just beautiful.

The Grill of Your Dreams

This is the heavy artillery.

When ordinary backyard smokers have lost their charm, and money is no object, do what the Pentagon does: Go shopping for big guns. This selection of barbecue monsters will give you an idea of what's out there. They may be designed principally for caterers and churches, but nobody's going to be checking your ID when you plunk down your cash. Tell them you're with the Church of the SubGenius. Tell them anything. Then pay your money and your shipping charges and wait to see the look on your neighbors' faces. Who cares if you have to park your Pinto at the curb just to make space? This is barbecue, Bubba. And the heavy hitters have to be ready to step up to the plate.

The Double-Door Smoker, BBQ, and Grill. It has 738 square inches of cooking surface. It has cast-iron, porcelain-coated cooking grates. It's made of heavy-gauge steel, with chrome-plated handles. It's a drum-style smoker with an offset firebox and a handy ash tray (and, of course, double doors). It looks like what you'd get if a gas-grill manufacturer got serious about making something for the backyard charcoal chef. Which is exactly what it is, made by Char-Broil of Columbus, Georgia. It's entry-level hot stuff for around $200. The Char-Broil folks are ready for you with a toll-free number, even: (800) 241–7544.

The Tejas Smokers 2040CC. The *j* in Tejas Smokers is pronounced like an *h,* as in "What in the joly jell is this contraption?" The answer is that it is one of the best-made barbecue smokers around. At 710 pounds, it's no lightweight, although it will lighten your bank account by about $1,500. It's an offset-firebox model, with a big, horizontal cooking cylinder in the middle and a firebox off to the right. On the left is an additional tall, vertical cooking chamber that looks a little like a sauna for short ribs. The 2040CC is made to burn real, 18-inch logs if you want to; it has a nine-gallon water reservoir; and it will feed at least twenty when it's fully fired up. Tejas Smokers can be found in Houston. Call them at (713) 932-6438 or surf on over to www.tejassmokers.com.

The Pitt's and Spitt's CB2436. After honing their designs in barbecue competitions in Texas, Wayne Whitworth and his brothers began selling grills to the general public, although there may be very little that's "general" about a burning desire for a $2,300 smoker/grill with side burners like this one. It has a carbon-steel cooking chamber with a built-in water reservoir and a firebox with a lifetime guarantee against burnout. The burners off to one side will keep your sauces warm while your buddies marinate in their own envy. The folks at Pitt's and Spitt's don't have a lot of truck with questions like, "Is that the deluxe model?" "All the grills we sell are deluxe models," they told us once. The company also sells mobile barbecue trailers, with the standard model starting at about $4,000 and custom, one-of-a-kind models rising in price as high as the hickory smoke. Pitt's and Spitt's, 10016 Eastex Freeway, Houston, Texas 77093. Swallow hard and give them a call at (800) 521-2947 or go online at www.pittsandspitts.com.

The Hasty-Bake Hastings 290. It costs almost $6,000, but your daughter doesn't really need that big church wedding, does she? Besides, you could serve the entire rehearsal dinner from this stainless-steel showpiece—with two individually controlled fireboxes that allow for simultaneous grilling and smoking. It has 1,194 square inches of cooking surface, dual thermometers, commodious storage, and a ten-year warranty. If your daughter's marriage lasts ten years, you can always apologize then. The Hasty-Bake folks hail from Tulsa, Oklahoma, and can be reached at (800) 426-6836. Online, they're at www.hastybake.com.

The WHAM Turbo Cooker WC-12. This is a cooker with a concept, indeed a whole philosophy, behind it—courtesy of inventor, restaurant owner, and champeen barbecue chef John H. Willingham of Memphis, Tennessee. His basic theory of barbecuing goes against the grain of a lot of traditional wisdom: Barbecue isn't flavored by "smoke," he says. Rather, it absorbs its pink color and distinctive smoky overtones from the "essence" of the wood, the unburned gasses that rise along with the smoke from the fire. "Smoke is nothing but ash suspended in a column of hot air," Willingham says. "How is ash going to penetrate meat? Ash would just land on the surface. You can't poke your finger into a piece of meat, and that has a lot more force behind it than ash." Operating on the theory that smoke is just a smoke-screen when it comes to good barbecue, Willingham designed his Turbo Cooker to burn clean, with almost no smoke at all—and then locked it up for six years until his patents came through. In its "backyard" version, it's a cartlike affair with a glass-enclosed greenhouse that accepts numerous racks of ribs, hanging and rotating in the hot "essence." The unit is designed with a Pel-Fire system that burns wood pellets, a technique that burns very efficiently and can be automated for long periods of time. Each $7,500 WC-12 is constructed of stainless steel and arrives with a plaque with the owner's name and date of construction. "This is built so you can pass it on to your grandchildren," Willingham told us, and allowed as how each buyer will be asked to sign a confidentiality agreement not to use the cooker commercially or reveal its secrets. If you're ready to take the pledge, write Willingham at P.O. Box 17312, Memphis, Tennessee 38187-0312; call him at (800) 737-9426; or visit www.willinghams.com.

Homely and Homemade

Homemade barbecue is the way all barbecue started out, and there's still something noble and uplifting about an ungainly, flat-black contraption smoking away out in the yard, producing delicious barbecue according to its inventor's intentions. It sort of makes you wonder where the Wright

Brothers might have ended up if they hadn't gotten off on that whole aviation thing.

The covered pit. The simplest homemade cooker to construct, of course, is the pit. All you need is a shovel, a pretty good pile of hard rocks, some gunny sacks, and chicken wire—and the sage advice of Pat and Bill Martin. Twenty years ago, at the Elk Mountain Hotel in Wyoming, Pat and Bill would barbecue 400 pounds of meat at a time on their own customized spit. Times have changed. Today you can get a buffalo burger or some fine osso buco at the Elk Mountain, but if you want an old-fashioned pig-out, it's strictly do-it-yourself. So here's how to do it yourself, according to Pat and Bill.

First, dig a craterlike hole in the ground a few inches wider than the hog in question (let's take an eighty-pounder as an example), making it about twice as deep, about 3 or 4 feet. Once you have put away your shovel, the real work begins: Cover the bottom of the pit with a layer of hard rocks (the rocks are there to absorb heat, not just to give you a terrific backache). Then build a healthy fire of wood or charcoal and let it burn way down until you have a thick bed of hot coals lining the pit.

Next, haul out a piece of chicken wire big enough to poke out opposite sides of the pit; this will help you lower the pig in and lift it out again. It'll also keep the pig out of the coals, and to help it do that, lay down some aluminum foil on top of the chicken wire where the pig will rest.

Now, a short digression on the pig itself: After it's dressed by your friendly butcher (don't have the pig skinned, and don't poke holes in it), wrap it in gunny sacks soaked with water and a mixture of spices—like sage, thyme, garlic, bay, and salt and pepper—or else soak the gunny sacks in barbecue sauce. Put the pig on the foil-covered chicken wire and lug it over to the pit, lowering it onto the hot coals and rocks. Cover it with more rocks, until the pit is sort-of leveled off, and then build another fire on top of those rocks. Let that burn down to coals, and then go have a beer; you've earned it. For the really fun jobs, like lifting and removing hot rocks and chicken wire, be sure to wear all the protective clothing and gloves your mother would want you to. As a bonus, during such back-breaking work you'll have plenty of time to wonder if maybe you shouldn't have put in a flower bed instead.

Eight hours later, pull the top layer of rocks off the pig with a rake or shovel, grab the chicken wire, and lift up a juicy, flavorful main course, adequate for feeding six to eight people. One of them may point out that the pig is technically not "barbecue," since it cooked in moist heat and not a stream of hot smoke. That person, while correct, should go home hungry.

The open pit. An open pit is a lot like the pit described above, except you go for a deep bed of coals (a foot deep, say) and steel yourself to turning the pig (or side of beef) while it cooks, basting it more or less continuously. Classic open-pit barbecue is a bit hard to find, and even harder to do at home since it requires a hefty spit arrangement that can be turned, in addition to a bucket brigade of basters willing to keep at it for twelve hours or more at a stretch. We're not trying to discourage you, but forget it, okay?

The cement-block pit. Many big-volume barbecuers, like church groups or contest entrants, use what is basically an aboveground pit made of cement blocks stacked up in a rectangle on some hard surface like a street or driveway (mind the asphalt, now). The blocks are stacked from two to five high, making walls on all four sides. The wood goes in the middle, and we're talking about a lot of wood here, in trip-to-the-sawmill type volumes.

At the International Barbecue Festival in Owensboro, Kentucky, monstrous versions of these cement-block pits send flames hundreds of feet in the air as they burn down to the requisite coals. Cooking this way requires a lot of tending and turning of meat, with a water hose handy to squirt on outbreaks of flames and somebody strong enough to yank a couple of cement blocks out of the wall when wood needs to be added. At Owensboro, most of the competitors use rough-cut planks of hickory, with a few other hardwoods tossed in for spice. Aside from the actual work of tending one of these pits, which will continue from the late evening of one day until the afternoon of the next, the hardest thing about cement-block pits may be scrounging the big metal grids that lie across the blocks and support the meat. You can try looking in scrapyards for big hunks of expanded steel.

But with all the scrounging, lugging, lifting, and tending, the cement-block barbecue tends to be the province of teams, usually of men, and frequently of men who can forget about how tired they are tending the fire at 3:00 A.M. if they just have another beer.

Drum smokers. The smaller scale of many homemade smokers doesn't lessen the ingenuity involved in building them. You will see smokers made out of segments of oil pipeline, out of refrigerators and stand-up freezers, out of welded sheet metal, and out of the favorite of the barbecuer on a budget, the fifty-five-gallon drum.

God must have loved the fifty-five-gallon drum; He made so many of them. Forget for a moment that most of them seem to turn up on the news surrounded by guys in white protective suits looking for toxic waste. Good, healthy, wholesome drums exist, and they can form the core of an impressive barbecue smoker that a reasonably stupid person can put together with an electric drill, a saber saw, a few hand tools, some bolts and rods, and angle iron. One of your reasonably stupid authors has done it.

First, get the right sort of drum, a drum that won't have you and your loved ones worrying about growing extra arms. Some fairly benign stuff comes in drums that can be found at your average factory, like soaps and other cleaning compounds. Such drums are available in reconditioned form at drum-supply places, too. A good washing should whip one of these babies into line. But the best drum, even better than a new drum, is one from a farm-supply store, should you be lucky enough to live near one. In many parts of the country, farmers will add bulk molasses to their livestock feed, and this sticky, sweet-scented stuff comes in, that's right, fifty-five-gallon drums. A drum like that you don't even want to wash out, and the last couple your authors have bought have had a little puddle of rich-scented residue still inside.

Once you have your drum, try your best to scrape away or sand off any loose paint. If you don't, the heat of the fire will make it peel off later. After you make sure such loose paint is gone, repaint the thing with some high-temperature paint, either the type sold at hardware or discount stores labeled "Bar-B-Q Black," or else the stuff they sell at auto stores that's made to paint headers and exhaust pipes. In this latter variety, you'll find reds and bright yellows, suitable for adding flames or other painted designs to your stoic black grill.

Next, decide whether you want a single-drum smoker or want to go all the way to full-bore double-barreled barbecue.

A horizontal single-drum smoker is simple to construct: You cut a drum in half lengthwise, add some hinges at the back, and a rack for the meat to rest on across the middle. Getting it up off the ground really is the trickiest part, but you can make legs by welding or bolting together angle iron; you also can just set it atop properly spaced columns of cement blocks for a quick but rather inelegant apparatus. With the lid open, this sort of horizontal smoker can be used as a grill by cooking directly over a fire made in the bottom; to use it as a smoker, build the fire in one end and cook the meat in the other, placing it over a drip pan if so desired and closing the lid.

A vertical single-drum smoker won't grill; it just smokes stuff, but it's probably the simplest drum smoker to make because it requires no legs to stand on. The fire is built in a separate pan set on blocks, and the drum (with one end removed) and its rack of meat are simply lowered onto the coals.

These are both fine ways to cook, but your authors admit to a fondness for what we term "double-barrelled barbecue" and a grill we call Big Baby. It may not be the ultimate drum smoker, but with both its smokestacks sending forth clouds of hickory and fire roaring out the front, it'll sure scare off your neighbor's dog. And that's nothing compared to what it'll do to your neighbor, who may in the past have harbored a few faint doubts about your cooking ability.

Big Baby and Double-Barreled Barbecue

The plans for Big Baby are on page 260. Memorize them and eat them (perhaps with a Kansas City–style sauce) before your friends see them. It is incalculably cool to be the first barbecuer on your block with a belching Big Baby in your backyard; however, showing up with the second one falls a bit short of overwhelming. Building one, if not exactly a breeze, is at least not one of those projects that requires the mythical "handyman." Basically, the Big Baby philosophy is to take stuff that's more or less lying around and turn it into a smoker that works on the same principles as the $2,000 jobbies that the pros sell.

The essential function of a top-notch barbecue smoker is to keep the meat entrusted to it comfortably separated from flames and direct heat and yet in the path of the hot air and smoke that give it its flavor. Big Baby does this by burning a hardwood fire in her bottom barrel and using the top barrel to contain the meat and direct the smoke. The top barrel also serves as a big, self-contained drip pan that catches meat juices. And the vents and dampers located all along the air path mean that the fire can be precisely controlled, keeping it from dying or flaring up.

Besides two fifty-five-gallon drums, the "trick" to the smoker is in making use of woodstove kits designed to convert such drums into cheap stoves for heating open work areas and such. The kits come with a cast-iron fire door, cast-iron legs on which to mount the smoker, cast-iron supports to connect the bottom drum to the one above it, plus flues to connect the two drums. From a hardware store or woodstove shop, you toss in some dampers and a couple of neat little smokestacks for each end to let the smoke escape from the top drum.

Building Big Baby

Before you get started, make sure you have the stuff you'll need. The used drums you should be able to find in your area for about $25 or so; you also can order brand-new fifty-five-gallon drums for about $100 from the totally smokin' Vogelzang International Corporation (616–396–1911; www.vogelzang.com).

The required stove kits are available at many bigger hardware and woodstove stores or by mail order from, say it with us now, Vogelzang! In fact, Vogelzang offers basic kits for the bottom barrel (about $70) and matching kits for adding the top barrel (about $55).

The two 22-inch grill surfaces usually can be had at a barbecue supply house for $25 apiece or so. Add some bolts, brackets, hinges, smokestacks, fire bricks, paint, and such, and you're up to a total expense of less than $300, more than the price of a simple covered grill but considerably less than the cost of a B1 bomber, which, by the way, does a simply horrible job on a rack of ribs.

The steps are simple: Paint the barrels first, then start cutting them with your saber saw. Use a fresh metal-cutting blade (ask the guy at the hardware store or tool-rental place for one), and prepare yourself for a violently annoying noise roughly akin to 500 colicky babies with the croup. Cutting through a hollow drum with a buzzing saber saw makes enough racket that you may want to consider earplugs. Or suicide. But persevere, and cut a hole for the fire door at one end of the bottom barrel and matching holes in both barrels for the flues that connect them. Cut the top barrel in half horizontally, setting the top half aside. Then do your drilling and mounting and bolting, referring to the directions in the kit whenever appropriate. Basically, you want to mount the bottom barrel on its legs (and we recommend connecting these to a couple of two-by-fours for a sturdier base), and then mount the fire door to it, followed by the connecting supports and the two flues (remember to insert the dampers before you bolt on the top barrel).

Then you add the top barrel, bolting together the supports and flues between the two. At this point, lay the top half of the top barrel in place and mark holes for the hinges and handles. After the lid is in place, you can drill holes and bolt in place the small chain that keeps the lid from falling over backwards. About now you can use the saber saw one last time to cut holes in either end of the bottom half of the top barrel and mount the two smokestacks (again, don't forget those dampers). Drill a hole for your thermometer (an inexpensive dial-type candy thermometer works fine, and it even includes a clip that will hold it in place). Line the bottom of the bottom barrel with fire bricks, which keep it from burning through. Then drill and mount the brackets that support the grill surfaces, slap those puppies

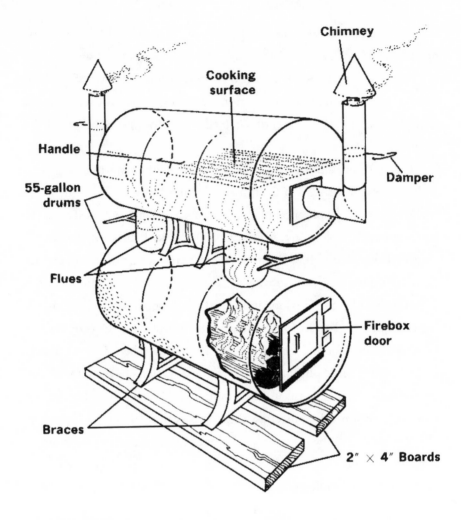

Chimney

Cooking
surface

Handle

Damper

55-gallon
drums

Flues

Firebox
door

Braces

2″ × 4″ Boards

Big Baby: The way Casey Jones would have cooked.

in place, and call one of those fellows who delivers wood. You're ready to barbecue!

It's best to operate this smoker over a nonflammable surface, from something as basic as packed dirt to concrete. The Babe sits a bit low to the ground, and her firebox gets more than a mite hot, so she will send any grass in the area to Turf Heaven almost immediately. For a neater look you could put down gravel and even border the area with bricks.

Cooking with Big Baby

Big Baby is designed to burn real wood, not charcoal. She'll be happy with just about any hardwood—hickory, oak, mesquite, whatever—but stay away from soft stuff like pine. Build a good-size fire in the bottom barrel and let it go for a while, maybe an hour or more, until it has formed a healthy pile of hot coals. Avoid cooking over a "fresh" fire, since such fires send up a lot of soot and creosote-like goo. Go for a hot bed of coals onto which you can toss the occasional log, keeping the temperature as even as possible. The exact temperatures you shoot for will vary with the recipes (see the following chapter).

Barbecue is not set-it-and-forget-it food; cooking it requires almost constant tinkering and tending to keep the heat even over a period of hours. But with a big base of coals for consistency and the proper combination of damper settings for the wind and outdoor temperature, the Babe will chug along at a constant heat for an hour at a time, certainly time enough to go out for more beer or CDs.

There will be very little in the way of barbecue that Big Baby can't handle, from a suckling pig to three twelve-quart stockpots of Not Really Patented But Nonetheless Reasonably Rare Chili-Q. But she's more than a simple smoker.

Big Baby is a sculpture in basic black, a lifestyle statement, a conversation piece, a badge of honor, and a joy forever. And on a hot summer day, even when you're not cooking anything, it still smells like barbecue.

Man's work: Cooking on a backyard smoker requires Attitude as well as Appetite. Especially at the wheel of a monster like the Babe, you will be joining an exclusive fraternity of pitmen, dedicated masters of the meat who stand ready to poke, prod, and ponder until an undistinguished piece of raw material completes its transformation into edible nirvana. To do this properly, you must realize that you have left ordinary men (and darned near all women, ordinary or otherwise) behind. You have become a semi-exalted creature, a Prince of the Pit. And you must learn to act the role.

First, realize that you have entered into one of the few remaining domains, outside of the NFL, where men still rule. The pitman's art is a manly art; even barbecue joints owned by women have male pitmen. And that's as it should be. It's not just a question of who's best at lugging logs and sucking smoke; it's preordained by history. From the caveman onward, women have been Joan of Arcs, good at inspiring fires but not at setting them. A man's rightful place is by his smoker; a woman's place is inside, making slaw. Accepting this fearless philosophy with confidence will mean forgetting what you heard on a lot of Dr. Phil shows, but you should at least make the effort. Women, it's a wonderful opportunity to feel his muscles and coo admiringly. Men, it's time to get down to business.

True, preparing for a barbecue feed will require you to be at your post for most of the day before an evening's guests arrive. But look at it this way: Tending a smoker is important work (if you're a man, don't miss this chance to refer to it as "man's work"). That means if you are forced to lounge in a chair within eyeshot of your smoker, sunning and sipping— well, maybe you'll just have to miss the vacuuming and dusting and errand running. It's a lonely job, but somebody's got to do it. It's only the main course. And you're the main man.

As long as you're out there, do it properly. If your religion permits, have a beer. Actually, have two; it's going to be a long day. And don't let any guilty feelings creep up as you watch the kids cut the grass or your girl-friend wash the car or whatever other mundane chores may happen to be in progress around you. Change the CD in your boom box. Holler up to the house for more ice. You're busy. You've got a job to do. Consider invit-ing a friend over, or even a couple of friends; they may need a big job to do, too, especially one that involves passing you another beer.

And some people wonder why barbecuing hasn't died out.

Backyard Barbecue: Mysteries of the Meat

Barbecue is Horatio Alger cuisine.

The big names of barbecue have grown almost without exception from a hole in the ground or a sliced-open fifty-five-gallon drum in the backyard to fame and (infrequently) fortune. That makes cooking up a batch of barbecue in your own yard a spicier proposition; you never know when your latest experimental technique or sauce might turn out something truly transcendental, catapulting you into the ranks of the masters and perhaps even the next edition of this book.

After all, if you're not expecting some bragging-good barbecue, what are you doing out in the lawn with your eyes full of smoke? You can get mediocre barbecue at the local Spee-D-Shop or Dairy Dollop; you can get it a lot quicker, and you won't smell like a Boy Scout Camporee when you're through. The only reason to cook backyard barbecue is to do it right. Here's how.

Go ahead and use the good stuff. Good barbecue comes from good meat. Though its origins connect it with wild game and its reputation with less desirable cuts, barbecue cooking properly done is a process that can enhance anything from the lowly brisket to the lordly tenderloin. In the competitive world of barbecue joints, owners don't skimp on the meat.

First Family Barbecue

In George Washington's diary for the year 1769 is this entry: "Went up to Alexandria to a barbicue. Back in three nights."

Even less celebrated cuts can vary considerably, and a good butcher can be invaluable in getting you the best basis for your barbecue. Get to know one. Tell him about your smoker, about the big weekend you have planned, and he'll usually be happy to keep his eye out for a particularly good cut. Remember that lots of finicky customers never really talk to butchers, probably because they're afraid they might have to shake hands with them. If you treat your butcher like an actual human being, he'll appreciate it. Don't give him the cold shoulder, and he'll give you a good one.

Be gentle. Despite the fact that the finished product may taste hot enough to strip the chrome off a '55 Chevy, barbecuing itself is a gentle process. That means it's best done over fairly long periods of time, without abrupt changes that will "shock" the meat.

Remember: Barbecue is your friend, even if it's your dinner, too. And you should treat it in a friendly fashion. Don't whip a hunk of meat out of a chilly refrigerator and toss it directly over a hot fire; wouldn't you complain if something like that happened to you? Besides, cold meat can cause condensation in a smoker, resulting in a bitter, smoky liquid.

So take it easy. Relax. Make your friend comfortable on the countertop, sit back, pop open a brew, and get to know each other. Start a conversation: "Been puttin' on a little fat there, bub?" It's okay to be a little familiar; after all, you're friends. Besides, later on you'll probably want to trim some of that fat and position the rest so that it "cooks through" the body of the meat when it's on the grill. Or you may decide to carve the cut into chunks of a particular size to influence your cooking time. Also, counter time is prime time for marinating or dry rubbing. In general, time spent getting to know your meat won't be wasted.

Keep your little buddy bundled up in freezer paper or plastic wrap so he won't catch a bug while he gets the chill out of his bones, and continue your chat while he does his best to hit room temperature. Perhaps he seems a bit nervous; there's a certain stage fright that comes from being the main course. But if he's been marinating overnight, keeping him tender shouldn't be a problem, unless you've been marinating overnight, too.

Marinades and Dry Rubs

To marinade or not to marinade? Soaking meat in an exotic concoction of liquids and spices is one of those things that just seem like fun, whether or not it does much good. Actually, the process of pit barbecuing is so effective at tenderizing that marinades aren't really needed for the reason most people use them—to soften up a tough piece of meat.

It's true that many marinades do have this effect, since the acid in them breaks down fibers and tissue. (Common acid ingredients in marinades include, in descending order of intensity, vinegar, citrus juices, dry wine, sweet wine or vermouth, and apple juice.) A number of professional pitmen, especially in Texas, will have nothing to do with marinading, however, or even basting, because they maintain that a marinade (especially a vinegar-based one) actually draws natural moisture out of the meat in the cooking process, leaving it with somewhat of a chalky texture and sometimes even a bit of a slimy feel.

When some chefs want to add flavor to the meat (the second reason to use a marinade), they tend to go with a "dry rub," a mixture of spices that coats the outside of the cut. Actually, if you like to marinade, there's no real reason not to. Just figure to marinade for flavor, not tenderness, and make sure to cut any vinegar in the recipe with something less acid to lessen its effect.

You can marinade for a couple of hours at room temperature or overnight in your refrigerator, but if you're having much in the way of barbecue, finding room to accomplish this can be a pain in the old Boston butt. Fitting odd-shaped cuts like a slab of ribs in any known pot or pan is difficult, and if you can find one, it's likely to be much too awkward to cram in the fridge. Okay—great chance to run down to the local discount emporium and get one of those stupid Gadgets You Can't Live Without: the Seal-a-Meal. This apparatus (or one of its cousins) will heat seal many cuts of meat in a custom-size freezer bag along with the marinade of your choice. A Seal-a-Mealed rack of marinating ribs fits nicely atop a couple of six-packs. You can stand them up or stack them with no fear of leaks. And you can carry them in their little plastic wrappers out to the grill under one arm, pitching the plastic after they're on the grill. And there are no pans to wash. It's great. Really. Just because you're cooking the old-fashioned way doesn't mean you have to live in the Stone Age.

Barbecue sauces make a flavorful base for marinades, especially with pork, and you can use your favorite. Some commercial vinegar-based sauces can be used as-is or cut with a little beer or cider to dilute their vinegar effect. Thicker tomato-based sauces require a little tinkering:

2 cups apple-cider vinegar

1 cup ketchupy barbecue sauce

2 tbs. lemon juice

1 tbs. dry mustard

1 tbs. cayenne powder

Simmer the mixture just long enough to make sure the flavors are mixed, then cool it down before using it as a marinade. If the strong vinegar flavor is not to your liking, substitute a couple cans of beer or even diluted lemonade. You can let the meat marinade for up to a day in the refrigerator.

A less store-bought approach is to take something that softens you up and use it to marinate the meat. Wine and beer are common bases for marinades, sometimes used straight, though you can find recipes that use gin and even bourbon (which may sound strange but beats the socks off wasting the stuff on a mint julep). There's really no need to follow a recipe; just start with a bottle of wine (light for pork, red for beef), some oil, vinegar (flavored or otherwise), and an available spice rack. To a bottle of wine, you can add in the neighborhood of a cup of vinegar, a half cup or so of oil, and pinches and teaspoons of spices, plus any garlic, Worcestershire sauce, or dry mustard that the moment demands. Trial and error is fun, and the errors are never so serious that a little fiddling can't fix them.

Aye, here's the rub. Massaging spices into a hunk of meat before barbecuing is an excellent way to add flavor or an undercurrent of heat. Some cooks maintain that a dry rub seals pores in the meat, making it retain its juices; some even theorize that a rub attracts moisture from the air and actually adds it to the meat. Whatever the explanation, the results speak for themselves: Dry rubs and smokers were made for each other. For the most part, rubs are simple mixtures of spices eminently suited to tinkering with, although some pitmen say that salt (although a frequent item in recipes) should be avoided because it tends to draw moisture out of the meat. But other ingredients can be used according to divine inspiration: chili powder, garlic powder, paprika, all types of pepper, mustard seed, a little sugar, even that bottled "barbecue seasoning." And increasing numbers of commercial rubs are becoming available as people realize that you don't need to soak meat in marinade with the right kind of grill.

A fresh cut of meat at about room temperature should bask in its spices for at least a half an hour before hitting the smoker. Frozen meat can be rubbed down when it's removed from the freezer; by the time it reaches room temperature, it will have absorbed sufficient spices. Also, you can rub meat, wrap it tightly, and stick it back in the fridge for a while.

Kansas City chefs often seem to like some sweetness in their rubs. Here's a basic formula once gleaned from barbecue guru Dr. Rich Davis, the man behind K.C. Masterpiece sauce, who now serves on the American Royal Board of Directors:

½ cup brown sugar
½ cup black pepper, coarsely ground
½ cup paprika
¼ cup chili powder
2 tbs. garlic powder

Down in Cajun country, there's more of a tendency to go for the jugular. The following red-white-and-black rub is nothing but hot and is based on a common cooks' aphorism in bayou country: Black pepper gives you the aroma, red pepper gives you the burn, and white pepper gives you the bite. This mixture bites your head off.

¼ cup black pepper, freshly ground
¼ cup white pepper, freshly ground
¼ cup hot red chile peppers (dried), finely ground

Acme Atomic Oil

A classic technique in grilling meats is to coat them with oil, which tends to keep them moist and seal in juices. It works in barbecuing, too. Olive oil is excellent for this since it doesn't burn easily. But in the midst of all the excitement attending a barbecue, using plain old olive oil (even the mild, expensive stuff) seems a tad boring. Luckily, olive oil is more than happy to take on the characteristics of various flavorings and spices dropped into it. Try rubbing and basting beef or pork cuts with the following recipe; for better effect, remove the label from the olive oil bottle. The resulting flask full of mysterious ingredients will amaze and astound.

1 bottle mild olive oil, pint size (about ½ liter)

1 clove of garlic

3 hot red peppers, dried

2 tbs. cracked peppercorns (black)

2 tbs. cracked peppercorns (white)

1 tbs. tarragon Cayenne powder (to taste)

Sopping and Mopping

Some barbecue cooks absolutely swear by basting; some won't be caught with a mop in their hands. Both sides can produce delicious meat to defend their positions. Hey, we don't care. If you do it, it won't make you go blind. Actually, basting is just a pleasant bit of cooking procedure; it's fun to peek at the progress of the meat while you dab it with your little cotton mop (available at most restaurant-supply stores). Done properly, it can add spicy heat and flavor to a mild meat like pork. But every time you open the lid of your smoker, you're letting hot smoke escape and wrecking the ovenlike conditions you worked so hard to create.

If you do baste, use a basting sauce (one without sugar or tomato, which burn easily). And keep your fire a little hotter to compensate for all the heat you're letting escape. Basting partisans baste a lot early, while the meat is open to suggestions. Also, adjust your basting recipes to conditions; a sauce like Frank's Sop (below) has a lot of oil—not appropriate for a cut of meat with lots of fat already. To lighten up on oil, add water or vinegar as part of the liquid. For hotter basting sauces, add Hungarian paprika, Tabasco sauce, Louisiana hot sauce, jalapeño peppers, black pepper, or cayenne.

Frank's Texas Style Bar-B-Que Sop

Frank Volkmer started out roughnecking on a drilling rig in Texas, but eventually he decided his fortune lay in barbecue. "I was going to semi-retire," he once told us. "I thought I'd found a gold mine." Aside from nearly going broke three or four times, he was more or less right. At the nuclear plant's open house in his hometown of Bay City, Texas, Frank served 20,000 people, including demonstrators. At the Exxon Day picnic he served 12,500. Then he moved to Denver, where he saw a city just waiting for some good Bay City barbecue. He opened up a catering business and a restaurant, and he kept expanding until darned if he didn't nearly go broke again. But he put Frank's Bar-B-Que & Catering Service in Denver on the map, where it remains today. He always resisted the clamor of Coloradans for hotter sauce than the mild Texas version he grew up with. "Hot is not good," he said. "Hot is to be put on the table and added." So when you dab this all-purpose sopping sauce on a slab of ribs, you won't be turning your pork into plutonium; it's meant to enhance the meat, not explode it. "It gives you distinctively flavored barbecue," he said. "It has a wonderful aroma."

1 stick

1 clean rag, torn

1 length of string

1 qt. Wesson oil

1 qt. water

2 lemons, sliced or quartered

1 large onion, chopped thumbnail size

1 oz. vinegar

2 tbs. salt

1 tsp. ground black pepper

¼ tsp. garlic powder

"First, take a stick off a tree," Frank told us. "Tie a rag around it with string. This is your sop stick." Then, he said, combine the remaining ingredients, bring them to a boil, and let them simmer for fifteen minutes. "Don't cook it," he cautioned, "just let it boil about a minute. Then keep it warm all day while you cook your barbecue." When your meat is about three-fourths done, start sopping. Keep doing it every fifteen minutes until the meat's done. Frank always had options for this sauce, and the first one is "nine-sixteenths imagination." With a caution ("In recipes, if a little is good, more is not better"), Frank allowed any of the following:

    1 can Coors beer
    1 small bottle ketchup
    1 oz. Worcestershire sauce
    2 or 3 jalapeño peppers, chopped
    1 oz. Tabasco sauce
    1 medium bell pepper

"Now, you can add Worchestershire sauce or beer or anything you want," Frank adds, "but the problem with that is, you like it and the neighbors maybe can't take it. A lot of guys put beer in it, get real drunk, and then say, 'It was in the sop!' I say, 'Keep it simple.'"

Barbecue Honey

In Kansas City, you'll find chefs who like to baste their slow-smoked pork and beef with honey, beginning a couple of hours before the end of its cooking time. Yes, it tastes a little sweet, they'll tell you. And, yes, it tends to burn a little—but who doesn't like slightly burnt barbecue? Indeed, "burnt ends," little snippets of beef from the end of the brisket, are a Kansas City staple. Just as with olive oil, however, it's possible to take a jar of honey into the lab and come out with something frightening: barbecue honey. Add pinches of cayenne or hot Hungarian paprika, even prepared horseradish. The combination of hot, sweet, and burnt is intriguing and unusual, the sort of thing that can set your barbecue apart from the pack.

Backyard Barbecue:
Making the Cut

Tenderloin

At the top of the list of backyard cuts is the tenderloin, a lean, tender, and boneless core of meat that runs along either side of the backbone in Mr. Cow and Mr. Hog. If you've ever been to a Southeast-style "pig-pickin'," in which guests help themselves to their meat of choice from a whole roast pig, you know about the tenderloin: It's what was already gone by the time you arrived. And beef tenderloin is familiar to diners in a variety of cuts that usually show up at the expense-account end of the menu, like filet mignon (from the head of the tenderloin), Chateaubriand (from the center section), and tournedos (from the tail).

Tenderloin makes impressive, fast barbecue, although we're including it here as sort of nouvelle version because it's served less than well done. It's not cheap, but it can be cooked relatively quickly into a spectacular main dish that is smoky and spicy on the outside but, when sliced, feathers into a plush, rosy pink in the center that is delicate, beautiful, and delicious.

Once you decide on a tenderloin, don't skimp; get a prime or choice cut. And ask the butcher to remove the sheath that encases the meat. It's possible to barbecue an entire tenderloin; the cut tapers at the each end, providing a range of "doneness" at any given cooking time. For less meat consider buying just the part of the tenderloin from the sirloin area of the beef; it's a thick cut that should feed about six to eight people.

County Line Smoked Tenderloin

Time: Forty-five minutes to an hour

Grill types: Any enclosed grill

This simple but spectacular recipe comes from Texas's County Line restaurants, which have grown from a single spot "On the Hill" in Austin to restaurants from Albuquerque to Oklahoma City to Houston. In a world of slow-cooked barbecue, this is a relatively fast recipe. The County Line folks may spend eighteen to twenty hours smoking their brisket, but this recipe for tenderloin will deliver a tender, spicy piece of the very best beef in less than an hour. Naturally, it's best on a smoker like Big Baby, but it can be cooked on a standard covered grill, also.

> 1 whole peeled tenderloin, graded choice, about 5–6 pounds
> Lemon-pepper seasoning
> Dab baste (melted butter, fresh lime juice, freshly squeezed garlic)

With the meat at room temperature, cover all sides of the tenderloin heavily with lemon-pepper seasoning. Place the meat on the rack in your smoker. (This meat can be prepared on a standard barbecue grill that has a lid; if the meat is to be close to the coals, you may want to place it in a foil "boat," which lessens the grilled effect but helps preserve juiciness.)

To a hot charcoal fire, add several chunks of hardwood that have been soaking in water for at least a half hour.

Cook at a grill temperature of 225 degrees. After twenty minutes, begin to check the tenderloin's temperature with an instant-read meat thermometer. Check it every ten to fifteen minutes. Since you're going to be opening the lid anyway, take the opportunity to baste the meat with a mixture of fresh-squeezed lime juice, melted butter, and fresh-pressed garlic (the exact proportions can vary according to taste; prepare it in advance).

When a meat thermometer registers 150 degrees, you will have arrived at a medium-done tenderloin, with the center a blushing pink. The meat can be served immediately, of course, but it also can be held at a reduced temperature of 120 degrees until your guests show up, as long as they're not coming from Fairbanks.

Like every barbecue recipe ever written, this one can be fiddled with. If the lemon-pepper flavoring isn't to your liking, try rubbing the meat with a fine coating of cayenne pepper; that will produce a slow, manageable glow in the mouth that goes well with barbecue sauces. Or try coating the cut with Acme Atomic Oil (see the Backyard Barbecue: Mysteries of the Meat chapter) instead of a dry rub.

Brisket: The Toast of Texas

What happens between brisket and a barbecue smoker is something akin to true love. The two simply were made for each other. Brisket is cut from the breast of a steer, just behind the foreleg, and it's made up of two main pieces of meat, surrounded and separated by seams of fat. It's this fat basting the meat during a long, slow barbecue that gives it such a rich, luxurious flavor—not as obviously smoky as pork, but moist and meaty, with a whisper of wood. Brisket is graded prime, choice, and select; any will do, but better is better. Often supermarkets will sell two versions of the wedge-shaped cut, one of them trimmed by the store to eliminate some fat (and sold at a higher price). Many pitmen recommend brisket with a maximum of ½ inch of fat on the outside. A ten-pound brisket can feed ten to twelve people; the meat will lose about half its weight while cooking. Actually, six- to eight-pound briskets are more common; also, smaller cuts are available, with the second cut (farther away from the shoulder) having fewer fibrous layers.

Beasy's Back Porch Brisket

Time: Nine hours

Grill types: Any enclosed grill

At Beasy's Back Porch Barbecue in Ashland, Oregon, the outdoor pit and the picnic tables used to overlook Lithia Creek. "We have one of the most beautiful summers you've ever seen," said Beasy McMillan, a happy refugee from the heat of Texas hill country. When he first headed north, he took his Texas-style brisket with him and gave Oregonians a taste of something besides fish. Although Beasy has moved on to Italian cuisine, here's his original recipe; with it, you can come close to Lone Star–level brisket on any backyard smoker big enough to burn a little wood and close a lid over it.

Dry rub:	Barbecue:
Cayenne pepper	Beef brisket, 8 to 9 pounds
Black pepper	Cut oak wood, pieces
Salt	Texas-style barbecue sauce
Chili powder	

Rub the meat with the dry-rub mix (using the ingredients proportioned to suit your taste). "Rub it in there good," Beasy told us. While you let the meat hit room temperature, build your fire of pieces of oak or hickory, as big as you can and still leave room for the meat to sit off to the side of the grill. When the wood has burnt to hot coals, put your meat on the grill ("Just as long as you can put it where the fire doesn't touch it, you're okay."). Keep the thermometer between 230 and 250 degrees. Make sure the fatty side of the brisket is on top. Cook for four hours, adding wood as necessary to maintain a constant temperature. After four hours, take the brisket out, wrap it in foil, and cook it for four more hours. Then remove the foil ("Save the juice; it'll come in handy in other cooking.") and put the brisket back in for hour number nine. ("That hour gives it its crispness on the outside.") After that final hour, take out the brisket and separate its halves "like a surgeon." The top half is used for chopped brisket. ("This is also known as the outside cut," Beasy said, and it can be shredded. "When you go to a barbecue restaurant, you can ask for the outside cut; it's like burnt ends.") The bottom half should be cut across the grain of the meat at a diagonal. This gives you 1½-by-6-inch slices, completely lean, with a beautiful red ring of smokiness around the outside. Serve with Texas-style sauce.

Ribs: Boning Up on Good Barbecue

Ribs and backyard cookouts are an American tradition, but the few ribs prepared according to the immutable laws of Real Barbecue get lost in all the hordes of sorry, smoking cinders that are either burnt black on a grill or else boiled in a pot of water first. This is not barbecue; this is meat abuse. Avoid it. First, get a good rib—loin ribs (from the back) or classic spare ribs from the chest. We prefer spare ribs, for philosphical reasons: Ribs should be eaten by hand, by people who don't care that they've just ruined their wardrobe; country-style "ribs" will tempt weaker souls to use a fork. No one, not even royal personages, can eat a spare rib with a fork. Small loin ribs, weighing less than two pounds, are favored by some pitmen as the meatiest and tenderest cut (they're often called "baby back ribs"). But others prefer spare ribs since real barbecuing works its wonders on them, making them plenty tender. (If they are trimmed of the flap of bone and brisket along one side, they're called "St. Louis style.") The best weight for spare ribs is generally agreed to be under three pounds—"three-down" they're sometimes called. Stay away from ribs that weigh much more than that; the bigger the rib, the older the hog and (usually) the tougher the meat. Also, stay away from ribs the "right" weight that have been heavily trimmed; they're probably bigger, tougher ribs that have been chopped to sell.

Floyd LeBlanc's Baton Rouge Ribs

Time: One hour or more

Grill types: Any enclosed grill

Jay's Bar-B-Q in Baton Rouge, Louisiana, is one of the best barbecue joints in America. Owner Floyd LeBlanc has passed away, but his son Milton can be found there most days at the Government Street location turning out delectable meat in his pit. Floyd told us years ago how he cooked the ribs in the backyard for his wife on Mother's Day.

> Pork spare ribs, 3-pound racks
> Barbecue sauce (your favorite)
> Fresh white onions (1 per rack)
> Salt (to taste)
> Pepper (to taste)
> Garlic powder (to taste)
> Charcoal (not quick lighting)
> Wood pieces (hickory, oak, or pecan)

Wash the ribs in cold water, then remove the tough skin on the back with a knife. Salt and pepper to taste and add a little garlic powder. Then go light the charcoal (being sure to use a closed grill) while the ribs sit at room temperature. After the charcoal turns white, put your wood chunks on it. ("I don't soak my wood," Floyd said, "because it kills the fire.") The smoke will start ten to fifteen seconds later. Cover the grill and get the temperature to about 200 degrees (or, if you have a lot of meat, 350 degrees). When you put the ribs on, the charcoal should just smoke, not flame up. If it flares, dampen it with water. Then close the grill again. "The slower you cook it, the better it is," said Floyd. "Don't cook it any faster than an hour. Do it so you can really enjoy it and don't have to rush." Sometime later on in the cooking process, when the spirit moves you, you can add a little more garlic powder. ("Garlic powder gives pork a real good flavor; it kicks out the meanness in the meat.")

Your meat will be ready when you can mash it in the seams between the ribs with your fingers. ("Your fingers will sink right through it. If you can, hold the meat with your fingers and squeeze it to test it.") As you approach that point, when your ribs are about three-quarters ready, put them in a pan and put barbecue sauce on them. ("Don't baste 'em: You lose too much sauce.") Put foil on top of the pan and let the ribs and sauce steam on the coals for a while. "I'm one of the few Frenchmen who doesn't like a lot of spice," Floyd told us, "but if you do, after you're done, slice up a fresh onion and spread the slices on the ribs. The juices will sink into that hot meat." Remove the onions before serving, with additional warmed barbecue sauce on the side.

Pork Shoulder: Superior Sandwich Stuffing

Around Lexington, North Carolina, if it isn't chopped, sliced, or pulled pork shoulder on a bun, it isn't barbecue. Although it isn't required by law, it's also the favored cut of many other places in the Deep South. Pork is graded differently from beef and lamb, but on the same grounds of flavor, tenderness, juiciness, and cutability (how much meat it has on its bones). For pork a grade of "U.S. No. 1" corresponds to "prime," and "U.S. No. 2" equals "choice." You can get by with "U.S. No. 3," a grade that corresponds to "select" (and usually the lowest grade sold in supermarkets), but if you're going to spend the next nine hours of your life cooking it to amaze your friends, you might as well spring for the good stuff, which has more fat running through the meat and makes juicier, tastier barbecue. Pork shoulder comes from about where you'd expect on a pig, and it's often cut and sold as "arm roasts" or "picnic hams." But you want the whole thing, bone and all. Look for light pink or white meat and fresh red-tinged bones, not dark ones. A shoulder of about sixteen pounds, even though it will cook down by about half, will feed about fifteen to eighteen people.

Buddy's Son's Shoulder

Approximate time: At least six hours

Grill types: Fifty-five-gallon barrel smokers work best, but as long as you can fit the shoulder in a closed grill and get the meat 12 to 16 inches above the coals, you'll probably be okay.

Buddy Halsell runs the Dixie Pig in Blytheville, Arkansas, where they barbecue mouthwatering pork shoulder. Buddy's brother Johnny, who also has put in his time in the restaurant business in Little Rock, once told us, "We cook the flavor in; we don't pour it on." So when Buddy's son Bob explained how to cook good shoulder, he didn't mention marinades or basting sauces. You could follow this basic procedure and baste your heart out, though. Just don't tell Bob about it. Or Johnny or Buddy.

> 1 pork shoulder
> Hot coals

First, start your fire (either with wood or charcoal); don't cook until it's glowing evenly. "Keep a side grill going," Bob said, "So you can add coals that are already hot." While the coals are getting ready, trim most of the fat off one side of the shoulder, leaving a little bit. "You want to leave some fat," Bob says. "It's good for smokin' and drippin'. Don't trim the knuckle skin off." (There's a bone joint that sticks out of a shoulder cut with membrane attached.) Put the shoulder on the grill trimmed side down first. Cook at least three hours—and as many as four or five hours. Now turn it. "You got to be very careful," Bob cautions. "You're going to turn it one time only." (If you turn it more often, the meat gets tough.) "Edge it up, or you'll pull the crispy pieces off. Jiggle it." Then let it cook maybe three or four more hours, maintaining a good bed of glowing coals. To tell if it's tender enough to be done, take a fork and lift the shank end of the bone; it'll just come apart at the muscle. Then slice or chop it immediately, dabbing with a rag or paper towel to soak up some of the grease.

Secrets of the Secret Sauces

Yes, we're revealing the recipes to some prize-winning sauces here, but we're also urging you to ignore them—or at least experiment with them. Good barbecue sauce is so completely a matter of personal taste that there simply isn't one that can't be "improved."

Half of the fun of whipping up sauces from scratch is the Mr. Wizard business of pouring in ingredients not covered in any written recipe. An eerie glow fills the room as you burst forth with a mad laugh, "Nyah, hah, hah!" and hold the beaker aloft, filled with a secret formula known to no one else. As the organ music rises, you impulsively take a sip, and . . . if you don't turn into a werewolf, you've probably got a tasty little sauce there, friend.

In fact, it's almost a matter of honor to add a hidden element to your homemade sauce. Face it: What's worse than having a secret sauce that's someone else's secret?

One technique is just to fiddle around with the proportions in these recipes: a little more cayenne and you can bring out the sweat beads on your guests' foreheads; a little more honey and you can lull them into a false sense of security. But more fun is to adopt a trademark secret ingredient that will add a distinctive character to the sauce you concoct, sort of a signature effect. A little imported hot Hungarian paprika will raise some eyebrows when dropped into the right recipe. An unexpected dash of balsamic vinegar or maple syrup can work some strange transformations, too. Just keep track of what you add as you add it, or it'll be a secret even to you.

At this point, the authors will reveal a favorite secret ingredient: single-malt Scotch whiskey, especially a pungent brand called Laphroaig. Its intense, peaty flavor will add an air of mystery to a sauce, and you don't need to add much (which is a good thing, because it costs more than a college education). But if Scotch is not for you, plenty of alternatives exist. The main thing is the quest. The only perfect barbecue sauce is the next one.

Memphis-Style Sauce

In Memphis, if your ribs aren't "dry," they're served with a sauce basically like this. Used full-strength, it's a typical table sauce. For a basting sauce, mix one cup of the recipe below with one cup of vinegar and one cup of water.

> 1 cup tomato sauce
> 1 cup vinegar
> ¼ bottle Worcestershire sauce
> 1 tbsp. butter
> ½ small onion, chopped
> Dash black pepper (more if you want it hotter)
> Dash red pepper
> 1½ tsp. salt
> ½ cup water

Mix ingredients together in large saucepan, bring to a quick boil, and let simmer for ten minutes. Figure out your own secret ingredient and dump it into the mix.

Western Kentucky–Style Sauce

Belinda Kirby is a native of Franklin, Kentucky, and offers this recipe:

½ cup brown sugar

½ cup ketchup

1 tsp. garlic powder

1 tsp. onion powder

3 or 4 dashes cracked pepper

2 tsp. soy sauce

3 tbsp. Worcestershire sauce

Pinch of oregano

1 tbsp. lemon juice

½ tsp. black pepper

2 or 3 dashes paprika

2 or 3 dashes chili powder

Combine ingredients until blended. Marinate meat in the stuff overnight. Baste the meat only during the last twenty minutes of cooking time. Save the rest of the mixture to use as a table sauce.

Kentucky Colonel Sauce

This recipe for a pork basting sauce comes from the Kentucky Home Pork Producers Association, which has been preparing barbecue for the Kentucky Colonels Derby barbecue since 1977.

2½ cups water

1 tbsp. sugar

3 tbsp. black pepper

2 tbsp. butter

¼ cup vinegar

3 tsp. salt

¼ cup onion, chopped

1 clove garlic, minced

1 tsp. red pepper

2 tsp. chili powder

1 tsp. red pepper sauce

1 tsp. dry mustard powder

3 tbsp. Worcestershire sauce

Combine all ingredients in a saucepan and bring to a boil. Reduce heat and simmer five minutes. Cool. Refrigerate overnight. Warm before using. Start basting meat at beginning of cooking and continue until pork registers 170 degrees on meat thermometer. For ribs this should take about twenty minutes.

Owensboro Black Dip

This is the original recipe for mutton dip used by the Moonlite Bar-B-Q Inn in the mutton capital of the world, Ownesboro, Kentucky. The barbecue restaurant no longer uses this recipe, but you can. It even goes with beef.

1 gallon water

1⅔ cups Worchestershire sauce

2½ tbsp. black pepper

⅛ cup brown sugar

1 tsp. MSG

1 tsp. allspice

1 tsp. onion salt

1 tsp. garlic

2 tbsp. salt

2 tbsp. lemon juice

1⅔ cups vinegar

Combine all the ingredients and bring to a boil. Baste and use the rest as a dip for chopped or sliced mutton.

Explosive Flavor

May this account serve as yet another apology to Colleen Endres, a sweet woman and wonderful neighbor who in no way deserved what she saw that summer day when she peeked through her curtains at the yard next door: Two armed men taking aim at a tree full of meat.

Actually, maybe we should back up a bit.

It all began innocently enough, with one of those casual brainstorming sessions that barbecue fanatics drift into—you know:

What if we add chipotle to the sauce? What if we add a steam chamber to the smoker?

Except this time it was: What if we load some brand-new shotgun shells with great seasonings and, instead of just rubbing our ribs, really let them have it with high-velocity spices? What could be better than barbecue shot from guns? Wouldn't it flavorize and tenderize?

We're not saying who loaded the shells and supplied the armament; let's just say he has since left the state. But he was definitely there that day, helping to suspend dozens of ribs from the low branches of a maple tree, where they dangled on bent coat hangers.

And he may even have fired the first shot, which, using lightweight spices instead of buckshot, had to be pretty close to point-blank.

More shots followed. Many more.

It was loud; it was exciting; it violated at least one city ordi-nance. But did it make transcendental barbecue?

The resulting ribs were indeed delicious—juicy, meaty, fla-vorful.

But they were exactly the same as every other rib we fix. The spices hadn't penetrated the meat; they'd just coated it like a regular rib rub.

Mrs. Endres didn't call the police that day, and more than ten years went by before she felt able to tell us about what she'd seen and the scare we'd given her. We apologized pro-fusely, and she said she forgave us.

But, before long, she moved away and sold her house to a lawyer.

Texas-Style Sauce

President Lyndon B. Johnson had a reputation as a man who was particular about his barbecue. It had to be like they had in Texas. This is one of 12,000 recipes that are said to be LBJ's favorite sauce.

½ cup butter
¼ cup lemon juice
¼ cup vinegar
¼ cup ketchup
¼ cup Worcestershire sauce
Dash of salt
Dash of pepper
2 tsp. Tabasco sauce
Dash of red pepper

Melt butter in saucepan. Add lemon juice, vinegar, ketchup, and Worcestershire sauce. Bring to a boil, then add seasonings. Refrigerate one to two days. Serve as a table sauce.

Down East–Style Sauce

In eastern North Carolina, they don't cotton to tomatoes. They don't think they're poisonous anymore, but they still don't use them.

1 gallon vinegar
¾ cup salt
2 tbsp. red pepper
3 tbsp. red pepper flakes
½ cup molasses (you may substitute 1 cup brown sugar)

Combine ingredients and allow to stand four hours. Serve as a table sauce.

Western North Carolina–Style Sauce

The meat of choice in western North Carolina is pork shoulder. The sauce of choice goes something like this:

⅓ cup cider vinegar

1 tsp. salt

1 tsp. celery seed

½ tsp. cinnamon

½ cup ketchup

½ tsp. chili powder

⅛ tsp. nutmeg

½ tsp. brown sugar

1 cup water

Mix ingredients and bring to a boil. Pour over meat. Use as a baste and save the rest to serve on the side.

Blondell's Barbeque Sauce

Joan Blondell was a city gal, born and bred in New York City. But as a teenager she worked with a stock company in Texas and once was named Miss Dallas. Our bet is that's where she picked up her barbecue recipe. (She died in 1979.) *Hollywood Studio* magazine said, "The dynamite lady was a gourmet cook before that phrase was invented and loved to entertain friends and family at home. She was devoted to her grandkids and a great lover of animals. At weekend barbecues, Joan would entertain pals such as Barbara Stanwyck, Nancy Sinatra Sr., Orry Kelly, Clark Gable, Bette Davis, Mary Astor, Ross Hunter and Jacques Mapes and dear friends and former restaurateurs Jerry Jerome and Cecil Hedrick.

"She often jumped into the kitchen of their famous La Cienega Blvd. boite, Ceejee Upstairs, to join in the cooking."

1 tbsp. bacon drippings (or vegetable oil)

½ cup onions, chopped

½ cup apple juice

2 tbsp. wine vinegar

¼ cup lemon juice

4 tbsp. molasses

1 cup chili sauce

1 tsp. ground pepper

1 tsp. French mustard

4 tbsp. tomato ketchup

Sauté the onions in the drippings or oil until brown. Add the rest of the ingredients and simmer for twenty minutes. To use, baste on meats or chicken to be barbecued (during their last fifteen minutes of cooking).

Mr. Vince's Hacking Sauce

I was mixing up some barbecue sauce, trying once again to capture that elusive taste, to create a sauce that would stand the test of time and thwart duplication. I had been playing around with a Lexington-style base, vinegar-thin with spices and herbs to enhance the natural flavor of the meat, but a hint of tomato and sugar to add a distinction. I wanted something delicate enough to seep through the meat but stout enough not to soggy up the bun. In short, the perfect sauce.

No matter what I did, every concoction seemed to just miss. If it had the right consistency, it lacked something in flavor. And when the flavor seemed close, everything else was wrong. I needed a secret ingredient. Every barbecue cook worth his salt pork has a secret ingredient. I dug around in the cupboard, when I spotted it on the shelf above the sink. No one was looking, so I sneaked it down, measured out a half teaspoon, and stirred it in.

I tasted it, and it was there; it was what I had been searching for.

A few days later I entered it, quietly, in a sauce contest. None of the thirty judges knew it was my sauce. In fact, they had no idea where any of the sauces came from. My Hacking Sauce didn't win—that honor went to Zarda's from Blue Springs, Missouri. But it did respectably and finished ahead of such well-known sauces as Maurice's of West Columbia, South Carolina; Ollie's of Birmingham, Alabama; and Demetri's of Homewood, Alabama.

And it was the only sauce in the contest—or in America—that would tinge your palate while soothing your throat. You see, my secret ingredient is cough syrup.

⅓ cup cider vinegar

1 tsp. salt

1 tsp. celery seed

½ tsp. cinnamon

½ cup ketchup

½ tsp. red pepper

1 tsp. chili powder

⅛ tsp. nutmeg

½ tsp. brown sugar

1 cup water

½ tsp. cough syrup, but not just any cough syrup. Most of them will make your sauce taste mediciney. The only one I found that works well in a sauce is a clear generic: elixir terpin hydrate with D-Metherphan; hydrate 40 percent alcohol. (Just ask your pharmacist for Terpin hydrate–D-M.)

Mix ingredients and bring to a boil. Let sit in refrigerator covered for five days to allow flavors to wed.

Bay of Pigs Sauce

This sauce was a one-time winner at the Memphis in May International Barbecue Cooking Contest, concocted by the Memphis Ad Ribbers team. It uses a little of this and that. If you don't have this, use that.

½ pound butter

1 qt. Heinz ketchup

24 oz. tomato sauce

40 oz. French's Worcestershire sauce

2 bottles Griffin's Hot-Sweet mustard

1 qt. Regina red wine vinegar

2 tsp. Tabasco sauce

8 tsp. brown sugar

4 tsp. paprika

2 tsp. garlic powder

4 tsp. Lowry's seasoning salt

4 tsp. lemon juice

½ tsp. chili powder

½ tsp. black pepper

½ tsp. cayenne pepper

2 oz. liquid smoke

Melt butter in a saucepan. Add the mustard, tomato sauce, and ketchup. Stir constantly. Add the vinegar and Worcestershire sauce. Stir constantly and add remaining ingredients. Simmer for thirty minutes. Brush on ribs at the end of cooking time and serve alongside.

Two-Shot Scratch Sauce

A lot of barbecue-sauce recipes consist of taking other sauces and combining them in deeply mysterious ways. There's no doubt that such tinkering is loads of fun: If you have a commercial sauce with a flavor you like but no horsepower, mixing in various hot elements can give you a new creation altogether. And if you can get lost in arguments over whether to add Heinz (wrong) or Brooks (right) when a recipe calls for ketchup, then you won't be missing the fun in assembling sauces from other people's bottles.

Still, it's possible to yearn for a sauce that starts at square one, with no Worchestershire, no ketchup, no Thousand Island dressing. This is such a sauce, based in the distant past on a Texas sauce recipe in a Time-Life cookbook. It has experienced the usual number of mutations, including a couple shots of unblended Scotch whisky, but it retains the characteristics that make it distinctive: It is chunky and rich with flavor that seems straight from the garden. It is thick to the point of being stubborn, thick enough to cling tenaciously to a rack of ribs (be sure to apply it only in the last fifteen minutes or so of cooking, or it will turn black and crusty). And finally, it has the characteristic that hard-core barbecue fiends insist upon: It is hotter than bare legs on black vinyl.

½ cup vegetable oil

3 cups onions, chopped

1 tbs. garlic, chopped

1 1-pound can tomatoes, drained and chopped

1½ cups tomato puree

2 tbs. crushed red pepper

2 tbs. chili powder

1 tsp. cumin

2 tbs. dry mustard

2 tbs. sugar

3 tbs. white vinegar

1 tsp. salt

½ tsp. Hungarian hot paprika

1 tbs. pure Vermont maple syrup

2 shots Laphroig unblended Scotch whisky

Cayenne pepper, to taste

Sauté onions in oil until soft. Add garlic and cook two minutes. Add tomatoes, tomato puree, red pepper, chili powder, cumin, dry mustard, sugar, vinegar, salt, paprika, maple syrup, Laphroig, and cayenne. Cook over low heat for about an hour. Cool and puree.

Side Dishes

Man cannot live by smoked meat alone.

But some dishes are better than others to serve alongside homemade barbecue. These can range from a sharp slaw that rejuvenates the old taste buds to the funky smokiness of Trixie's Baked Beans, which conspire rather than compete with a slab of ribs.

Some sections of the country practically insist that certain side dishes be served alongside barbecue, dishes with traditions almost as long as those of the main course. If you haven't whomped up a pot of Brunswick stew or burgoo, ladled any hash over rice or stuffed down a second helping of sweet potato pie, then you're missing a treat. Keep reading, though; your days of deprivation are about to end.

Most of the recipes included here are family recipes, with family-size proportions that serve a dozen or so semi-starving, semi-polite people without starting too many fights in the serving line. For your nutrition-conscious guests, we have included a number of incredibly sweet or unconscionably unhealthy dishes and desserts that should serve to make them feel much better about eating the barbecue itself.

Trixie's Baked Beans

Trixie is a party animal, and these are party beans, made to be eaten out-doors under a blue sky with hot barbecue and cold beer. The recipe makes a few concessions to modern life, like using canned instead of dried beans; such shortcuts keep the things from being such a chore that you shy away from making a mess on fairly short notice.

There's chopped (or pulled) pork in the recipe, which you'll have to cook or buy in advance, so there's a little bit of planning. And part of get-ting the taste right involves letting the beans simmer for a while as you tamper with the precise formula on the stovetop. Start cooking 'em on the morning of the day of a party; the pungent perfume from the kitchen will keep you in the right mood. You also can stick a stockpot full of Trixie's finest on a fifty-five-gallon drum barbecue smoker; they'll cook up with an extra suffusion of smoke, which you can increase by gently stirring the beans frequently.

2 cans (40 oz. each) pork and beans

2 cans (15½ oz. each) white beans

6 oz. chopped or pulled smoked pork

3 medium white onions, cored and quartered

2 tbsp. spicy mustard

2 tbsp. white vinegar

½ cup Brooks (or very tangy) ketchup

¼ cup dark brown sugar

¼ cup pure Vermont maple syrup

1 tsp. horseradish

1 shot unblended Scotch whiskey

¾ cup hot barbecue sauce

Generous splash of hot sauce (to taste)

Drain beans. Mix all ingredients as gently and as little as possible. Adjust seasoning hotter or sweeter to taste. May be cooked in a Crock-Pot, on the stove, or in a smoker. As beans cook, stir periodically. Simmer covered for two hours, then uncovered for one hour.

The Rib Joint Roadhouse's Black Beans and Rice

The Rib Joint Roadhouse Restaurant is a 1930s log cabin built into a hill along the Coast Highway in Dana Point, California. The license plates are gone now and the walls have been repainted, but Sam Ibreighith, who has been running the restaurant since 1980, is still there. Sam came from South Jerusalem himself, and his unique perspective resulted in this excellent side dish, perfect for anyone a little bored with baked beans. This mixture is tasty, funky, and just fine with ribs.

> 1 pound long grain white rice
> ½ pound black beans, soaked in cold water overnight
> 4 slices bacon, chopped
> 1 onion, chopped
> 1 celery stalk, chopped
> 4 crushed bay leaves
> Cracked pepper and salt to taste
> 1 tbsp. ground cumin
> ½ tbsp. garlic, chopped
> ½ tbsp. ham base
> 2 beef bouillon cubes, crushed
> 1 tbsp. oregano

Soak beans in cold water overnight. Drain, then cook in a large pot of boiling water for one and a half hours, or until beans are soft when squeezed between your fingers. Drain the beans. Bring five cups of salted water to boil. Add rice, cover, reduce the heat, and cook twenty minutes or so until all liquid is absorbed. Heat the bacon in a skillet until it releases its fat. Add the onions, the celery, and the four crushed bay leaves and sauté until soft. Add the cooked rice to the drained cooked beans. Add the sautéed bacon mixture and the remaining ingredients. Bake covered in preheated 350-degree oven for twenty to thirty minutes. Serves eight as a hearty side dish. Be sure to offer hot sauce.

Leo & Susie's Famous Baked Beans

This recipe came from Leo & Susie's Famous Green Top Barbecue Cafe in Dora, Alabama.

> 6 slices bacon
> ½ medium onion, chopped
> Chopped bell peppers to taste
> ¼ cup of your favorite barbecue sauce (Green Top, if you've got it)
> 1 32-oz. can pork and beans

A secret source at Leon & Susie's once gave us the secret: "Sauté the bacon, then add the onion, bell peppers, and sauce. Put all this in a big pot, add the beans, and cook them real slow until they're tender. Don't bake them."

Johnny Cakes

This recipe may be about as old as barbecue itself. The name is a corruption of "Shawnee cakes." These would be cooked up by Shawnees on hot, flat rocks. It's okay if you use a stove.

> 2 cups white cornmeal
> 1 tsp. salt
> 3 cups boiling water
> Shortening for frying

Mix cornmeal and salt in a deep earthenware bowl. Slowly pour boiling water into it, stirring constantly to scald all of the meal. This may take a little more or a little less than three cups of water, depending on the texture of the meal. When mixture is well stirred, allow to set for ten to fifteen minutes, with bowl covered. The meal should then be so stiff that it has to be pushed off a spoon onto a hot greased griddle. With a pancake turner, pat the meal into flat cakes, about ⅜ inch thick. When one side is a rich brown, beginning to turn darker, turn and cook the other side. The two sides should have a thick, nutty crust, and the inside should be cooked through. Butter, honey, and maple syrup have been known to associate with Johnny Cakes.

Cheesy Corn Bread

This is a bridal-shower recipe, which means two things: (1) It's good enough to give as a gift, and (2) it's hard to louse up. Although bland, white Wonder bread is served alongside much of the great barbecue at joints across America, and corn bread makes a good accompaniment, too. Yes, you can eat it by the wedge, hot and steaming with a pat of butter. But you also can shove the leftover crumbs around on the plate where the sauce is and pick up a sloppy fingerful of spicy, cheesy corn bread that doesn't need butter to send you back for more.

1½ cups yellow cornmeal

1 14½-oz. can cream-style corn

⅓ cup vegetable oil

1 cup sour cream

1 egg, lightly beaten

1 tbsp. baking powder

1 tsp. salt

2 jalapeño peppers, finely chopped

2 tbsp. green bell pepper, minced

2 tbsp. onion, minced

1 cup sharp cheddar cheese, grated

Stir the cornmeal, baking powder, and salt together in a bowl. Add everything else except the cheese. Mix. Pour half the mixture into a hot, greased, 10½-inch-round iron skillet or pie pan. Sprinkle half the cheese over this. Add the remaining mixture and cover with the other half of the cheese. Bake at 350 degrees for forty minutes. Serves six.

Moonlite Burgoo

Owensboro's Moonlite Bar-B-Q Inn came to fame under Ken Bosley, along with his three brothers and sister. Four generations of Bosleys have specialized in cooking mutton: "We take hickory wood and build a fire in our pits and keep it under the meat at all times," Ken told us. "We cook mutton about sixteen hours, basting it a little after it's turned."

For side dishes, Ken suggested serving potato salad, coleslaw, barbecue beans, or burgoo. Burgoo is a native Kentucky stew, not unlike the Brunswick stew favored in the Carolinas and Georgia. Here is the Moonlite's burgoo recipe:

> 4 pounds mutton, on the bone
> 1 to 3 pounds chicken
> ¾ pound cabbage, ground or chopped fine
> ¾ pound onion, ground or chopped fine
> 5 pounds potatoes, peeled and diced
> 2 cups fresh corn (or 2 17-oz. cans corn)
> ¾ cup ketchup
> 3 10¾-oz. cans tomato puree
> Juice of 1 lemon
> ¾ cup vinegar
> ½ cup Worcestershire sauce
> 2½ tbsp. salt
> 2 tbsp. black pepper
> 1 tsp. cayenne pepper
> Water

Boil mutton in enough water to cover. Cook until tender, about two to three hours. Throw out broth and bones. Chop meat fine and set aside. Boil chicken in two gallons of water in a large kettle until tender. Remove chicken. Add potatoes, cabbage, onion, corn, ketchup, and one gallon of water to the chicken broth. Meanwhile, chop chicken meat. Discard bones and skin. When potatoes are tender, add the chicken, mutton, lemon juice, salt, pepper, cayenne, Worcestershire sauce, vinegar, and tomato puree. Let this simmer for two hours or longer, stirring occasionally as it thickens. Yields three gallons.

The Moonlite is one of the few barbecue restaurants that sells its own cookbook. You can order the *Moonlite Bar-B-Que Inn Cookbook* for a little over twenty bucks from the Web site www.moonlite.com.

Barbecue Coleslaw

This is coleslaw made with the same stuff that's used to baste barbecue in western North Carolina. The amounts aren't real exact; experiment a bit.

    1 medium head white cabbage, grated
    ¼ head red cabbage, grated
    1 tbsp. onion, grated
    3 tbsp. granulated sugar
    1 cup cider vinegar
    ⅔ cup ketchup or thick barbecue sauce
    ½ cup water
    ¼ tsp. cayenne pepper
    Salt and freshly ground pepper to taste
    Hot pepper sauce to taste

Mix the cabbage. (This may be covered with cold water and stored in the refrigerator for several hours before using. Drain before mixing with other ingredients.) Cook sugar and vinegar in a saucepan until the sugar dissolves. Add the remaining ingredients and simmer for ten minutes. Pour over the cabbage, toss, drain well, chill, and serve.

Maple Syrup Pie

There's no particular reason for this subtle, luxurious pie to show up in a book about barbecue, but it's so good that the recipe ought to appear in every book published, including new editions of *War and Peace*.

The recipe (actually for *Tarte au Sirop D'Erable*) comes from Aux Anciens Canadiens, a restaurant in old Quebec that specializes in down-home up-North Canadian cuisine. Since the eastern provinces seem to be constitutionally unable to produce good barbecue, this recipe is sort of a consolation prize for our neighbors to the north. And some consoling! This pie is simple, but it's simply divine, rich enough to make you beg for more and light enough to let you eat it.

The recipe makes three pies, which will barely be enough.

1 cup pure maple syrup
1½ pounds brown sugar
1½ cups whipping or heavy cream
2 tbsp. soft butter
4 eggs
3 unbaked 9-inch pie shells
Additional whipping or heavy cream for topping

Combine all ingredients and beat together. Pour into the pie shells and bake for forty minutes at 350 degrees. Serve with a small amount of additional warmed cream ladled over the slices.

Mama's Hot and Greasy Fried Pies

One accoutrement that seems to cross barbecue style lines is the lowly fried pie. We found it, or commercial versions of it, on sale in barbecue places from North Carolina to California and from New England to South Florida. The first fried pie we ever had hooked us. It came right off the top of a pot of boiling grease. It was made by Jerry Woods's grandmother Mama (that's what Jerry called her). Mama lugged out a skillet as big as she was, dumped in enough grease to keep Elvis's hair in place for a year, fired it up to the boiling point, and dropped in half-moon-shaped pieces of dough with apple filling inside. She fried them until they turned the color of red clay, then fished them out, dabbed the grease off with a paper towel, and handed each of us one. That was almost fifty years ago.

Mama said this was how she used to make her famous pies. "You need one or two pounds of dried apples. You can also use either dried apricots or dried peaches or mix all three. Wash the fruit real good. Soak it in water overnight. Put it in a large pot and cook it in a small amount of water on low heat until it's tender. Stir it occasionally and don't let it stick. Add sugar to your taste. Continue to cook it until it begins to thicken. Keep stirring. When it gets thick, remove it from the stove. When it cools down enough, mash it with your hands or with a sieve. Let it stand until it's cool. Any extra you can freeze."

Now for the crust:

1 cup sweet milk (whole milk)
2 cups plain flour
½ tsp. salt
½ tsp. baking soda
1 tbsp. vinegar
½ tsp. baking powder
2 tbsp. Crisco

Mix the milk, flour, salt, soda, vinegar, and baking powder until there are no lumps. Gently fold in the Crisco. Put in the refrigerator until chilled. Pinch off in little balls and roll them out on a floured board. Put one tablespoon of fruit on each piece of dough, then roll the dough over and seal the edges. Fry in a skillet of Crisco until golden brown.

Wilber's Banana Pudding

Wilber's in Goldsboro, North Carolina, is famous in the Down East barbecue belt for its barbecue and its banana pudding. Wilber Shirley, the owner, wouldn't give away his secret sauce recipe. But he agreed to part with the banana pudding secrets.

"People think it's a complicated recipe, and I don't tell them otherwise," Wilber told us once upon a time. "There ain't nothing to it. My granddaughter could make it if she didn't eat all the cookies first." Here it is:

> 1 package vanilla pudding
> Bunch of bananas
> Box of vanilla wafers

"Mix up the vanilla pudding according to the directions on the box. Then stir in the bananas and vanilla wafers to taste. We like to use a lot of wafers to give it a kind of cakey taste."

Aunt Esther's Sweet Potato Pie

Vince's Aunt Esther Shanks, who lives in Leesburg, Tennessee, says, "My people all come from over around Shelby, North Carolina. They raise a lot of sweet potatoes over there. Too many sweet potatoes. They got to figure out ways to eat them." Here's a good way—the sweet potato pie recipe passed down through four generations of the Sutherland family of Shelby, North Carolina.

> 2 unbaked pastry shells
> 5 or 6 medium sweet potatoes, peeled and sliced thin
>   ("I like the white sweet potato.")
> 2 cups sugar
> 2 tbsp. cornstarch
> 1 stick margarine
> Dash nutmeg
> 1½ cups water

Put one of the pastry shells in a 13-by-9-inch pan. Then put your sliced sweet potatoes in the pastry shell. Mix the sugar and cornstarch and sprinkle over the potatoes. Dot with margarine and sprinkle with nutmeg. Pour the water over this. Now put the second pastry shell on top as the crust. Bake at 350 degrees for forty-five minutes or until the sweet potatoes are done.

Collectors' Items:
Mail-Order Masterpieces

Heaven forbid, the day may come when you and your buddies finally have finished battling over the best ribs in town. And popular acclaim is the worst thing that can happen to a barbecue joint, transforming a lovely secret into a boring certainty. Worse still is uncontested local dominance; it's a barbecue fanatic's nightmare—no more sticky-fingered arguments, no more sudden Saturday trips to settle the issue beside a smoking pit, nothing but succulent, perfect barbecue, day after day, night after night, forever.

Should you find yourself trapped in such epicurean ennui or, worse still, in a blighted area of our great nation that's shy on smokers altogether, don't despair. There's an exciting cure for the barbecue blahs: Start a sauce collection. To do that properly, you've either got to do a lot of traveling, or else you've got to get it delivered. Short of bringing the stuff home with you after a barbecue safari (still the recommended way to acquire sauces), mail or online ordering is the best bet.

It's true that there are barbecue sauces sold in the grocery store, and it's also true that some of these go beyond the ketchupy predictability of supermarket sauces past. (The mass-marketing of what once had been a good regional sauce, K.C. Masterpiece, was an example of how the store shelves began showing signs of shaping up.) Still, any grocer worth his salt won't be filling up his valuable shelf space with a smorgasbord of sauces for you and your finger-licking friends. For true variety you'll have to go elsewhere.

Luckily, a crowd of chefs stands ready and eager to send you sauces through the U.S. mail or via various package-delivery outfits. You can mail order what is arguably the best sauce made in Missouri, as well as a mustard-based masterpiece from Georgia that's arguably better. Note that the operative word here is *arguably*.

The magic of mail order can plunge you back into the fray of the barbecue wars, clashing with your compatriots over the merits of a clingy, ketchupy sauce from Texas versus a vinegar-based concoction from the Carolinas. Your acclaimed local (or backyard) barbecue may be the reigning champeen, but it becomes merely the arena for Round Two: namely, the battle over the Best Sauce in America. And that, we confidently predict, is a mighty struggle with no peace treaty in sight.

Care and Feeding and One-Upmanship

Barbecue sauce is not tender stuff, but it ought to be refrigerated after you open it. Sauce left to sit out indefinitely undergoes some, shall we say, "interesting" transformations (check out the prehistoric, sedimentary stuff in the windows at Arthur Bryant's, for instance), but while it may acquire a certain cachet as an objet d'art, it loses a lot in subtleties of flavor and good, old-fashioned, Home Ec–approved safety.

A minor problem with chilling your condiments is that cold barbecue sauce is in an unnatural state and must be brought to room temperature before it's served. (Actually, for the proper temperature, just match whatever the thermometer read at 4:00 P.M. last August 12 wherever you live.)

On the plus side, refrigerated sauces are the best justification imaginable for the little shelves that refrigerator-door manufacturers put in refrigerator doors. There is absolutely nothing like the sight of row upon row of secret sauces revealing themselves when that door slowly swings open, any of them ready for a curious sniff or fingertip. It's a poetic vision that simply crushes the nearest social climber who has invested all of his stock certificates in an expensive, effete wine cellar stocked with wines that have to "rest" for another seven years before they may be delicately decanted.

Of course, it's perhaps a bit unfair for a member in good standing of the Carnivore Club to lay such a shot of one-upmanship on a feeble, undernourished sort whose passions are restricted to fermented grape juice, for God's sake. The only truly worthy victims of a sauce-collection smackdown are alleged barbecue connoisseurs unfortunate enough to have disagreed with one of your considered opinions on the subject.

There is a literally delicious moment that comes when you casually swing open the door to the fridge and inquire, "By the way, what do you think of that Everett and Jones Super Q sauce?" You will watch as your slack-jawed acquaintance stares in miserable awe at your assemblage of sauces, salivating slightly in spite of himself. Try that with a dusty bottle of Bordeaux.

Naturally, there's a friendly side to all of this, too. A sort of Christmas-morning excitement attends the arrival of a new carton of mail-order sauce. Since many are sold in twelve-bottle cases, it helps to have some similarly afflicted friends to share the cost—and the sauce. And there are those wonderful surprise phone calls, too: "My Willingham's came in today; want to come over for ribs?"

Mail-Order Mania

The available variety of mail-order sauces is staggering—and ordering them can be habit-forming. After you've been at it for a while, you may find yourself wondering about maybe getting ahold of a second refrigerator, just a plain white job down in the basement or out in the garage, just big enough to contain the collection. At least that way there might be room enough for your children to have milk again.

Here are some swell sauces available through the mail. Shipping charges vary, and the sauce prices themselves may change, of course. But this is no time to start worrying about money. You can make car payments later; we're talking sauce here.

Arthur Bryant's Barbecue Sauce. At last—you can order the ultimate health food—a fat-free, low-sodium pack of Sweet and Hot Sauce from this Kansas City institution of good eating. The three-pack costs $29.50, shipping included. You might also want to mix and match a twelve-pack of the eighteen-ounce bottles, with four of the Original sauce, four of the sweeter Rich and Spicy, and four Sweet Heats for $59.50, shipping included. The two-pack Meat and Rib Rub and the two-pack Poultry and Fish Rub cost $17.50 each. Their Web site is www.arthurbryantsbbq.com.

Craig's Original Barbecue Sauce. The sauce's inventor, Lawrence Craig, developed it while working on a riverboat on the mighty Mississippi, before he opened up his family restaurant in DeValls Bluff, Arkansas. The sauce itself boasts an insinuating sting, with a smoky touch and a lot of tiny, tasty unidentified floating objects (shake well). You can order it from the Craig Brothers Café, P.O. Box 272, DeValls Bluff, Arkansas 72041. A case of twelve bottles will cost you $33.48, plus about $25 for shipping. Send a check or money order. Call the cafe at (870) 998–2616 for information.

Curley's. This stuff is the lava flow of barbecue sauces, dark, oozing, seriously smoky, and molasses-sweet. People who consider chicken to be barbecue have been known to eat Curley's on it. If you're searching for a sauce with about as much smoke as Mount Saint Helens, Curley's has Smoky, Hickory, and Mesquite versions. There's also a hot-and-spicy style that sends in its zing after a brief grace period, and even it has enough liquid smoke to set off your home alarm. You can get Curley's in cases of twelve twenty-ounce bottles. The price is $38, UPS shipping included. Orders (and checks) are welcome at the Legacy Foods, P.O. Box 1099, Hutchinson, Kansas 67501, or you may use a credit card and order by phone by calling (800) 835–5006. You may also order the sauces on their Web site, www.legacyfoods.com.

Demetri's "America's Best" Gourmet Barbecue Sauce. Almost four decades ago, Demetri developed a sauce with wonderful properties. His wife, Helen Nakos, used to say, "It's a Cadillac product; it's perfect. It's not a hot sauce, it's not sweet, not faked or gooped up. It has pure ingredients, no stuffers." Those ingredients include a little tomato, a little Worchestershire sauce, a little mustard, and some vinegar, lemon juice, and margarine. The result is a concoction that's long on flavor and short on singe, good enough to have been carted back to Sweden by traveling barbecue lovers. When you receive a bottle, it arrives with a half-hour barbecued chicken recipe that involves Coca-Cola and a frying pan. The pint bottle is $2.95, shipping extra, no minimum order. Check out the Web site at www.demetris-bbq.com, or talk to Sam at Demetri's Barbecue Sauce by calling (205) 871–5420.

D. L. Jardine's Barbecue Sauce. With individual bottles priced from $3.00 to $7.00, you can travel the Texas barbecue world. Check out the 5-Star BBQ Sauce, Blazin' Saddle Habanero XXX Hot Sauce, Mesquite Sauce, Chik'n-Lik'n BBQ Sauce, Texas Pecan Sauce, and Killer BBQ Sauce. Consider the priciest of the sauces, Buckin' Berry, which includes red raspberry and roasted chipotle peppers. You can peruse the sauces, marinades, and spices on the mind-boggling Web site, www.jardinefoods.com, or order by phone: (800) 544–1880.

Everett and Jones "Super Q" Barbecue Sauce. Contrary to what you read in the papers, California is not just a land of sprouts and sushi. There is Real Barbecue there, too. This sauce has won praises for its sweet but zingingly hot taste, as well as its luxuriously thick texture, suitable for slapping on ribs (at the last minute, please). It comes in Mild, Medium, and Hot. The Medium is mildly hot, so the Hot should be mildly amazing. Order a case of twelve eight-ounce jars for $42, plus shipping, by calling (888) 368–1200, or order online at www.super-que.com. Or, you might want to stop in at Matt & Jeff's Car Wash in Novato, California, to pick up a few bottles—but hurry, because Matt's not sure how many he's got left.

Gates' & Son's Bar-B-Q Sauce. In Kansas City's pedigreed barbecue scene, there is Arthur Bryant's and there is Gates' & Son's. Bryant's may have garnered more ink in the press, but Ollie Gates's sauce has soaked its share of napkins at several locations around the city. The stuff is packed with a balanced flavor that incorporates tomatoes, spices, a touch of vinegar, and a lot of hot. There are four versions available—Original, Extra Hot, Sweet and Mild, and Mild. It's sold by the case of twelve eight-ounce bottles for about $20, plus shipping and handling. You can also order a combo pack of two eighteen-ounce bottles, plus one eight-ounce container of seasoning, either Sweet and Mild or Extra Hot. Order by phone by calling (800) 662-RIBS (7427) or online at www.gatesbbq.com.

Golden Secret Recipe BBQ Sauce. Big Joe Bessinger taught this recipe to son Melvin, who retired from the barbecue biz in 2004. But third-generation David Bessinger now runs the company that still will ship you any of the sauces that got things rolling. You can create your own six-pack for $21.95 plus shipping of original 1933 Golden Secret, Southern Hickory, Southern Honey, and/or Southern Red. Dry rubs and meats also are available, at www.melvinsbbq.com.

Hayward's Pit Bar-B-Que Sauce. One of the semi-innumerable sauces duking it out in the Kansas City area, Hayward's will ship six bottles (eighteen-ounce size) for $28.70, shipping included. There's only one flavor, the one that Hayward Spears started cooking up almost forty years ago, now served in one of the fanciest barbecue joints anywhere, complete with etched glass and a professionally tended lawn. The sauce itself is sweet and very tomatoey, containing both ketchup and tomato paste, but it has a delicate zap at the end. Call (913) 451-8080 to order, but also check out the restaurant Web site at www.haywardsbbq.com.

Johnny Harris Famous Barbecue Sauce. This peach of a Georgia sauce has something for everybody—a little shot of smoke, a splash of Worcestershire, a dab of ketchup, and a mouthful of down-home flavor in a sauce that splits the difference between a mustard recipe and a traditional ketchup style. Slapped on near the end of smoking time, it cooks up a pretty golden color. A little on the side at the table gives a tang that cuts through the smokiness of barbecued pork or chicken, the meats of choice. It would be derelict not to mention that this stuff won the 1985 Diddy-Wa-Diddy Barbecue Sauce Contest in Olathe, Kansas. The sauce also is available in a Hickory Smoke and a Carolina Mustard version, but the original is the preferred item. It is sold, appropriately enough, by Johnny Harris Famous Barbecue Sauce Co., and it will run you $15.99 plus shipping for a three-pack of twelve-ounce bottles. You can mix and match sauce types and add in some rubs and spices. The phone number is (888) JH SAUCE (547–2823), ext. 221, and the Web site is www.johnnyharris.com.

M & S Meats Barbecue Sauce. This place sells a Flathead Valley, Montana, sauce that's like sucking on a sagebrush. The vinegary sauce has a dash of sweetness and an unusual flavor that will make you say, "Boy, I bet this stuff'd go great on an order of boneless bison roast." Which is convenient, since M & S sells that, too, as well as a chub (one pound) of elk Thuringer (mild-flavored meat). The company will pony-express you some $5.00 bottles of the sauce. Just call (800) 454–3414, or visit their Web site, www.msmeats.com. You're on your own with the buffalo.

Maurice's Gourmet Barbecue Sauce. For proof that pork and politics don't mix, you needn't look much further than Maurice Bessinger. His unreconstructed defense of states' rights and the Confederate flag has landed him in court and in the headlines, branded as a racist. Perhaps a good rule is: Don't open your mouth unless you're putting barbecue in. And Maurice's is a pretty good thing to put in there. You can order not only his mustardy, greenish gold "heirloom recipe" sauce, but also packages of barbecued ham, country hash, turkey, and ribs (see the next section on mail-order barbecue). Maurice's is a masterful mustard-based sauce, unabashedly yellow and proud of it, but cut with a pleasingly complex mix of all-natural ingredients like apple cider, soy sauce, herbs, spices, and a dollop of ketchup, just to confuse the issue. A four-pack of eighteen-ounce bottles costs $25.95 plus shipping, but you can also buy gallon jugs of the stuff. You don't have to buy the philosophy. Call (800) MAURICE, ext. 12, or check out the Web site at www.mauricesbbq.com.

Missouri Classic Bar-B-Que Sauce. This rich tomato sauce is subtly smoky and not too sweet, perhaps because it makes use of brown sugar and honey. It may have a "classic" name, but it comes from plain ol' Johnny's Smoke Stak in Rolla, Missouri. Wendy, who used to work there but is now retired, once commented, "We've got kids that put it on everything 'cept cereal." (Actually, it might go rather well with corn flakes.) In a major blow for decisiveness, it comes in only one variety, available in thirty-two-ounce bottles in batches of six for $3.85 a bottle, plus shipping. Call (573) 364–4838 or visit www.johnnyssmokestak.com.

Moonlite's Bar-B-Que Sauce. If you're planning to have barbecued mutton soon (and who isn't?), this is the place to write for truly authentic barbecue dip. Smack in the middle of muttondom in western Kentucky, the Moonlite is the largest restaurant in Owensboro, a town which at one time wolfed down anywhere from 30,000 to 100,000 pounds of mutton a week. Ken Bosley, who works the restaurant with three brothers and a sister, and some of their kids, says, "After the meat is cooked, we serve a combination of three sauces: black dip, a tomato-based sauce that is sweet, and a hot sauce." They're available online, as well. The Thick & Spicy Bar-B-Que Sauce, sweet, flavorful, and tomatoey, is $3.19 for eighteen ounces. The Barbecue Dip, a watery Worcestershire-and-brown-sugar concoction suitable for basting or flavoring mutton or beef, is $2.99 a pint. The Barbecue Sauce, a middle-of-the-roader recommended for pork, costs $3.05 for eighteen ounces, and the Very Hot Sauce, which is suitable for chemical warfare, costs $3.39 for eleven ounces. This last variety is made of pepper, more pepper, and vodka, and it will turn you into a contralto in ten seconds. All the prices are subject to change, of course, since their last update in 2005. Call (800) 322–8989 or visit the chatty and charming Web site at www.moonlite.com.

Pepperheads Hot Sauces. This mecca of online sauce shopping will dazzle even the most adventurous collector. Want a Kentucky sauce? Try Pappy's

XXX White Lightnin'. Going tropo? There's a Caribbean Health Choice Bananas and Honey barbecue sauce. Ready to travel? The Beechwoodhouse Ginger Wasabi will take you there. The site is worth it just for the titles (Dave Badlands, Pain is Good Barbeque Batch 114). The prices vary from bottle to bottle, but most will set you back about $7.00 each plus shipping. Check out www.pepperheads-hotsauces.com.

Rendezvous Barbecue Sauce. The Rendezvous is rightly named for its leagues of Memphis-area fans. It sells mild or hot sauce for $6.50 a bottle—and dry seasoning for the same price (minimum orders of four). Garlic and chili powder stand out in the latter, which you can apply to ribs, chicken, or sausage just before serving. The sauce is more flavorful than resolutely hot, thick yet tangy with vinegar. Call the toll-free line (888) HOGS FLY (464-7359) or order online at www.hogsfly.com.

Rudolph's Barbecue Sauce. A lot of Chicago's ribs never make it into the mouths of Windy City residents, since tons of them are shipped each year to the Minneapolis home of the barbecue chain founded in 1975 by Greek immigrant Jimmy Theros. Rudolph's is named after the silent-movie star, not the reindeer, by the way. Victorious in 1983 and 1985 at Cleveland's National Rib Cook-Off, the restaurant's approved technique is to rub ribs with spices that are allowed to marinate for about three days before cooking. The sauce doesn't go on until the last minute. The sauce also goes out through the mails, thanks to Trudeau Distributing. One fan of the stuff described the appeal: "It's not tomatoey, there's some vinegar, and it doesn't make you sweat." To buy a case of twelve nineteen-and-a-half-ounce bottles, send a check for $55 (this includes shipping) to Trudeau Distributing, 25 West Cliff Road, Burnsville, Minnesota 55337, attn: Rob Eversman. Put a note in the letter that you want Rudolph's Barbecue Sauce, and where you would like it shipped. Rob will pack it for you himself. He sends out about a case or two a week.

Santa Cruz Chili Barbecue Sauce. Considering its pedigree, it shouldn't be surprising that this slow-simmered sauce rides in with chiles blazing. Its

Mexican heritage should offer an interesting change of pace to anyone who grew up with gringo-'que. Buy a case of twelve twelve-ounce bottles for $35 plus shipping. Call (520) 398–2591.

Scott's Famous Barbecue Sauce. This is a lively North Carolina–style sauce cooked up originally by the Reverend A. W. Scott and patented in 1946 by his son, Alvin Martell Scott. It features lots of tart vinegar and absolutely no ketchup. You can call Scott's at (800) 734–SAUC (7282). The ten-ounce bottle costs $1.50, or you can splurge for the 128-ounce bottle at $11.50. A case of Scott's costs $16.50 for twelve ten-ounce bottles. UPS shipping charges will be determined by the size of the order and your location. You may order online at www.scottsbarbecuesauce.com.

Show-Me BBQ Sauce. If you've been looking for a sauce with a pH of 3, here's your baby. It's mixed up in "the only basement approved by the Missouri Department of Public Health" by retired professor and veterinary pathologist Harry H. Berrier. Actually, the pH, like everything else about this dense, smoky sauce, is carefully considered. "Bacteria, including the kind that causes botulism, will not grow in a medium of pH 4.6 or below," he explained, so the sauce needs no refrigeration, even after opening. He was also quick to point out it has no extenders, not even a drop of water. As a result, it's a dusky, ketchupy sauce that's almost a concentrate. Aside from being rich and delicious, it's worth ordering just to read the recipes on the label, which are printed in type that is one atom tall. Lina Berrier, Harry's wife, oversees the high school and college students who help with the shipping. You can't order online. (Lina said, "We sold our computer. I never even learned to turn it on.") So you'll have to send snail mail to Harry H. Berrier, 1250 Cedar Grove Boulevard, Columbia, Missouri 65201, and tell him what you want. You also may call (573) 442–5309. The sauce is $2.50 a pint, but you save a little money on a case of twelve pints for $24.00. Gallon jugs are $12 each. Once you've let Harry and Lina know your order, they'll figure out the UPS shipping cost and add that to a $2.00 packing charge. An invoice with the sauce shows you how much to send back.

Texas Firehouse Sauce. What household is safe without the Texas Firehouse Emergency Survival Kit? You can mix a three-pack of Mesquite sauce, with its hint of brown sugar and honey, some Chipotle Pepper sauce, and the Three Pepper Sauce, with a smoky combo of habanero, serrano, and chipotle peppers that's bound to spark your taste buds. The pack is $19 for the sixteen-ounce jars, plus shipping. Call (800) 347–3431, or buy online at www.texasfirehouse.com.

Wicker's Barbecue Cooking Sauce. We're talking *real* "cooking" here, as in slapping sauce all over a slab of meat while it basks in the inferno of a barbecue grill. Old Peck Wicker's sauce is custom made for that, mixed without a pinch of sugar or a dab of tomatoes, so there's nothing to burn into a coating of cinders on the meat. The recipe for this Missouri boot-heel basting favorite takes a vinegar base and adds spices (secret, of course) until arriving at a sharp and sincere medium-hot. Its watery consistency makes it a good choice for marinades, as well as for basting. However, the company doesn't take any chances, also recommending Wicker's for everything from tenderizing meat and making gravy to boiling shrimp and goosing a Bloody Mary. You may do with it what you like; you could even drink the stuff straight with a clean conscience. It's available in a three-pack of the original marinade (sixty-four ounces) for $25.06. Also available are Wicker's Thicker, which is just as devoid of sweetness as the original, and just as vinegar-spicy when its afterburners kick in, and gourmet, hickory, and mesquite-flavored original sauces. If you want to try all the sauces, and toss in a bottle of the Black Label Steak Marinade, you could get a Variety Pack Assortment for $34.78 (shipping included.) Orders may be phoned in at (800) 847–0032 or purchased online at www.inetba.com/wickers.

Wilber's Barbecue Sauce. The motto on the concoction created in 1962 by Wilber Shirley is "It's Spicy Good," and Wilber is not a man to lie. The sauce is a North Carolina vinegar-based style, so the first impression is a pleasantly sour taste, followed shortly thereafter by a puckery tartness and finally a little fire. The various red and black peppers are used with discretion; this is a well-balanced and reasonably civilized splash of a sauce, suited for basting as well as tasting. In fact, there's a recipe for basting a turkey printed right on the label. It's available with no minimum order in ten-ounce bottles for $2.50 each plus shipping. Just call Jamie or Dennis at (919) 778–5218.

Willingham's WHAM Sauce. This sauce can claim back-to-back victories as Grand Champion of the Memphis in May barbecue festival, not to mention a near-sweep and Grand Champion award at the American Royal contest in Kansas City. And anytime you can get judges in Memphis and Kansas City to agree on anything, that's news. There are several varieties of sauce, a flavorful Mild, a lively Cajun Hot, a scalp-tingling Hot Sauce for Big Kids Only, and a chocolate, butter, and molasses tinged Sweet 'n' Sassy. If you're really brave, consider the Cool Breeze, which on a heat scale of 1 to 10 is a 20. Prices range from $5.00 plus some change to $7.00 for a bottle of sauce, with rubs in the $8.00 and $9.00 range. A five-gallon jug of Cajun Hot Sauce costs $101. If the Web site is being finicky, call (800) 737–WHAM (9426) to place your order. The online address is www.willinghams.com.

Mail-Order Barbecue

Mail-order barbecue hasn't won enough converts to have the reputation of, say, mail-order brides or mail-order dentures. In fact, it doesn't have much of any reputation. But several places are trying to give it a good one— including Gridley's, Charlie Vergos' Rendezvous in Memphis, and Maurice's Piggy Park in West Columbia, South Carolina, as well as Melvin's Legendary BBQ in Charlestown, South Carolina. There's even a way to get vacuum-packed beef brisket from Texas.

Up front, we have to tell you: Mail-order barbecue is not the same as being there. But it is the next best thing to being there. Plus, we must consider our friends in North Dakota and Wisconsin who don't have barbecue to speak of.

Charlie Vergos' Rendezvous. These folks are in the sauce biz (see the previous section), and they'll also overnight Federal Express ribs—orders will arrive fully cooked and frozen. Two slabs of ribs, which will serve a family of four, cost $89, and the order comes with eighteen ounces of mild sauce and four and a half ounces of seasoning, and popcorn. An order of four slabs costs $139. You may add on more sauce, seasoning, or maybe a tub of pork shoulder and some coleslaw. The ribs come with directions for heating on the grill, in the oven, or the microwave. Call the toll-free line (888) HOGS FLY (464–7359) or order online at www.hogsfly.com.

Fiorella's Jack Stack Barbecue. Whether it's turkey, brisket, or any of your classic barbecue options, you probably can get it from the Web site, www.jack stackbbq.com, or call toll-free at (877) 419–7427. If regular ribs seem too mundane, opt for the Kobe Beef Rib Indulgence. You get seven or eight "enormous" ribs, with bean and corn bake sides, for $79.95 plus shipping.

Gourmet Grocery. This online site includes a Kobe Beef Burnt Ends extravaganza for $119.95 plus shipping that includes two pounds of the beef, thirty-two ounces of Hickory Pit Beans, and an eighteen-ounce jar of KC Original BBQ Sauce. Call (866) 682–1052 or visit www.gourmet groceryonline.com.

Gridley's. Gridley's is pure Memphis-style barbecue: pulled pork topped with a tomato-and-vinegar-based sauce that is tangy without being tart. The sauce was developed in the early seventies by the late Clyde Gridley, his wife, and five daughters. Before opening his own barbecue restaurant, Gridley had worked for Loeb's Barbecue in Memphis. Gridley's will ship you pork for $7.99 a pound and ribs for $16.99 a slab. You may also want to order the original or hot barbecue sauce for $2.99 a bottle. The ribs are sent packed in dry ice by two-day UPS, and the pork is sent frozen. Back when Gridley's had an 800 number for ribs, one of the first customers was Memphis native Cybill Shepherd. Call (901) 377–8055 and ask for Camille; she'll calculate the shipping for you.

Maurice's Flying Pig Barbeque Service. Maurice Bessinger's country hash contains pork, pit-cooked barbecue ham, mustard, brown sugar, potatoes, onions, and bell peppers. Four pints will set you back $36.00, or you can try the $69.95 special order of a rack of ribs, a pound of ham, a pint of hash, and a free bottle of sauce. If you want to put together lots of different options, calling is a good idea. The number is (800) MAURICE, ext. 12. According to the Web site, www.mauricesbbq.com, there are just too many choices for a measly computer to handle.

Melvin's Legendary BBQ. Here David Bessinger is the third-generation purveyor of Carolina-style sauce and meat. Ribs and hand-pulled pork are shipped two-day or overnight. Consider the Rib Event, two slabs of ribs with a bottle of the sauce (see Golden Secret Recipe BBQ Sauce in the previous section) for $47.99 plus shipping, or go for broke with the Backwood Bar-B-Que combo of three sauces and six pounds of hand-pulled pork for $79.99 plus shipping. The Web site is www.melvinsbbq.com.

Ranch House Mesquite Smoked Meats. Do not visit this site when you're hungry. These fourth-generation Texans smoke their brisket eighteen hours. You can order a half or a whole (two to four pounds), rubbed with salt, pepper, and spices, for $30 to a little more than $50, plus shipping. You can get it chopped, sliced, or whole, You can serve yourself and a friend with one pound of sliced for $11, or invite a dozen or more people to share that four-pounder. The company also offers a spicier version of the brisket, called "West Texas Wild Brisket." The orders come vacuum-packed, and you may want to add a bottle of Ranch House Barbeque Sauce. If you keep perusing the site, you may have to get some ribs, or even lamb. The number is (800) 749–6329, and the Web site is www.brisket.net.

Mail-Order Wood

City dwellers with a taste for wood-smoked cooking had better have their sources for the raw materials. After the bunk beds are burned up and the credenza is gone, it's generally not considered good citizenship to start skulking around likely looking trees in the park late at night.

Look, nobody made these people move to the city, and if they finally have arrived at the point where they have to mail order wood to fuel a halfway decent barbecue, well, that's just too bad, isn't it? You wouldn't believe how inconvenient it is for someone in Lexington, North Carolina, to see a good opera. It all averages out. At any rate, mail-order wood for barbecue junkies is definitely available.

Wood by the truckload? One of the most complete sources for wood, and other nonedible barbecue products, is the Web site www.barbecue wood.com.

Let's say you want to experiment with wood chunks. You can order apple, pecan, white oak, maple, cherry, and hickory. How about forty-five pounds of apricot wood chips for $36? Two cubic feet of alderwood chips cost $36, and ten pounds of apple chunks go for $14.97. Of course, you'll have to add on the cost of UPS shipping. In addition to chips and chunks, you can order Hickory Chimney Wood, twenty-five pounds for $24.98. If you're really serious, check out the 500 pounds of wood delivered by freight truck. Calling (800) DRYWOOD (379-9663) will get you to a cheerful operator who might convince you that the freight-truck delivery is really the best buy.

If you're in the market for boutique wood, consider the all-natural, no additives Chigger Creek Products. Wood is offered in chunks, logs, and chips, and is delivered sealed and labeled. Varieties include pear, sassafras, persimmon, and even apple/hickory blends. Prices are posted online, but about six pounds of hickory chunks cost $31.50. A case of 12-inch or 16-inch sugar maple logs costs $24. You may call (660) 298-3188 to calculate shipping charges and place your order, or e-mail from their Web site, www.chiggercreekproducts.net.

One last note—there are some passionate devotees of wood pellets. There are cookers designed to operate with wood pellets, and some backyard experimenters even will argue that pellets can enhance traditional smoking flavors. If you're curious about these people and their pellets, look up www.bbqrsdelight.com. The site gives recipes and suggestions for cooking with pellets, as well as offering one-pound bags for $4.99 in savory (a blend of herbs), pecan, apple, and cherry. There's even a product called "Smoke Stix" for $2.99. Call Candy at (877) 275–9591 for more information.

Barbecue: A Dying Art?

They may cook pork shoulders or beef briskets. They may pull the meat or slice it, drown it in a sweet sauce or serve it unadorned. But one strand unites the dedicated pitmasters we told you about in this book. They are practitioners of a dying art: cooking barbecue.

Technology has made the barbecue process easier, but these artists refuse to take the shortcuts. "When you start cutting corners, finding a faster way to do it, you're hurting yourself," said Monk, who was the owner of Lexington Barbecue No. 1 in Lexington, North Carolina. Monk built his sauce from scratch, never using a commercial product when he could make it up himself. He shook his head when told about cooks who use Worcestershire sauce as a base for their barbecue dip. "You don't have to use that stuff. You can make it yourself." Early Scott of Lexington, Tennessee, grew all the vegetables for his sauce. And when he was cooking, Scott slept in his smokehouse so he could keep the fire at exactly the right level.

Why do they still cook barbecue the old-fashioned way, the hard way, when it would be much easier to use commercial ingredients and modern conveniences? Simple. As Early Scott told us, "You see that sign out there? That's my name on that sign." That's what this book has been about: the kind of pride that produces a personal art. The teenager who slings hamburgers at the local burger franchise doesn't care if that's the best hamburger he can make. With barbecue people it's different. It's not just cooking barbecue—it's cooking the best barbecue. And that isn't a science. Temperature probes, oven gauges, and heat-flow diagrams can't take the place of a cook who cares.

"It's not something you learn in a day, either," said Hugh Knoth of Knoth's Barbecue in Kutawa, Kentucky. The barbecue artists we talked to didn't learn to cook barbecue by reading a book or a manual. They learned by cooking. And they learned to trust themselves more than a gauge. "Most of these boys around here go by how long they can hold their hand on the fire," said Dennis Rogers, columnist for *The News & Observer* in Raleigh. "They know if they can't hold it on more than, say, two seconds, then it's ready."

"We didn't have no thermometers in the old days," recalled Leo Phelps of Oak Ridge, North Carolina, who cooked barbecue for half a century.

PORKLORE

"Barbecue don't go high class."

Jonathan Weld, an Englishman, visited the young United States in 1799 and wrote to his friends back home, "The people are extremely fond of an entertainment which they call a berbecue. It consists of a large party of people meeting together to partake of a sturgeon or pig roasted while in the open air, on a sort of low hurdle, over a slow fire; this, however, is an entertainment confined chiefly to the lower ranks."

"We just felt the fire." Jack Dempsey of Ty Ty, Georgia, said, "I open the door and put my hand on the barbecue. That's how I can tell if it's ready."

There are gauges to tell when to add one ingredient, electric motors to turn the meat, and automatic brushes to baste it. But they haven't invented a machine yet that can taste. That's where the art comes in. And the only way the art of barbecue will be saved is if it is valued.

It's that love of good barbecue that will keep the flame burning a while longer.

Acknowledgments

No book is an island. If it were, you'd have to pay a lot more for it, plus closing costs and points. We had the help of a great many people in researching and writing this book. A great, great many.

We'd like to acknowledge and thank Maureen Brown, our never-tiring research assistant; Susan Johnson, who made more phone calls and traveled more miles than her original wedding vows ever had hinted at; Judy Staten, who always believed; Chris Wohlwend, who introduced us to the lady who turned this project from a burnt end into a main course; Kris Dahl, that lady; and Hugh Van Dusen, our editor for the first edition.

We'd like to thank our parents, George and Margaret Johnson and Lyle and Margie Staten.

We would also like to acknowledge Will Staten for sharing his dad with the barbecue world; and Juliet Johnson, who was gnawing on rib bones before she could talk, but who has since gone over to the Other Side as a vegetarian. There's always coleslaw, sweetie pie.

Our thanks also to Adam Guenther; Kurt and Andrewe Guenther; Marc, Stephanie, and Erin Guenther; Bruce and Rosie Haney; Herb Shankel; Bob and Karen Moody; Tom Jester; Robin Beard (America's number one barbecue lover); Rusty and Mary Brashear; Lois Hunt; Rod Irvin for the surf; Margy Clark; and Dan Pomeroy.

And Lisa Anne and Mike Milhorn, Susan Patterson and George, Brenda and Arnold Fowler, Charlotte and Andy Smith, Tom and Marsha McNeer again, Pete Fornatale and Susan Van Metre, Sharon and Dave Harris, the back table at Kathy's Korner, Darrell Perry, and Claude Russell.

And John and Dale Reed, who provided advice, encouragement, and the Texas photos.

And Mary Caldwell, who doesn't know anything about barbecue but wanted her name in the book anyway.

And especially to our editor Mary Norris and to Chris Grimm, who rediscovered us.

We'll stop here, before this gets longer than the Academy Awards show.

A love of real barbecue is a lifetime thing. For your authors, it has been burning since at least 1988, when the first edition of this revised and updated book was published by Harper & Row Publishers, New York. We thanked a bunch of people then, and we don't want to unthank them now. But to help save the Earth's precious resources, we won't print the whole list again in this new book. As before, we want to close with special thanks to all of the barbecue pitmen and dedicated chefs who still are hard at work out there, cooking barbecue that's as good as we've ever eaten.

Index of Restaurants and Locations

About the Authors

Vince Staten's many and varied careers have included freelance writer, author, columnist, movie critic, lecturer, professor, and restaurateur. He says that one of these days he'll settle down and pick a career. He's currently the Metro columnist for the *Kingsport Times-News* and was awarded Best Columnist in Tennessee by the Tennessee Press Association in 2005. As a freelance writer his articles have appeared in more than one thousand publications, including the *New York Times, Boston Globe, Dallas Times Herald, Baltimore Sun, Food & Wine, Satellite Orbit, Video Review, Saturday Review, Icon,* and *Bon Appetit*.

Vince is the author of twelve books, including *Kentucky Curiosities* (Globe Pequot Press) and *Jack Daniel's Old-Time Barbecue Cookbook* (Sulgrave Press).

Here are some other facts about Vince:

Age: Same as David Letterman and Almond Joy (the candy bar, not the striptease artist)

Co-owner: Vince Staten's Old-Time Barbecue in downtown Prospect, Kentucky

Education: Bachelor's degree with worthless major in psychology from Duke University; Master's degree in journalism from University of Tennessee

Civic organizations: Commissioner of the City of River Bluff, Kentucky (population 356), 1989–1996. Never indicted.

Honors: Eighth-grade Twist Champion, Ross N. Robinson Junior High School; Homecoming Queen, University of Tennessee, 1970 (never crowned, ruled ineligible due to graduate student status)

Greg Johnson is the features editor at the *Courier-Journal* newspaper in Louisville, Kentucky, a former restaurant critic for the *Louisville Times,* and the recipient of numerous journalism awards.

In case you were wondering, here's how you can tell Greg from Vince:

Greg has the beard: In fact, hair on the head of any sort probably is good evidence you're not talking to Vince.

Vince is the queen: He was voted homecoming queen at the University of Tennessee in a still-controversial election.

Cholesterol: Greg's is actually going down. Vince did the eating for this latest edition; Greg updated information by phone.

Greg has a daughter in a private college: Julie, at Boston University. Tuition is increasing; please consider buying two copies of this book.

Vince actually opened a restaurant: Vince Staten's Old-Time Barbecue.

Greg actually was a restaurant critic: For the *Louisville Times*. He never officially critiqued Vince's restaurant. But he loves it.

Greg is a closet Yankee: He was born in Chicago and grew up in Indianapolis. (Please don't tell the pitman at the Old Hickory.)

Vince has written a bunch of books. Greg has read those books.

Land speed record: Greg's is 140 mph, indicated, in a Plymouth Barracuda. That's another story.

Greg knows better than to submit any list without mentioning his wife of thirty-plus years: There you go, Susie.

Greg has won journalism awards: But wouldn't you rather read about barbecue?